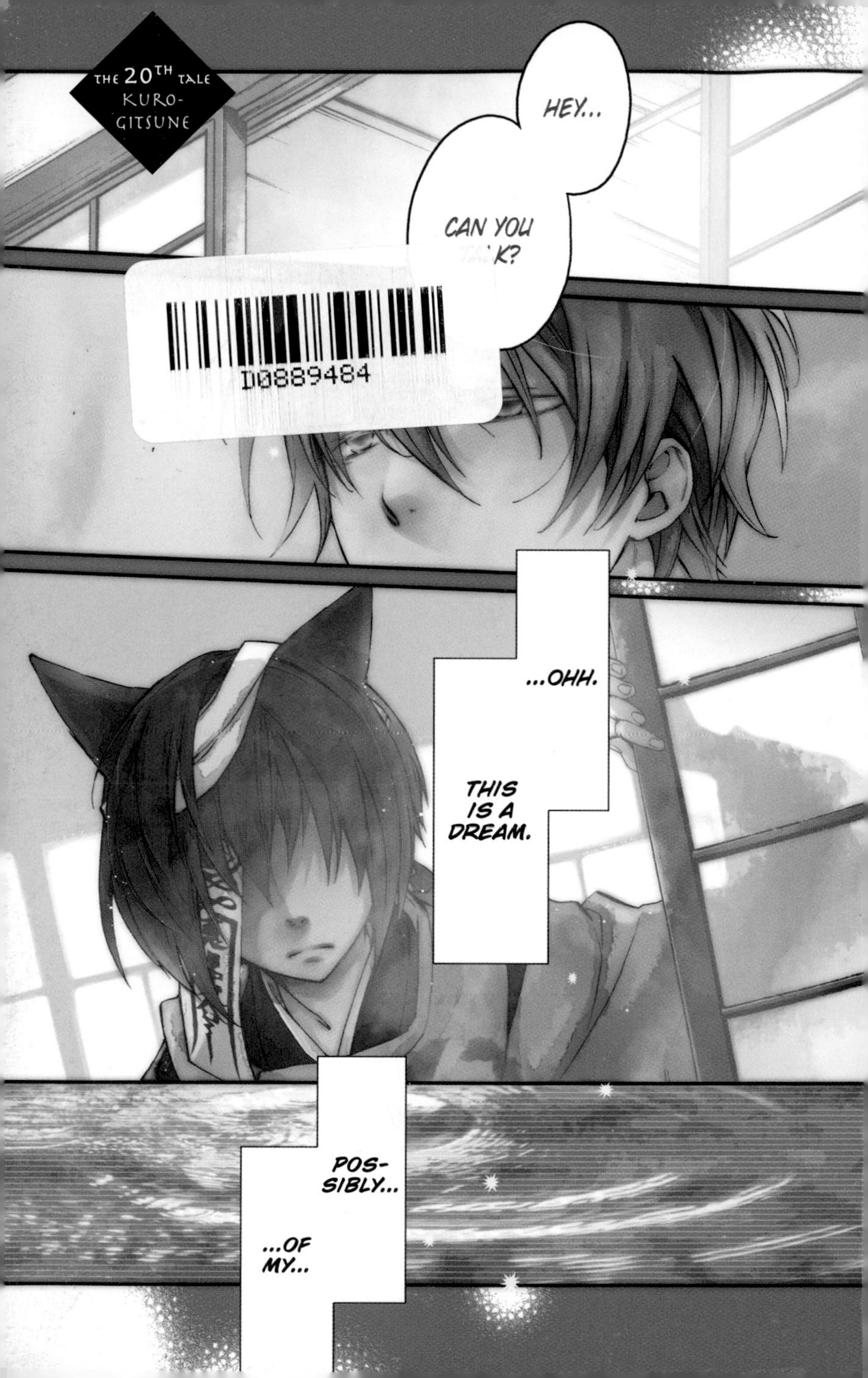
THE 20TH TALE
KURO-GITSUNE
HEY...
CAN YOU
...OHH.
THIS IS A DREAM.
POS-SIBLY...
...OF MY...

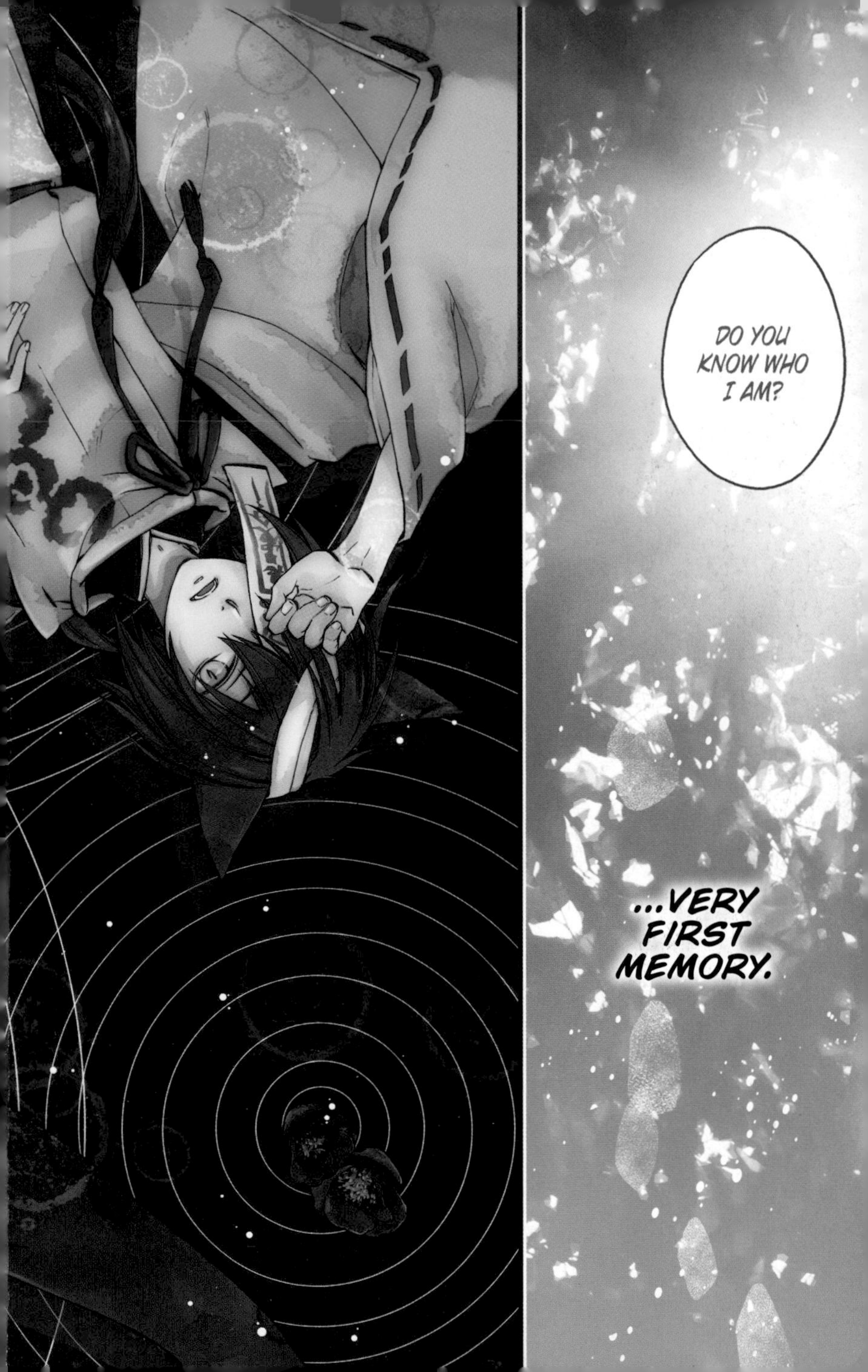
DO YOU KNOW WHO I AM?
...VERY FIRST MEMORY.

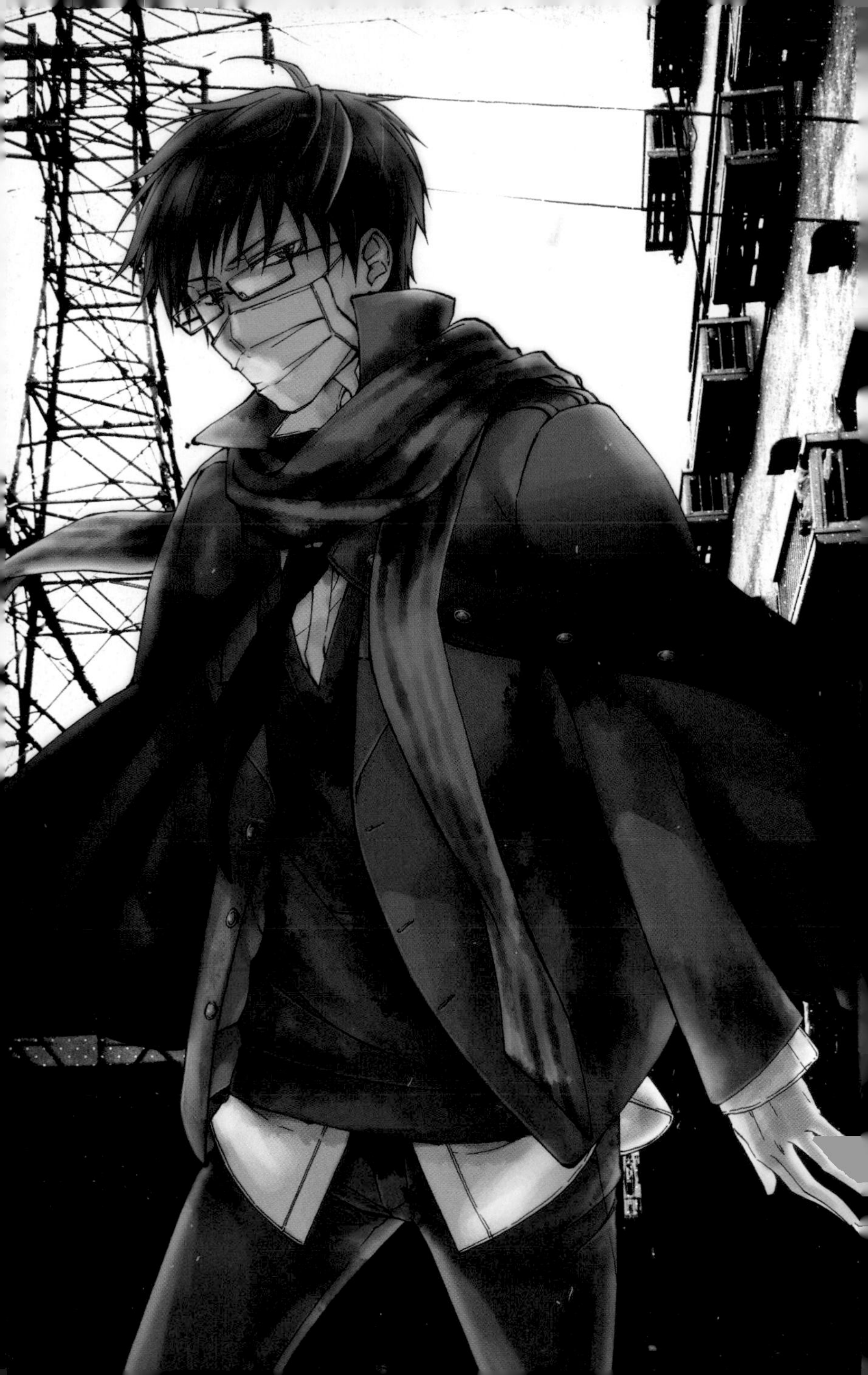

CONTENTS

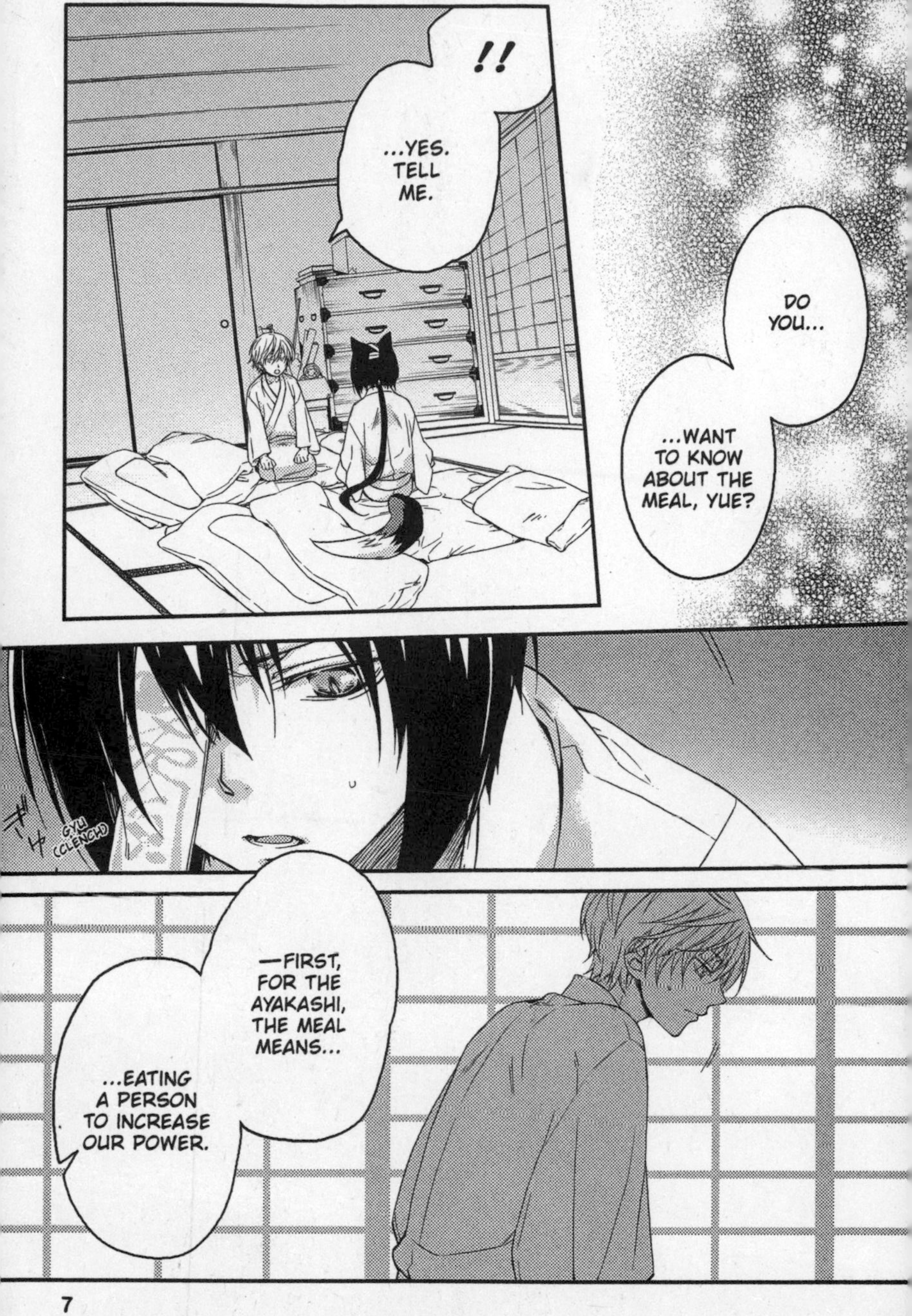

DO YOU...
...WANT TO KNOW ABOUT THE MEAL, YUE?
!!
...YES. TELL ME.
ギュ
GYU (CLENCH)
—FIRST, FOR THE AYAKASHI, THE MEAL MEANS...
...EATING A PERSON TO INCREASE OUR POWER.

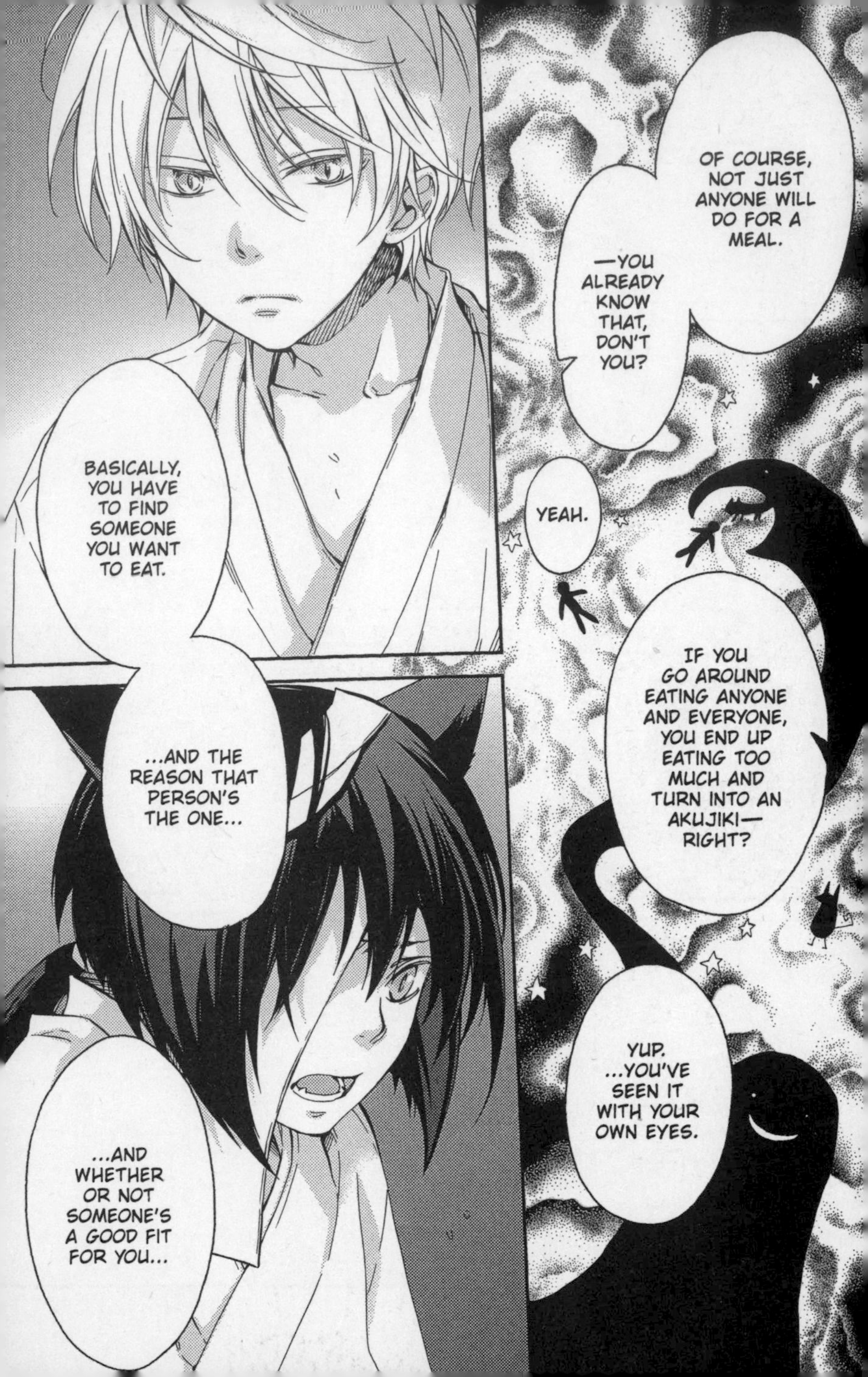
OF COURSE, NOT JUST ANYONE WILL DO FOR A MEAL.
—YOU ALREADY KNOW THAT, DON'T YOU?
YEAH.
IF YOU GO AROUND EATING ANYONE AND EVERYONE, YOU END UP EATING TOO MUCH AND TURN INTO AN AKUJIKI—RIGHT?
YUP. ...YOU'VE SEEN IT WITH YOUR OWN EYES.
BASICALLY, YOU HAVE TO FIND SOMEONE YOU WANT TO EAT.
...AND THE REASON THAT PERSON'S THE ONE...
...AND WHETHER OR NOT SOMEONE'S A GOOD FIT FOR YOU...

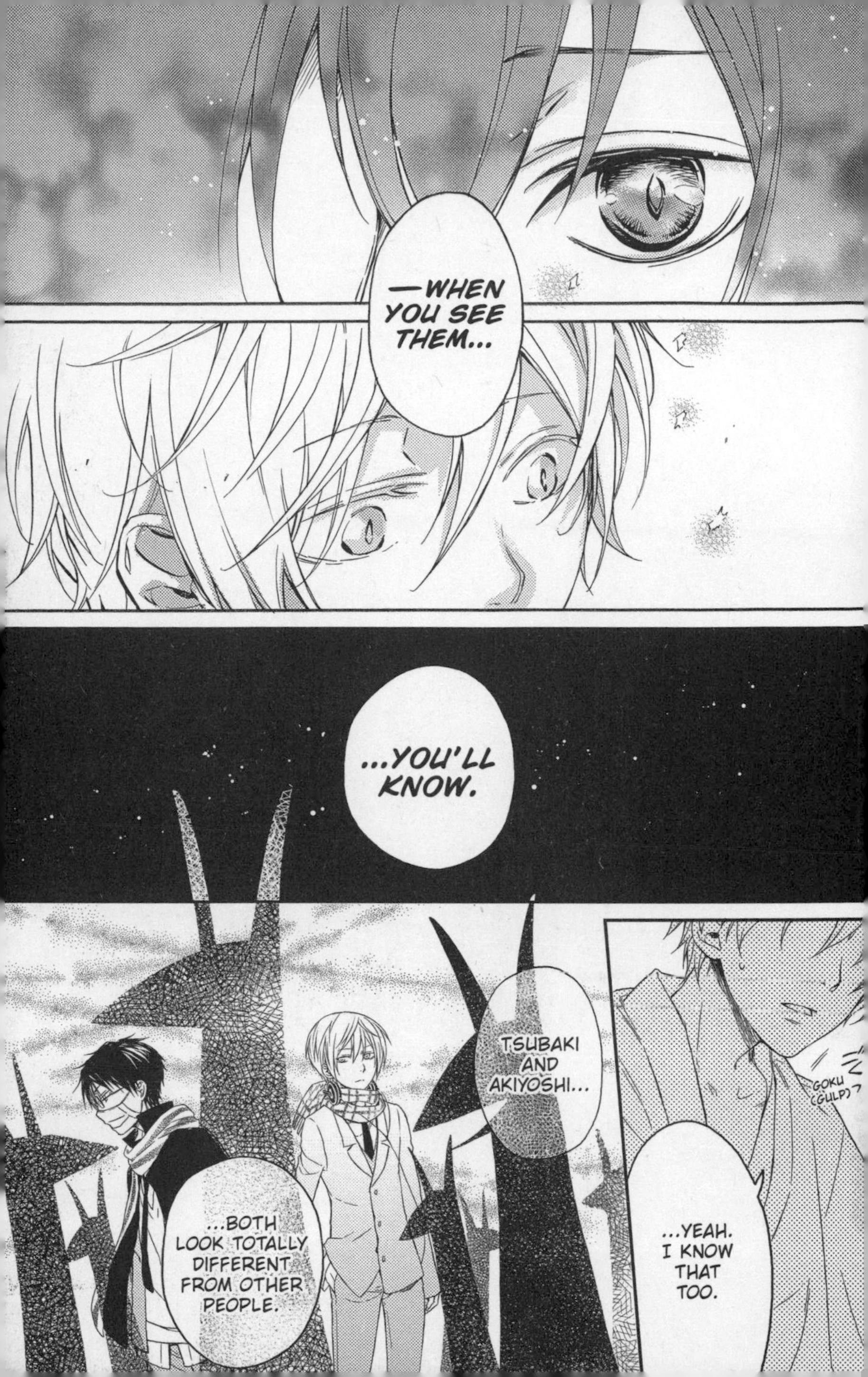
—WHEN YOU SEE THEM...
...YOU'LL KNOW.
GOKU (GULP)
...YEAH. I KNOW THAT TOO.
TSUBAKI AND AKIYOSHI...
...BOTH LOOK TOTALLY DIFFERENT FROM OTHER PEOPLE.

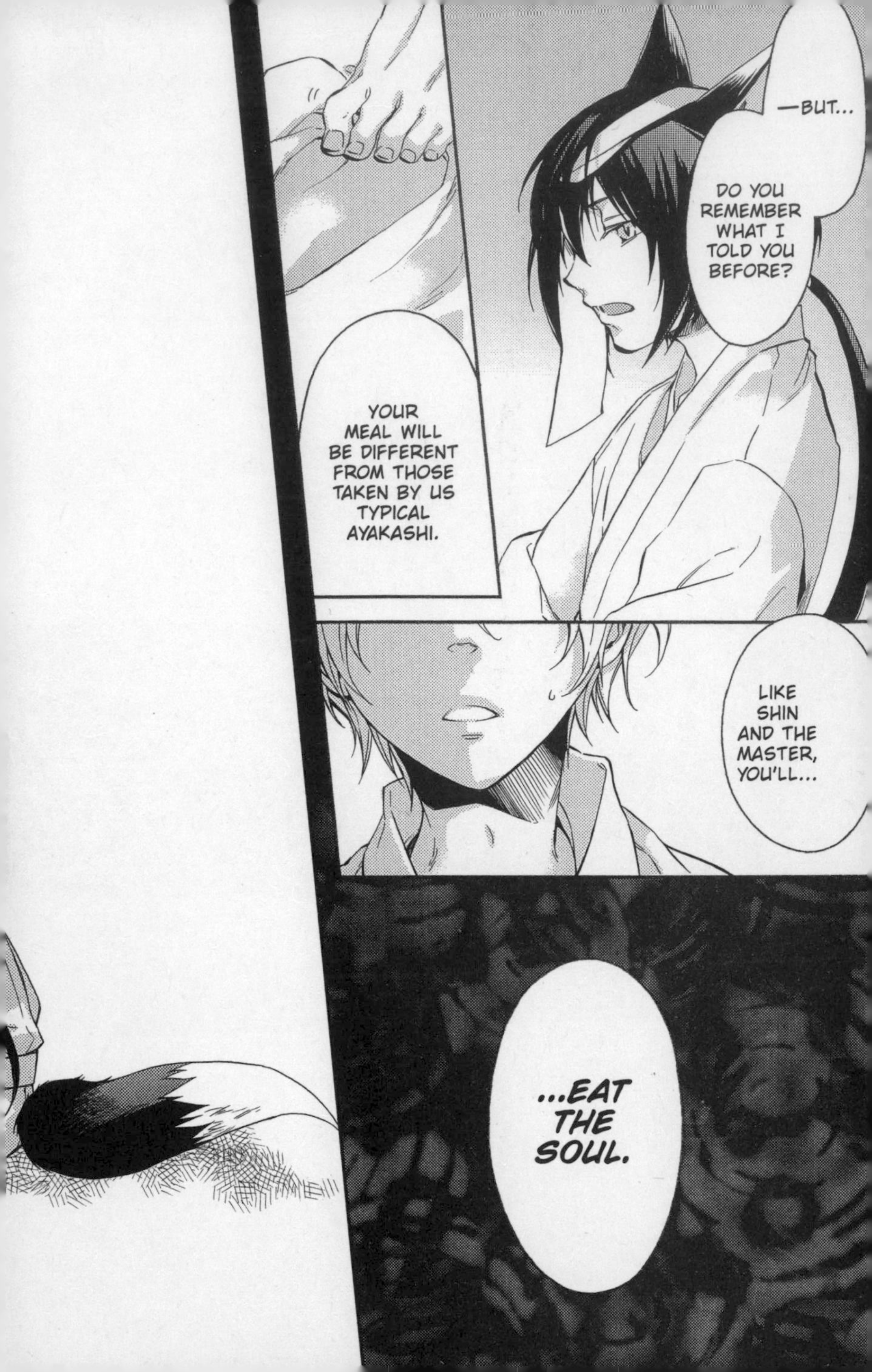
—BUT...
DO YOU REMEMBER WHAT I TOLD YOU BEFORE?
YOUR MEAL WILL BE DIFFERENT FROM THOSE TAKEN BY US TYPICAL AYAKASHI.
LIKE SHIN AND THE MASTER, YOU'LL...
...EAT THE SOUL.

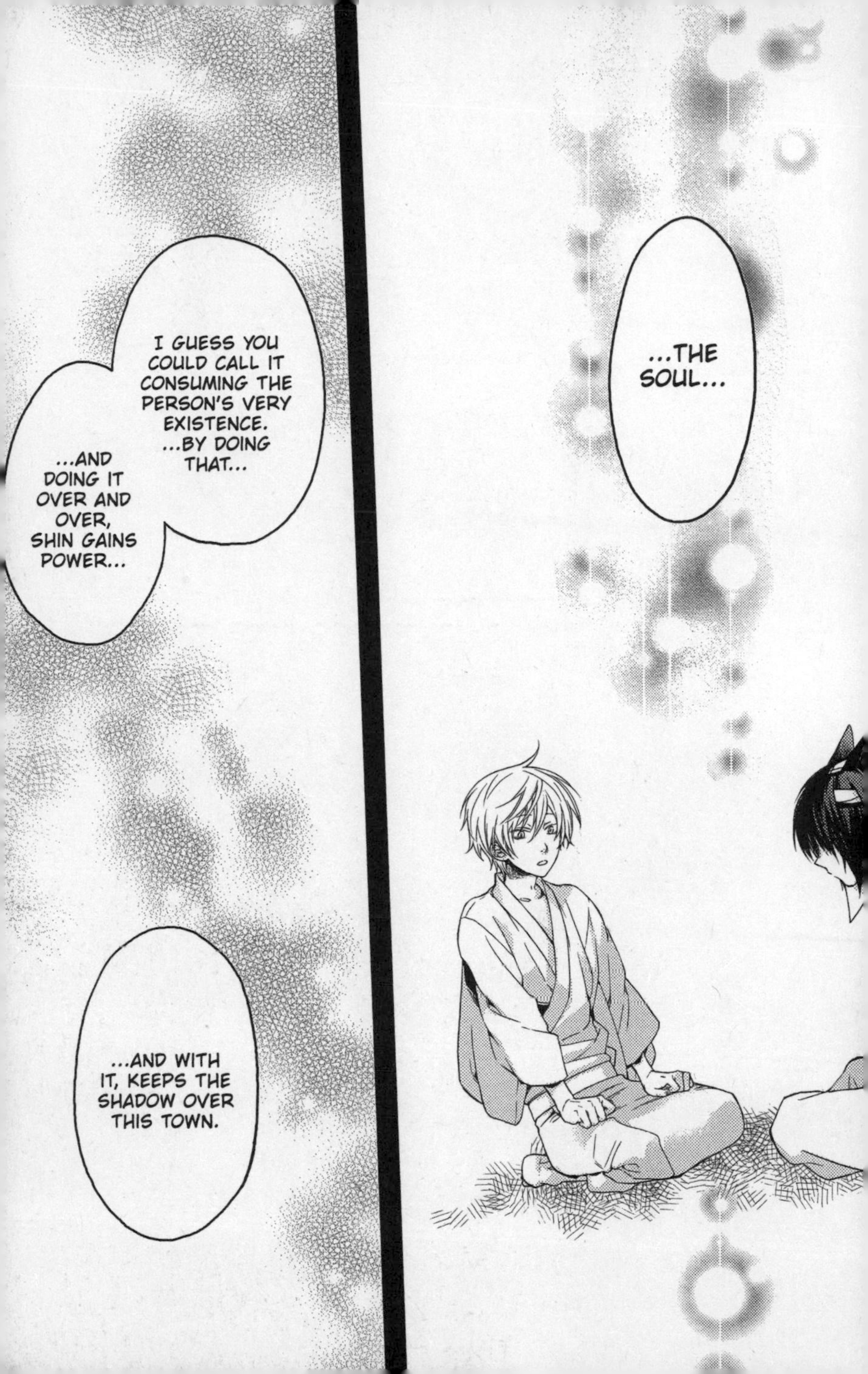
...THE SOUL...
I GUESS YOU COULD CALL IT CONSUMING THE PERSON'S VERY EXISTENCE. ...BY DOING THAT...
...AND DOING IT OVER AND OVER, SHIN GAINS POWER...
...AND WITH IT, KEEPS THE SHADOW OVER THIS TOWN.

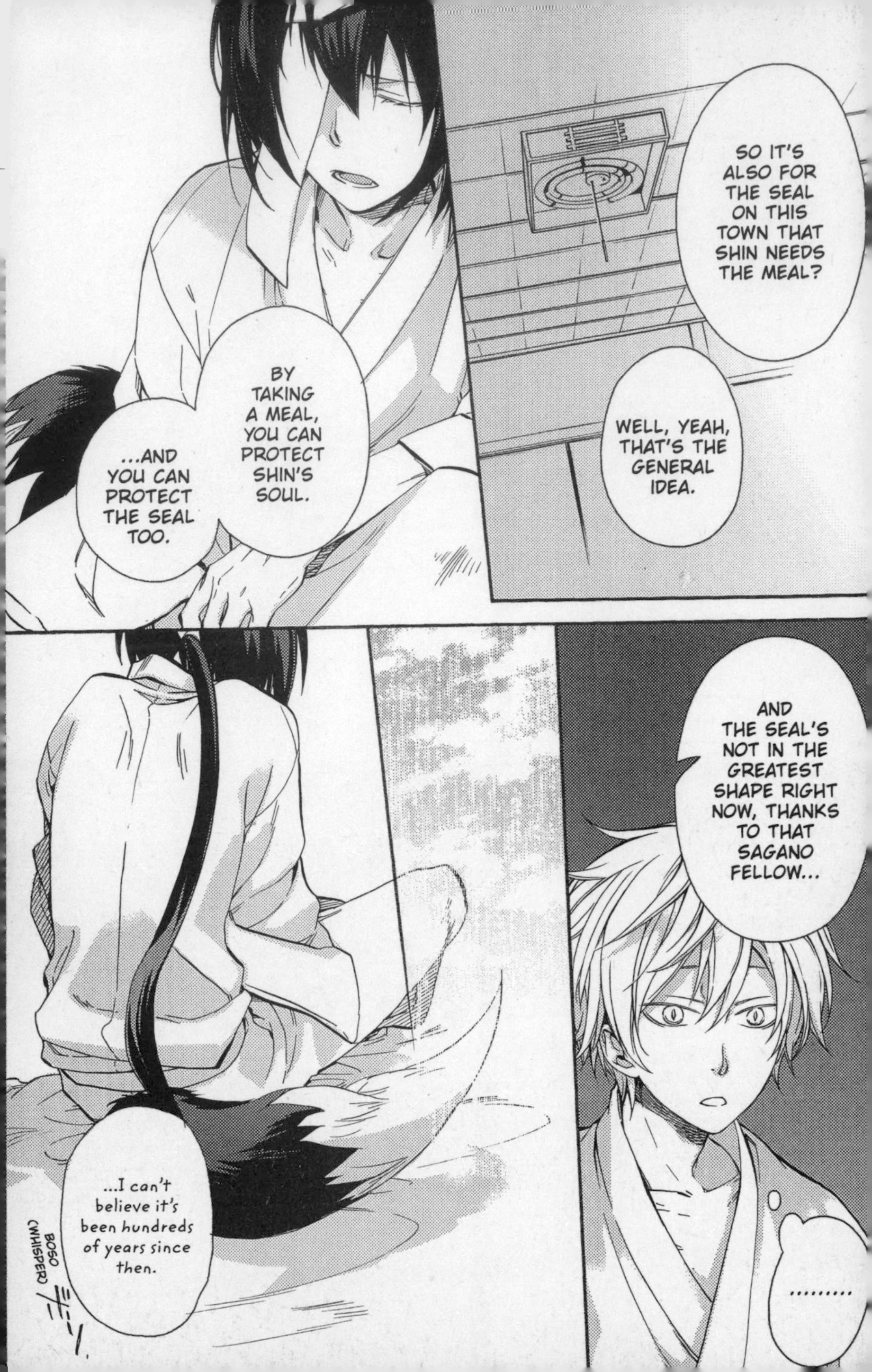
SO IT'S ALSO FOR THE SEAL ON THIS TOWN THAT SHIN NEEDS THE MEAL?
WELL, YEAH, THAT'S THE GENERAL IDEA.
BY TAKING A MEAL, YOU CAN PROTECT SHIN'S SOUL.
...AND YOU CAN PROTECT THE SEAL TOO.
AND THE SEAL'S NOT IN THE GREATEST SHAPE RIGHT NOW, THANKS TO THAT SAGANO FELLOW...
....
...I can't believe it's been hundreds of years since then.
BOSO (WHISPER)

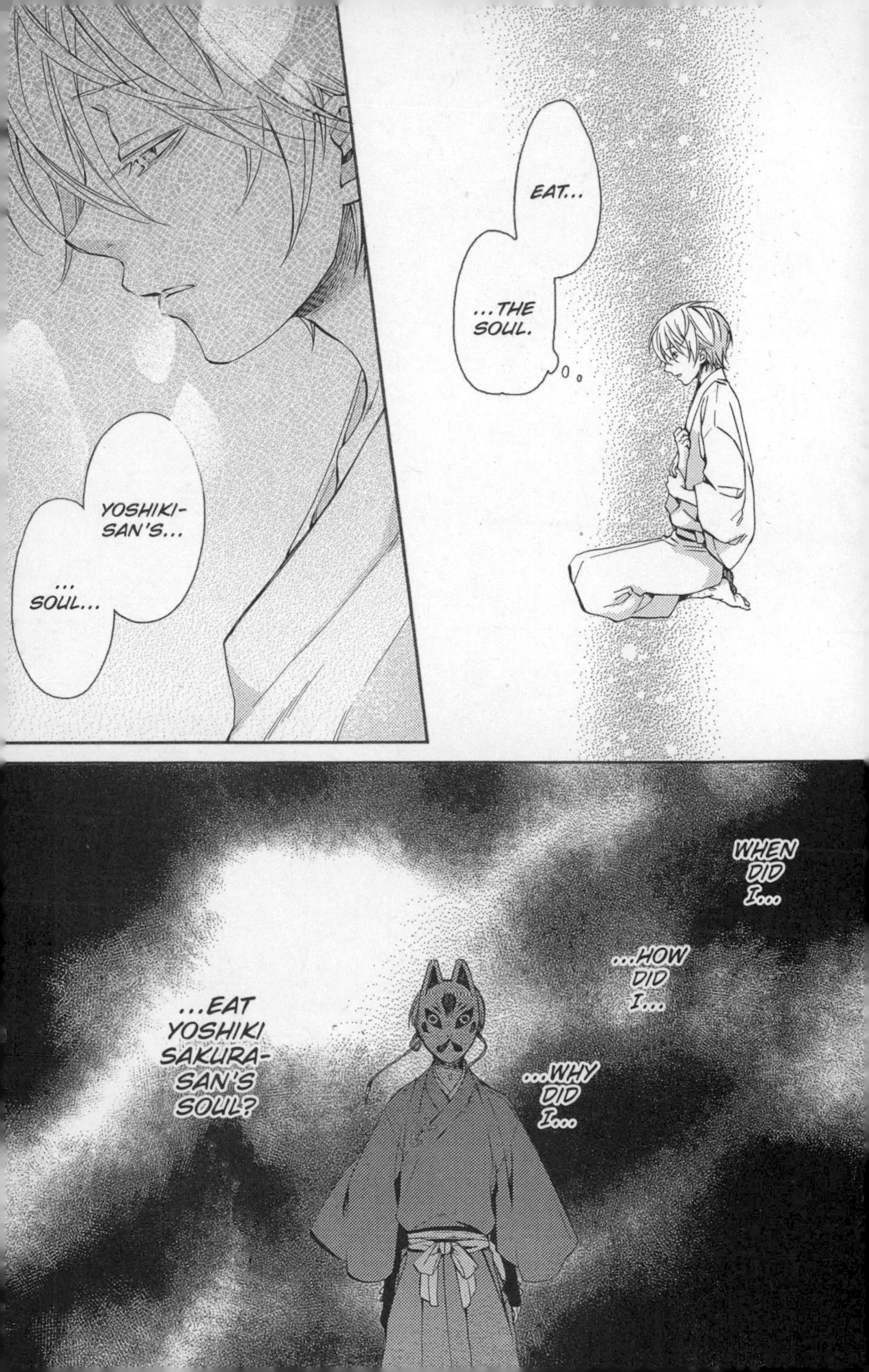
EAT...
...THE SOUL.
YOSHIKI-SAN'S...
...SOUL...
WHEN DID I...
...HOW DID I...
...WHY DID I...
...EAT YOSHIKI SAKURA-SAN'S SOUL?

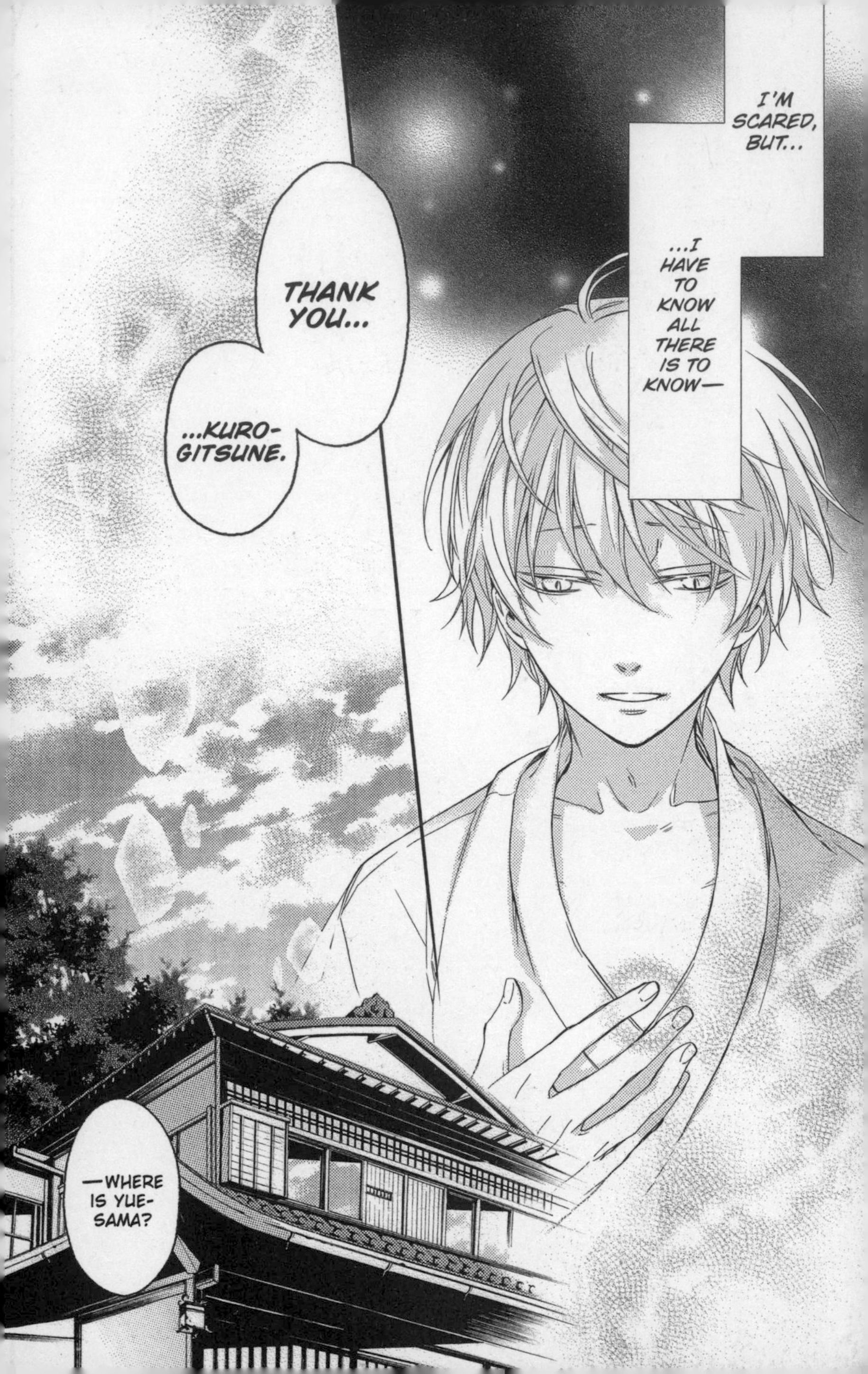
I'M SCARED, BUT...
...I HAVE TO KNOW ALL THERE IS TO KNOW—
THANK YOU...
...KURO-GITSUNE.
—WHERE IS YUE-SAMA?

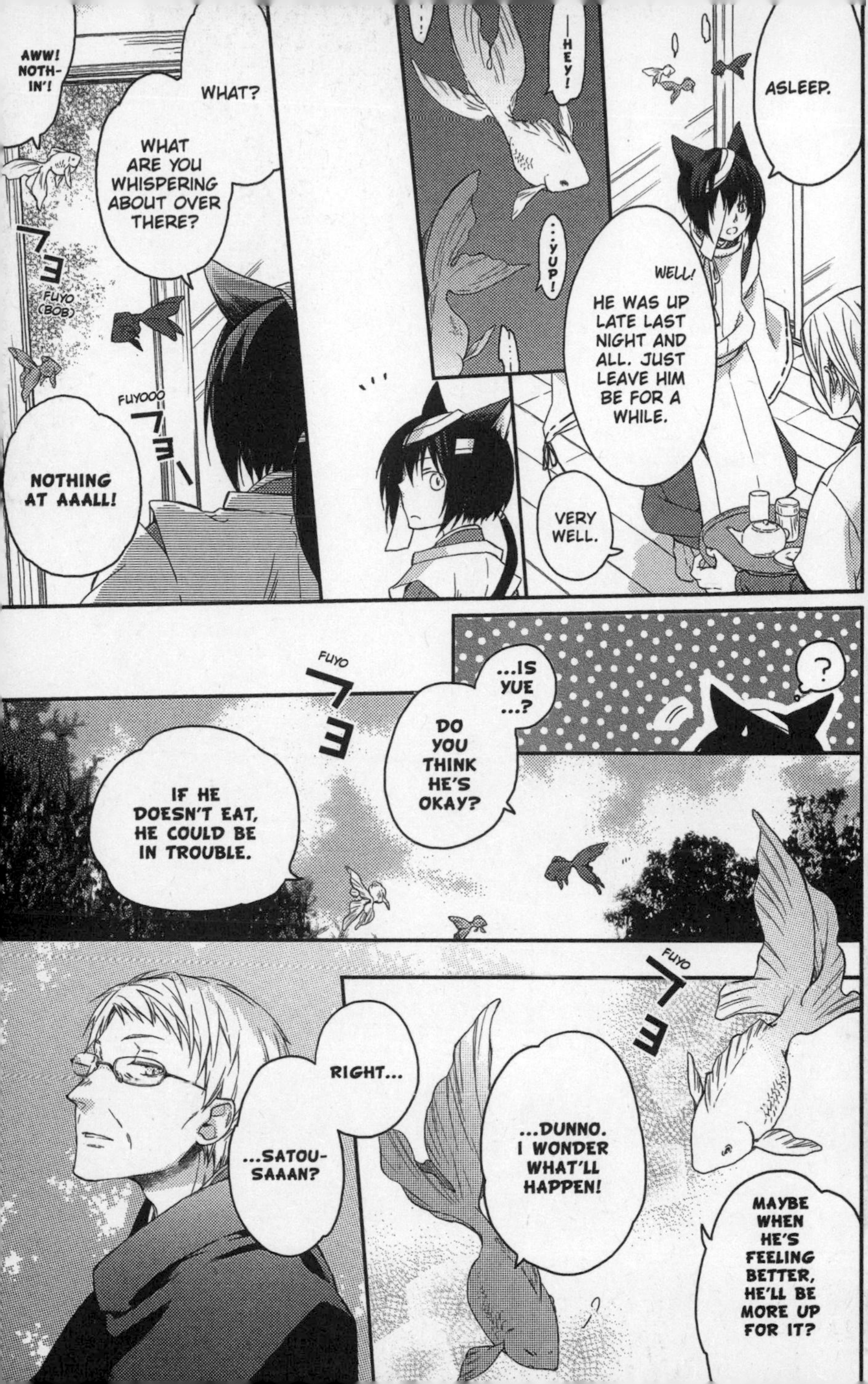
ASLEEP.
WELL!
HE WAS UP LATE LAST NIGHT AND ALL. JUST LEAVE HIM BE FOR A WHILE.
VERY WELL.
...
—HEY!
...YUP!
WHAT?
WHAT ARE YOU WHISPERING ABOUT OVER THERE?
AWW! NOTHIN'!
FUYO (BOB)
FUYOOO
NOTHING AT AAALL!
?
...IS YUE ...?
DO YOU THINK HE'S OKAY?
FUYO
IF HE DOESN'T EAT, HE COULD BE IN TROUBLE.
FUYO
MAYBE WHEN HE'S FEELING BETTER, HE'LL BE MORE UP FOR IT?
...DUNNO. I WONDER WHAT'LL HAPPEN!
RIGHT...
...SATOU-SAAAN?

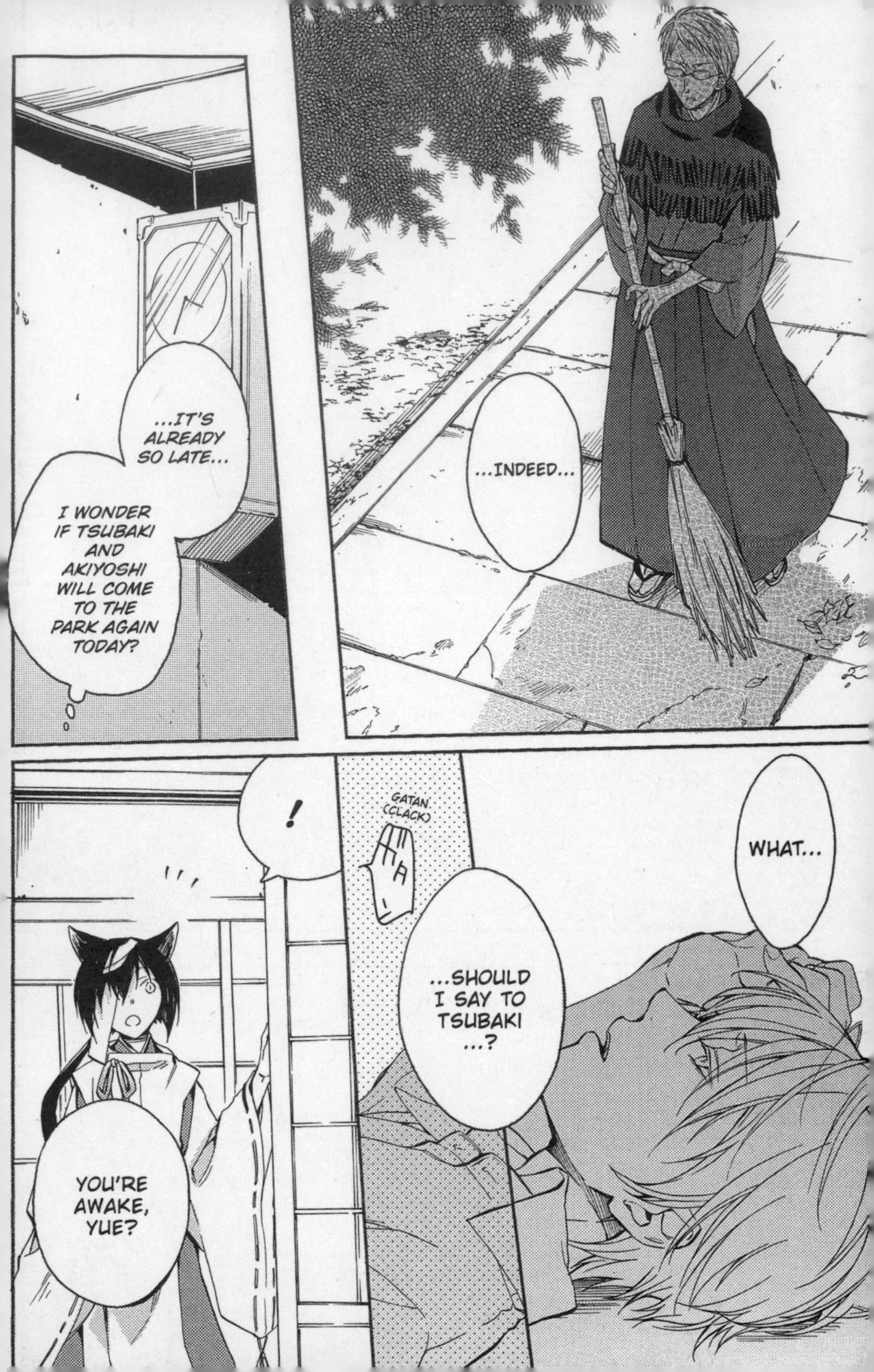
...INDEED...
...IT'S ALREADY SO LATE...
I WONDER IF TSUBAKI AND AKIYOSHI WILL COME TO THE PARK AGAIN TODAY?
WHAT...
...SHOULD I SAY TO TSUBAKI ...?
GATAN (CLACK)
!
YOU'RE AWAKE, YUE?

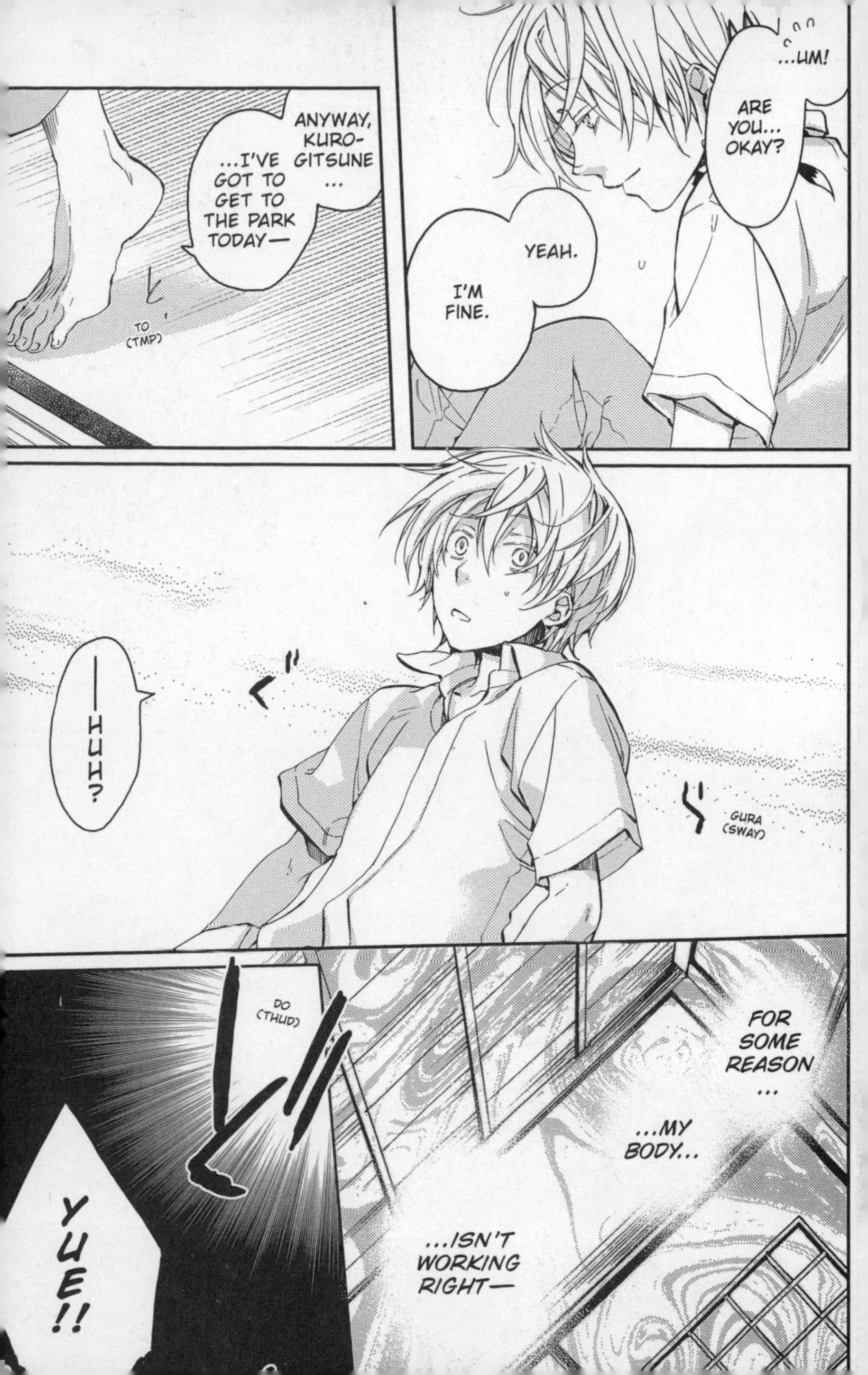
...UM!
ARE YOU... OKAY?
YEAH.
I'M FINE.
ANYWAY, KURO-GITSUNE...
...I'VE GOT TO GET TO THE PARK TODAY—
TO (TMP)
—HUH?
GURA (SWAY)
FOR SOME REASON...
...MY BODY...
...ISN'T WORKING RIGHT—
DO (THUD)
YUE!!

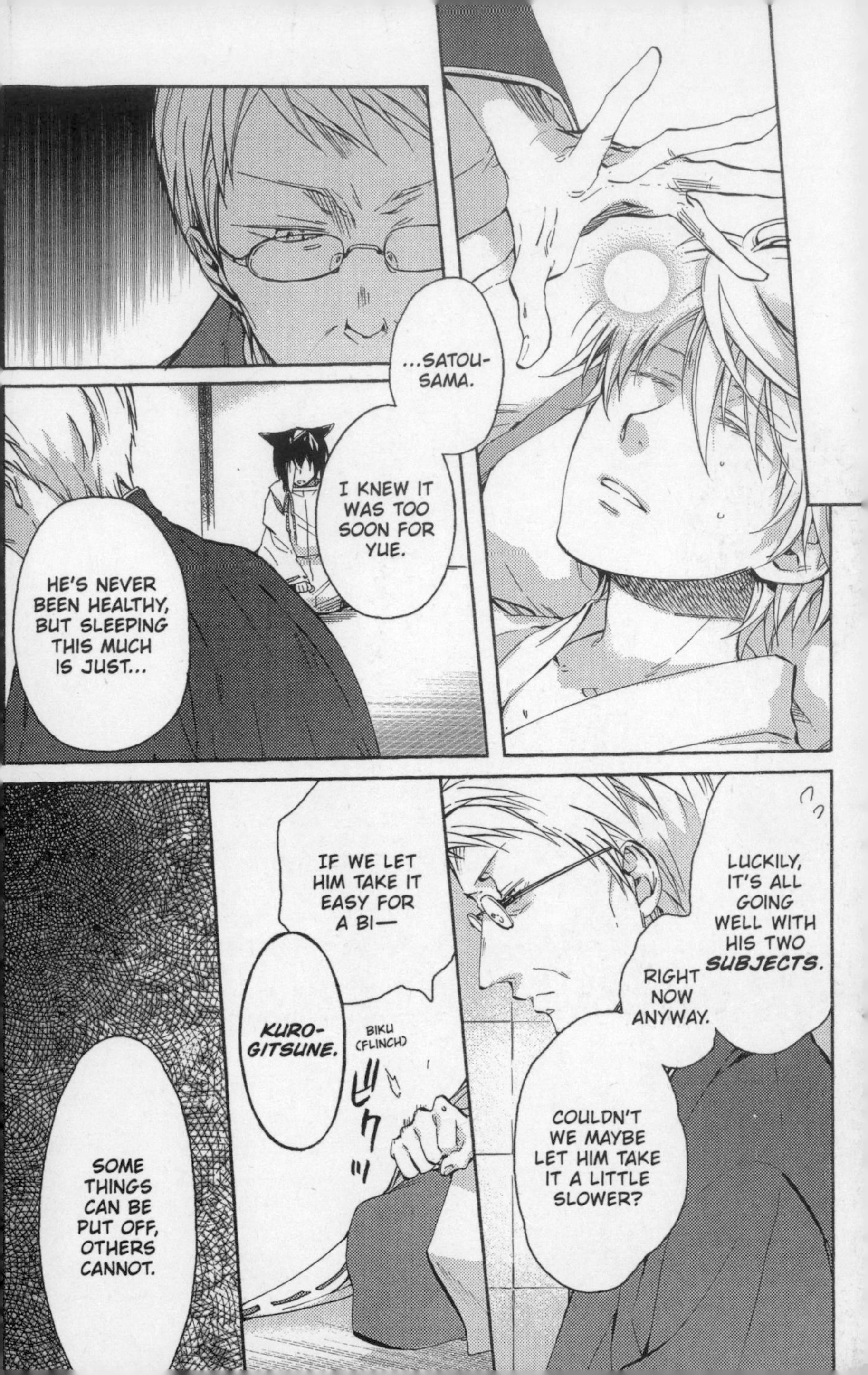
...SATOU-SAMA.
I KNEW IT WAS TOO SOON FOR YUE.
HE'S NEVER BEEN HEALTHY, BUT SLEEPING THIS MUCH IS JUST...
LUCKILY, IT'S ALL GOING WELL WITH HIS TWO *SUBJECTS*.
RIGHT NOW ANYWAY.
COULDN'T WE MAYBE LET HIM TAKE IT A LITTLE SLOWER?
IF WE LET HIM TAKE IT EASY FOR A BI—
KURO-GITSUNE.
BIKU (FLINCH)
SOME THINGS CAN BE PUT OFF, OTHERS CANNOT.

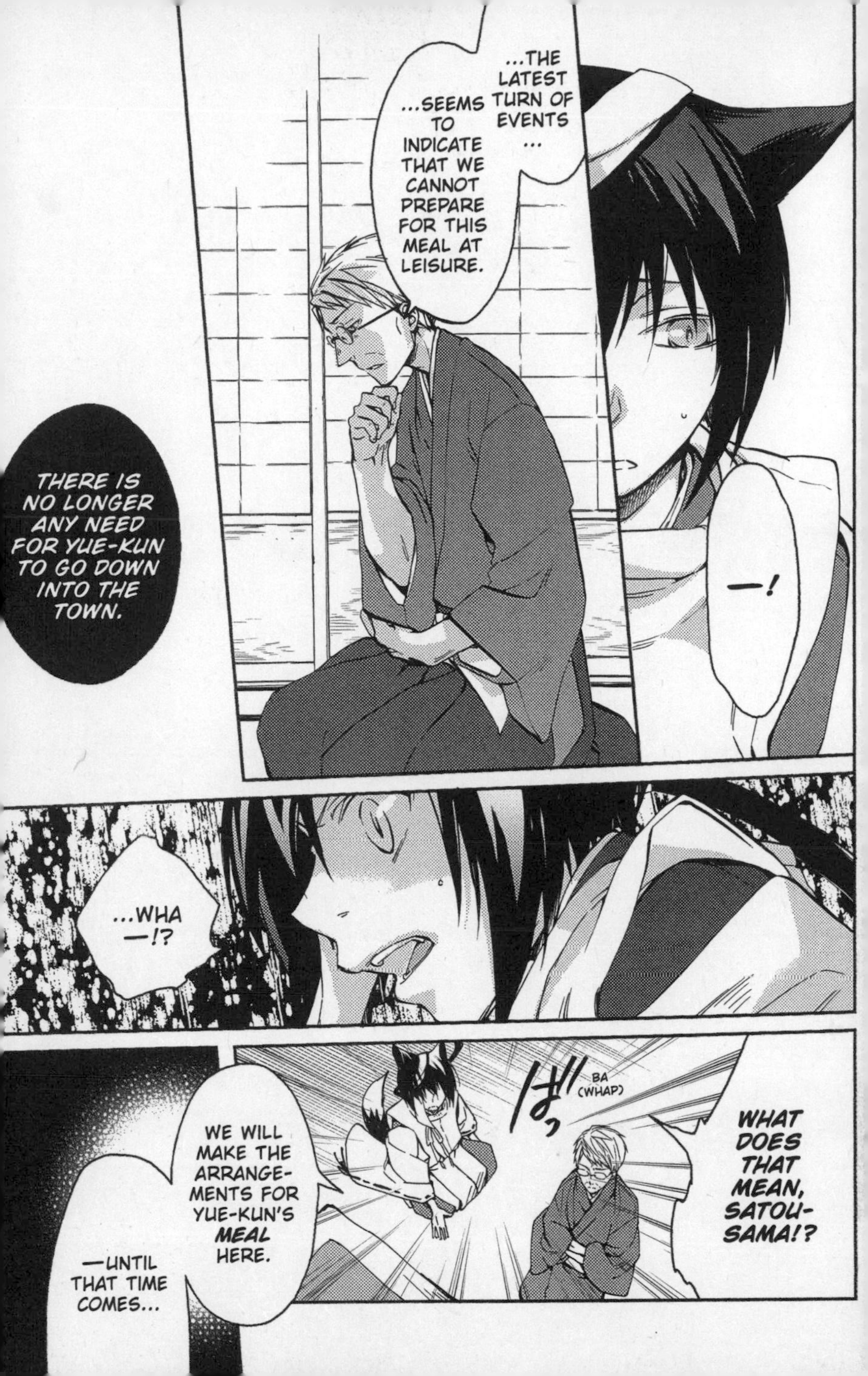
...THE LATEST TURN OF EVENTS ...
...SEEMS TO INDICATE THAT WE CANNOT PREPARE FOR THIS MEAL AT LEISURE.
THERE IS NO LONGER ANY NEED FOR YUE-KUN TO GO DOWN INTO THE TOWN.
—!
...WHA —!?
WHAT DOES THAT MEAN, SATOU-SAMA!?
ばっ
BA (WHAP)
WE WILL MAKE THE ARRANGE-MENTS FOR YUE-KUN'S MEAL HERE.
—UNTIL THAT TIME COMES...

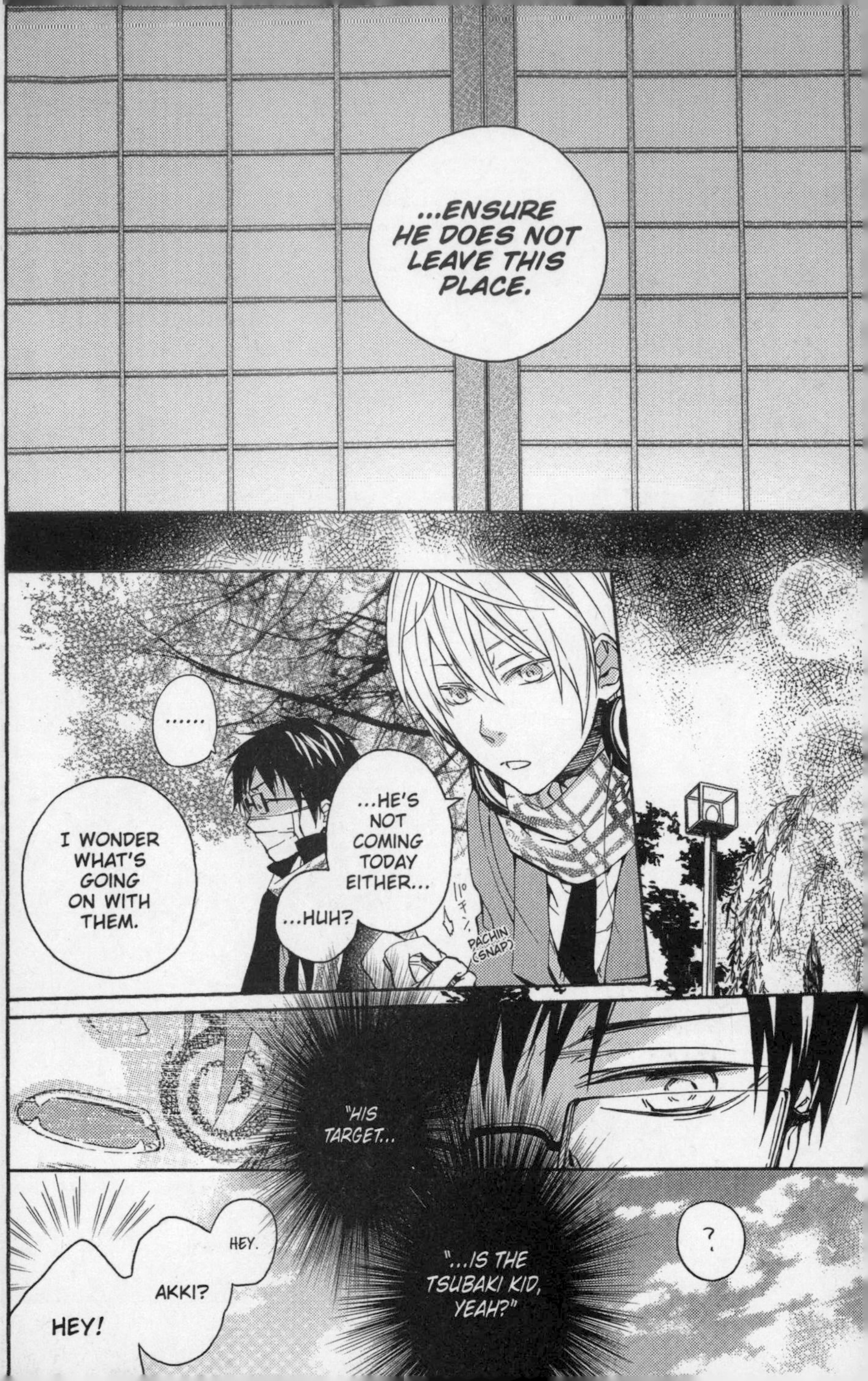
...ENSURE HE DOES NOT LEAVE THIS PLACE.
...HE'S NOT COMING TODAY EITHER...
PACHIN (SNAP)
......
I WONDER WHAT'S GOING ON WITH THEM.
...HUH?
"HIS TARGET...
?
"...IS THE TSUBAKI KID, YEAH?"
HEY.
AKKI?
HEY!

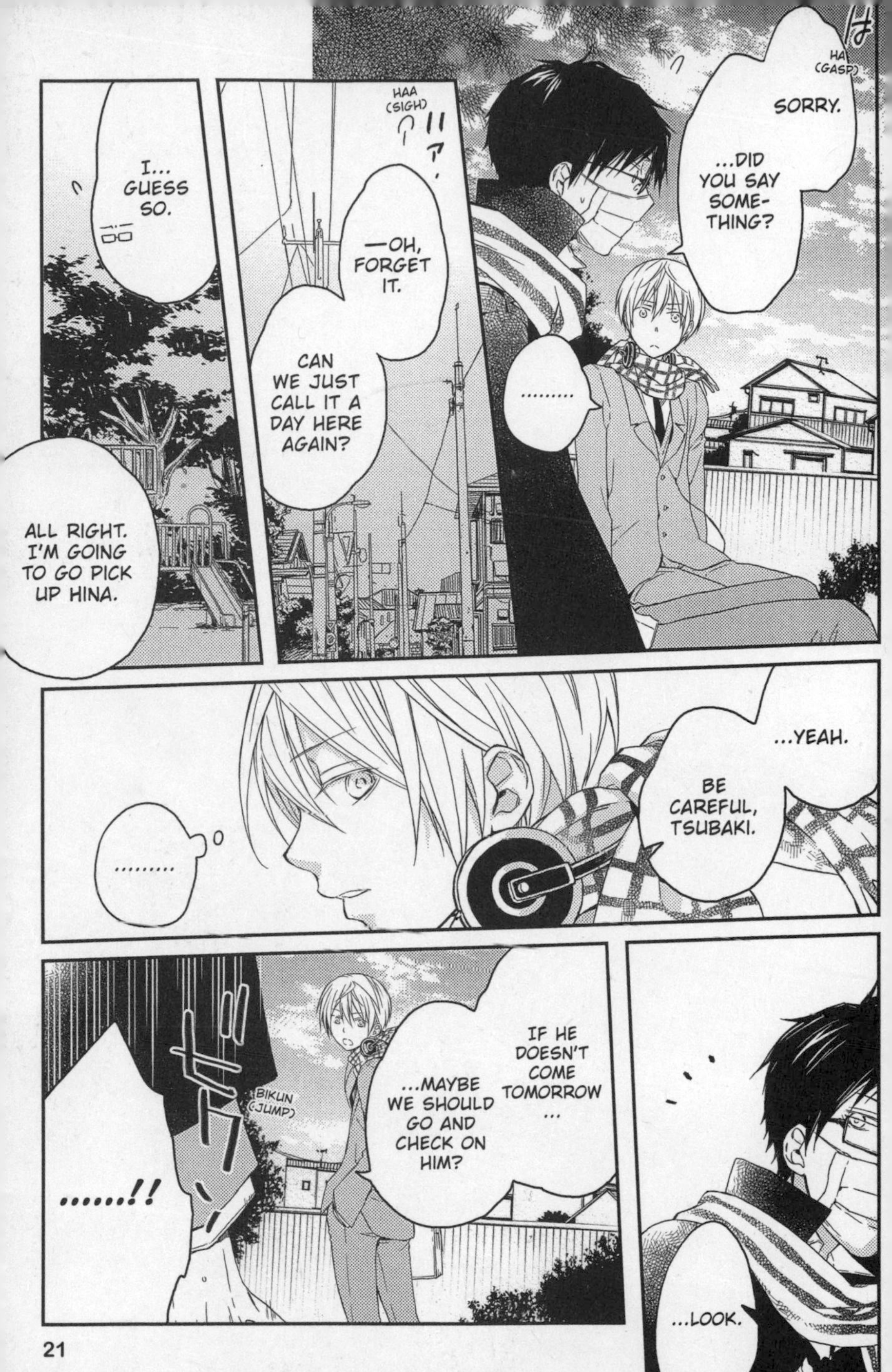
HA (GASP)
SORRY.
...DID YOU SAY SOME-THING?
....
HAA (SIGH)
—OH, FORGET IT.
CAN WE JUST CALL IT A DAY HERE AGAIN?
I... GUESS SO.
ALL RIGHT. I'M GOING TO GO PICK UP HINA.
...YEAH.
BE CAREFUL, TSUBAKI.
....
...LOOK.
IF HE DOESN'T COME TOMORROW ...
...MAYBE WE SHOULD GO AND CHECK ON HIM?
BIKUN (JUMP)
......!!

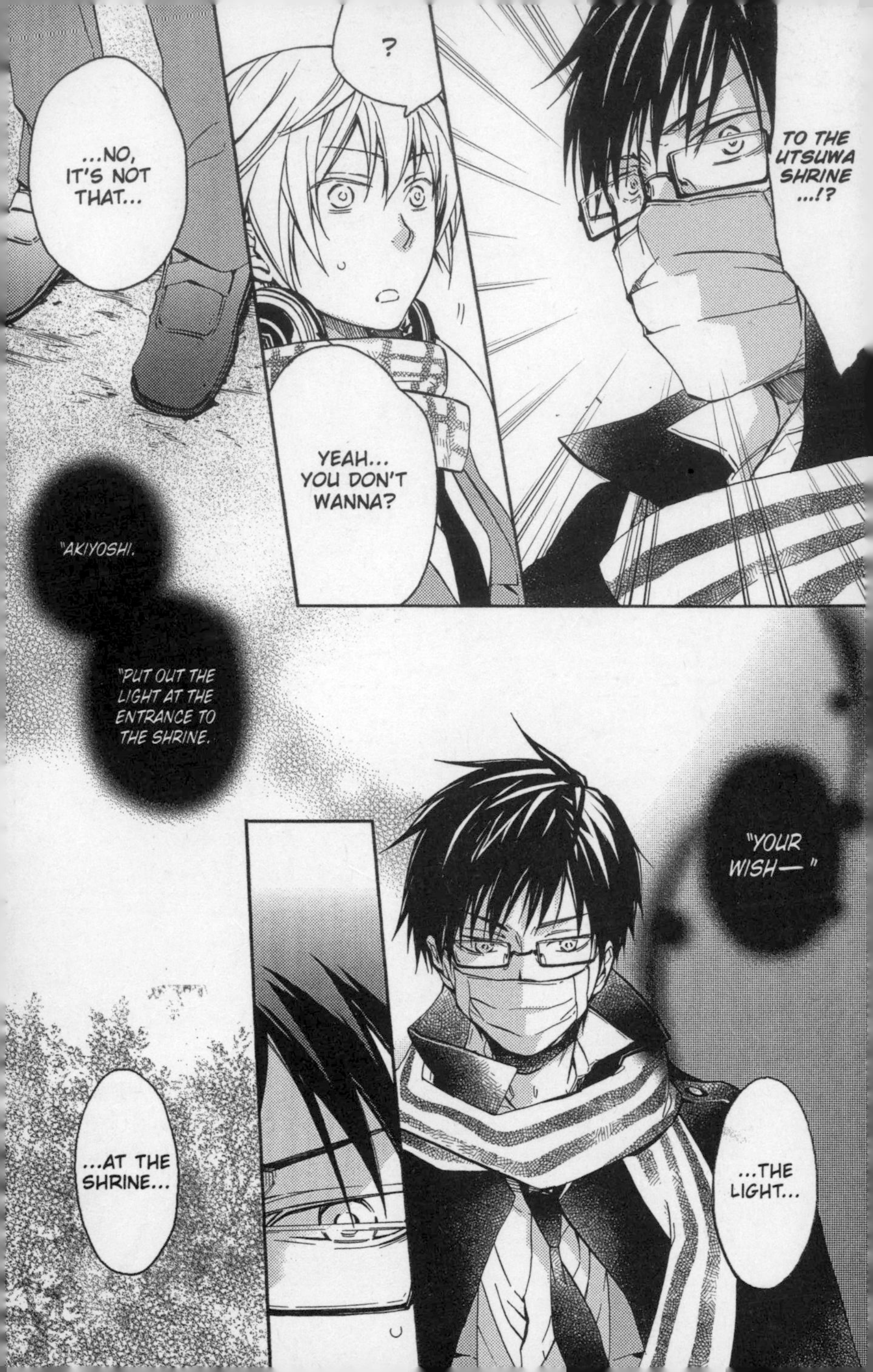

TO THE UTSUWA SHRINE ...!?
?
YEAH... YOU DON'T WANNA?
...NO, IT'S NOT THAT...
"AKIYOSHI.
"PUT OUT THE LIGHT AT THE ENTRANCE TO THE SHRINE.
"YOUR WISH—"
...THE LIGHT...
...AT THE SHRINE...

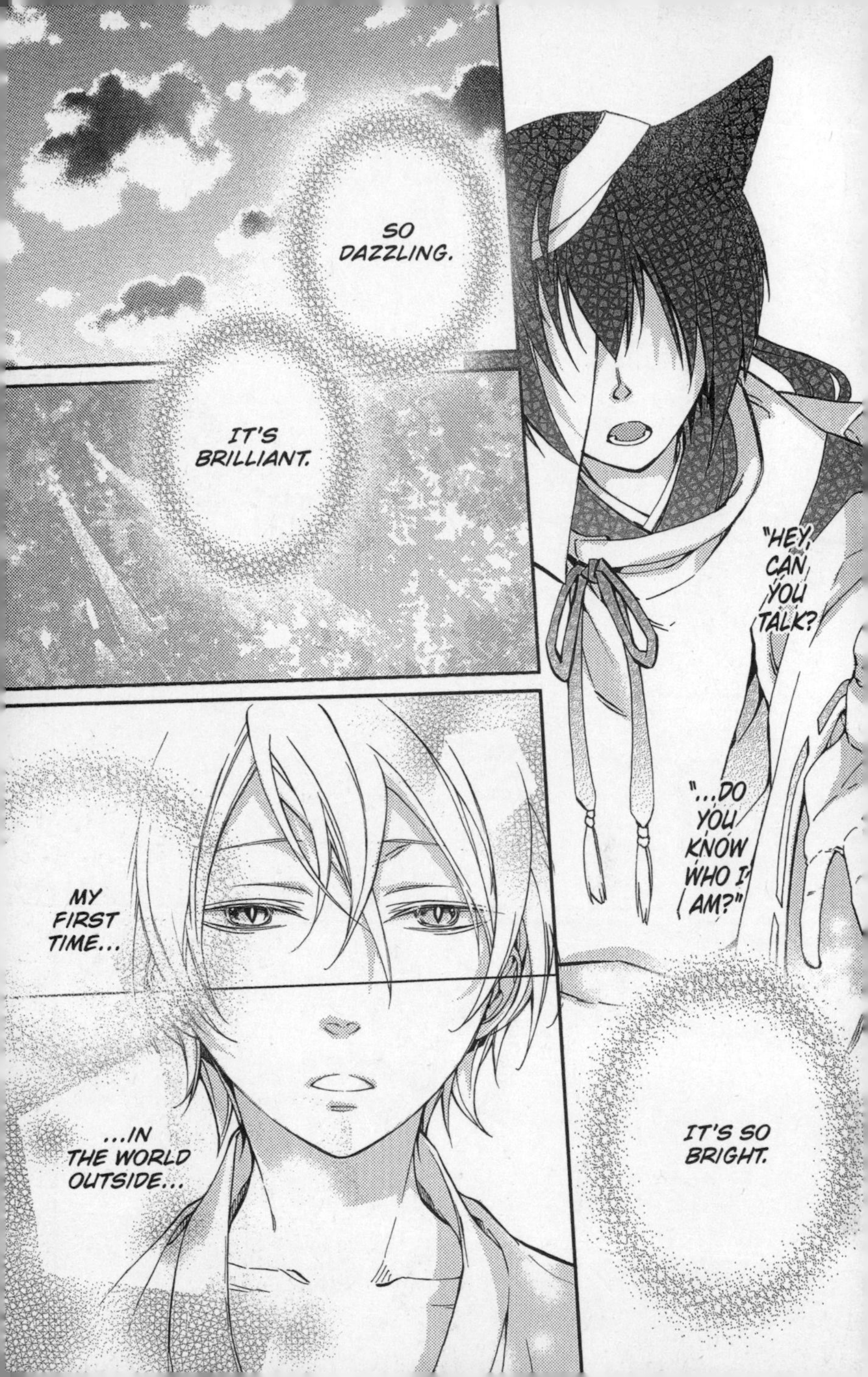
"HEY, CAN YOU TALK?
"...DO YOU KNOW WHO I AM?"
SO DAZZLING.
IT'S BRILLIANT.
IT'S SO BRIGHT.
MY FIRST TIME...
...IN THE WORLD OUTSIDE...

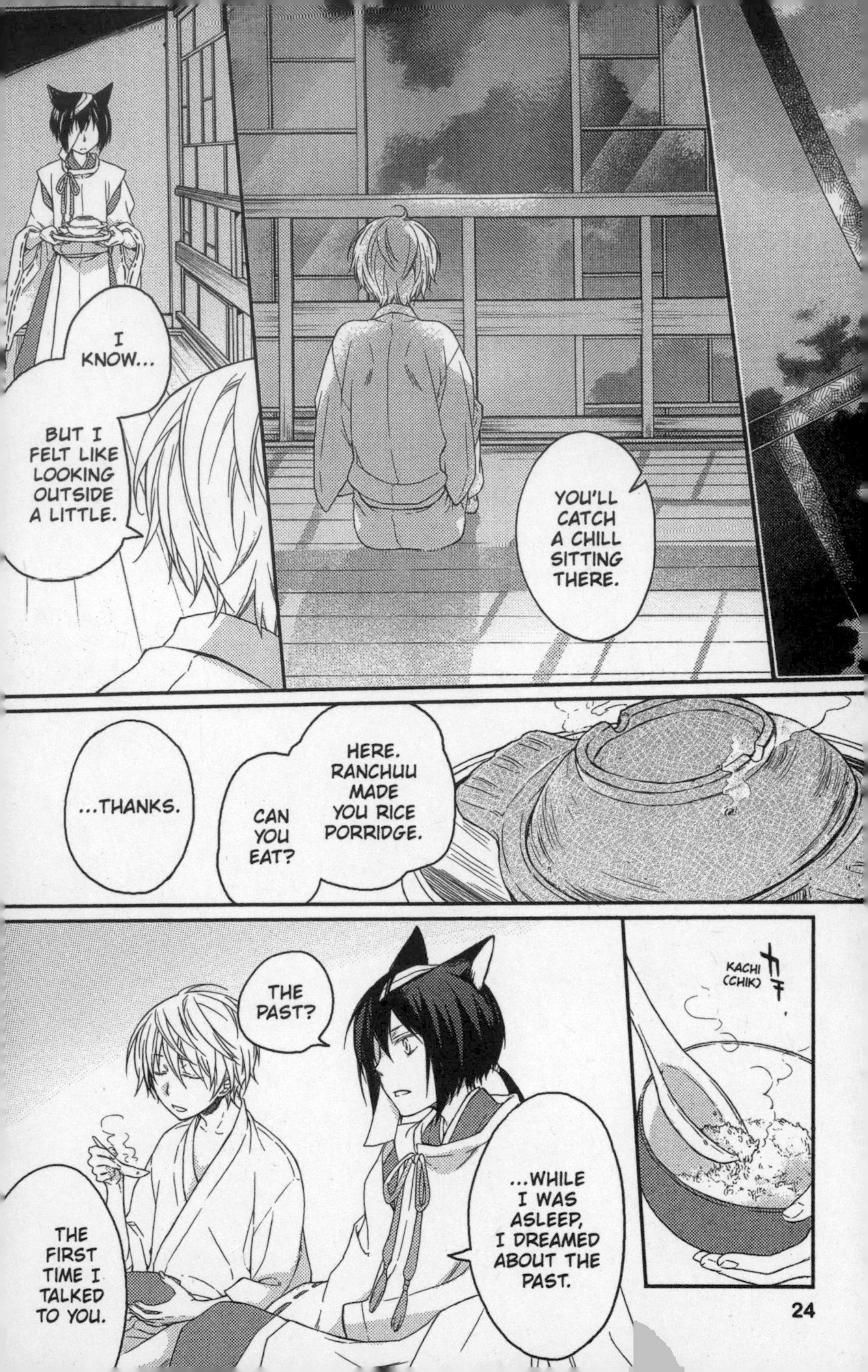
YOU'LL CATCH A CHILL SITTING THERE.
I KNOW...
BUT I FELT LIKE LOOKING OUTSIDE A LITTLE.
HERE. RANCHUU MADE YOU RICE PORRIDGE.
CAN YOU EAT?
...THANKS.
カチ
KACHI (CHIK)
...WHILE I WAS ASLEEP, I DREAMED ABOUT THE PAST.
THE PAST?
THE FIRST TIME I TALKED TO YOU.

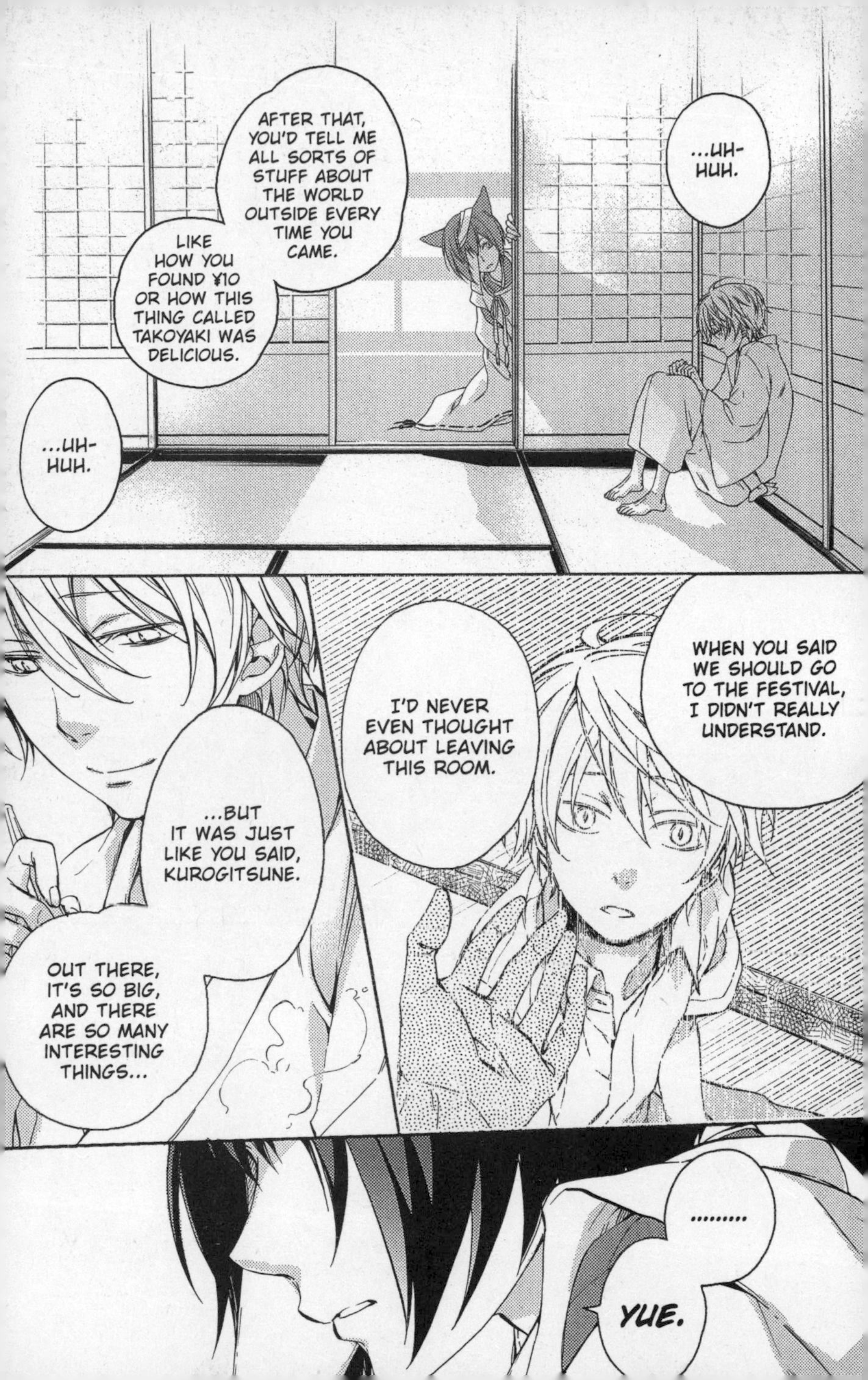
...UH-HUH.
AFTER THAT, YOU'D TELL ME ALL SORTS OF STUFF ABOUT THE WORLD OUTSIDE EVERY TIME YOU CAME.
LIKE HOW YOU FOUND ¥10 OR HOW THIS THING CALLED TAKOYAKI WAS DELICIOUS.
...UH-HUH.
WHEN YOU SAID WE SHOULD GO TO THE FESTIVAL, I DIDN'T REALLY UNDERSTAND.
I'D NEVER EVEN THOUGHT ABOUT LEAVING THIS ROOM.
...BUT IT WAS JUST LIKE YOU SAID, KUROGITSUNE.
OUT THERE, IT'S SO BIG, AND THERE ARE SO MANY INTERESTING THINGS...
....
YUE.

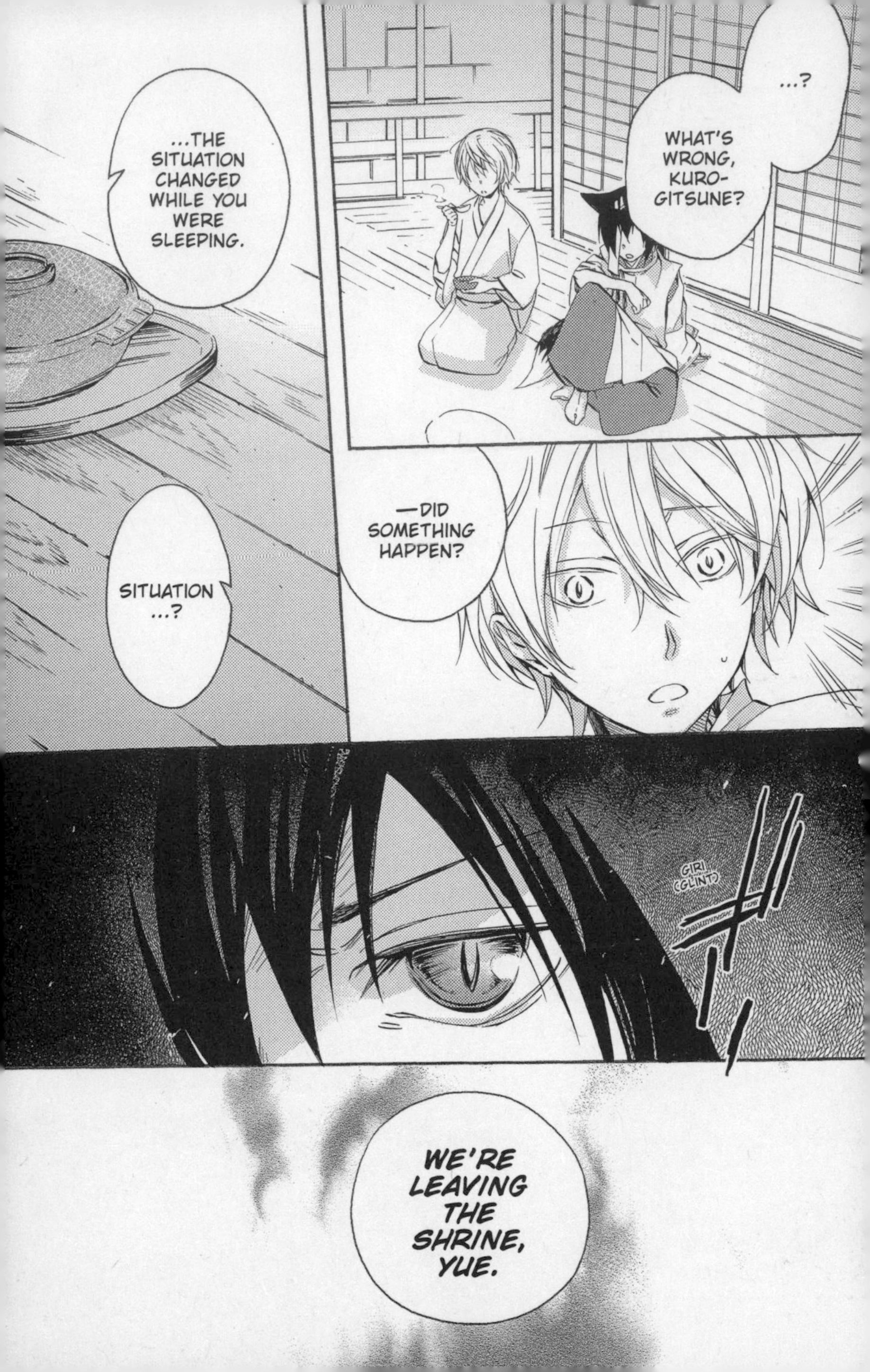
...?
WHAT'S WRONG, KURO-GITSUNE?
—DID SOMETHING HAPPEN?
...THE SITUATION CHANGED WHILE YOU WERE SLEEPING.
SITUATION ...?
GIRI (GLINT)
WE'RE LEAVING THE SHRINE, YUE.

I NEVER THOUGHT...

—HUH?

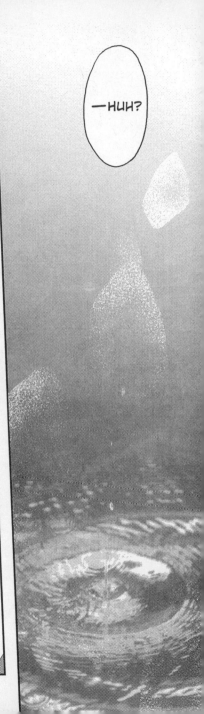

...THE DAY WOULD REALLY COME WHEN I...

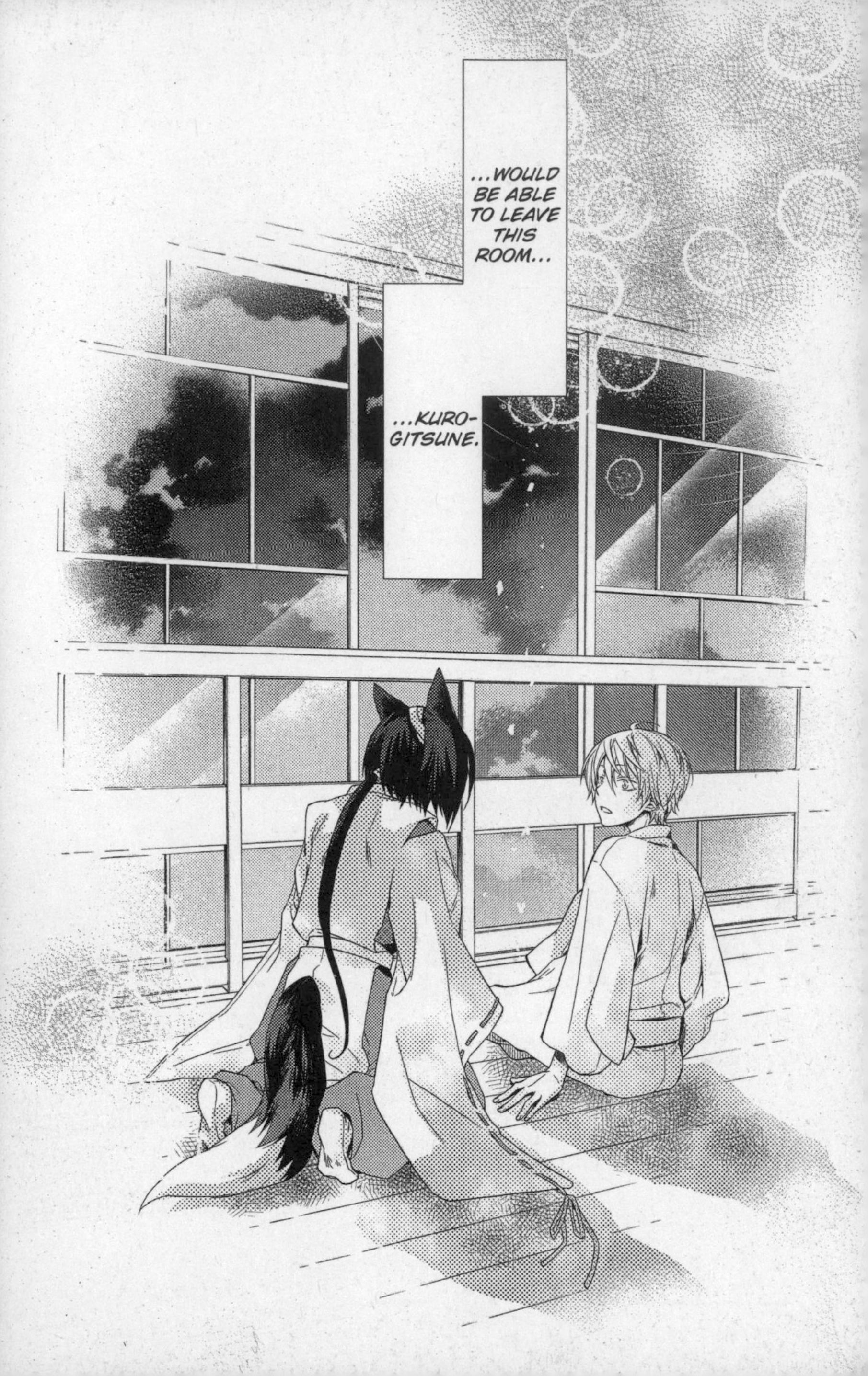
...WOULD BE ABLE TO LEAVE THIS ROOM...
...KURO-GITSUNE.

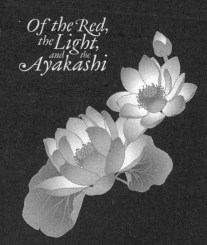

*Of the Red,
the Light,
and the
Ayakashi*

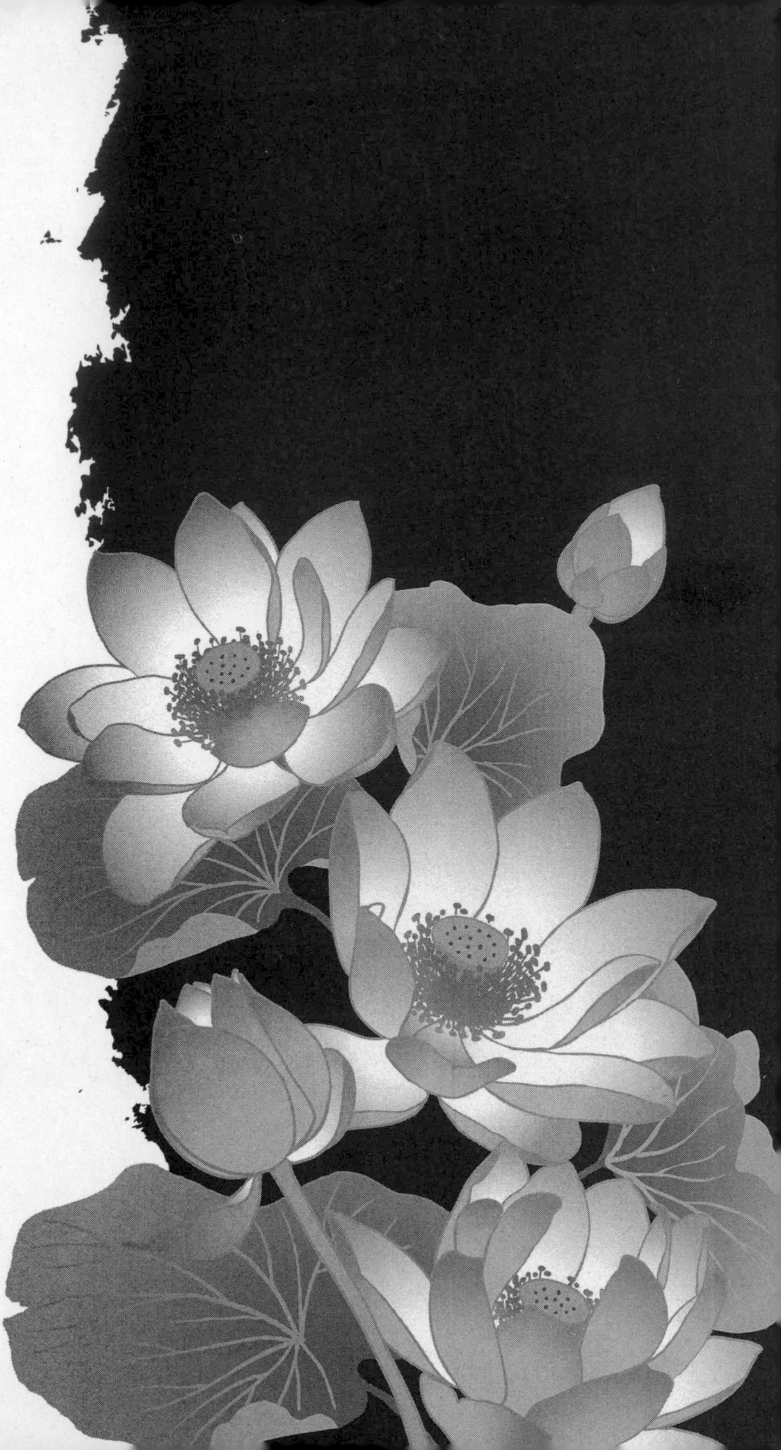

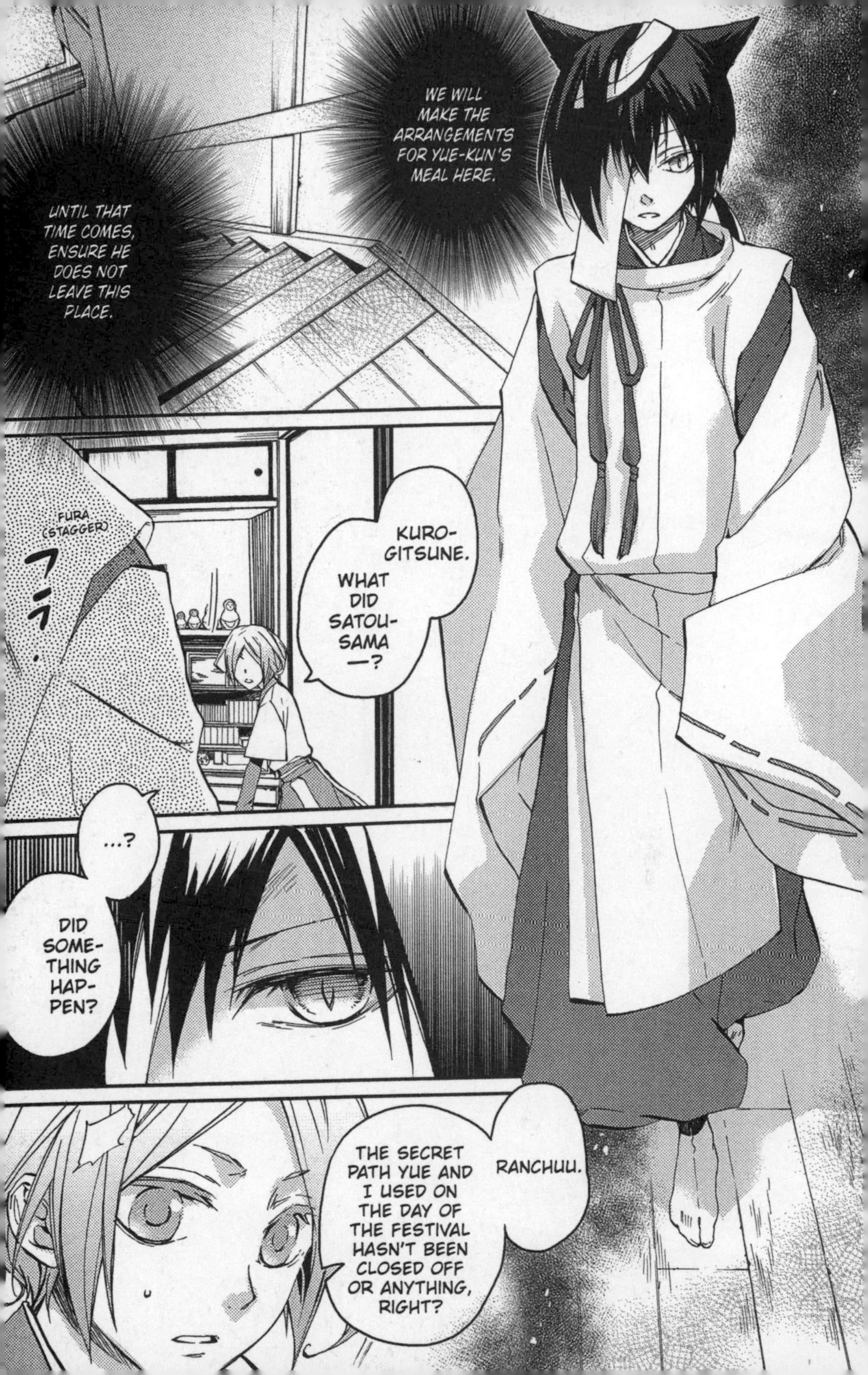
WE WILL MAKE THE ARRANGEMENTS FOR YUE-KUN'S MEAL HERE.
UNTIL THAT TIME COMES, ENSURE HE DOES NOT LEAVE THIS PLACE.
KURO-GITSUNE.
WHAT DID SATOU-SAMA—?
FURA (STAGGER)
...?
DID SOMETHING HAPPEN?
RANCHUU.
THE SECRET PATH YUE AND I USED ON THE DAY OF THE FESTIVAL HASN'T BEEN CLOSED OFF OR ANYTHING, RIGHT?

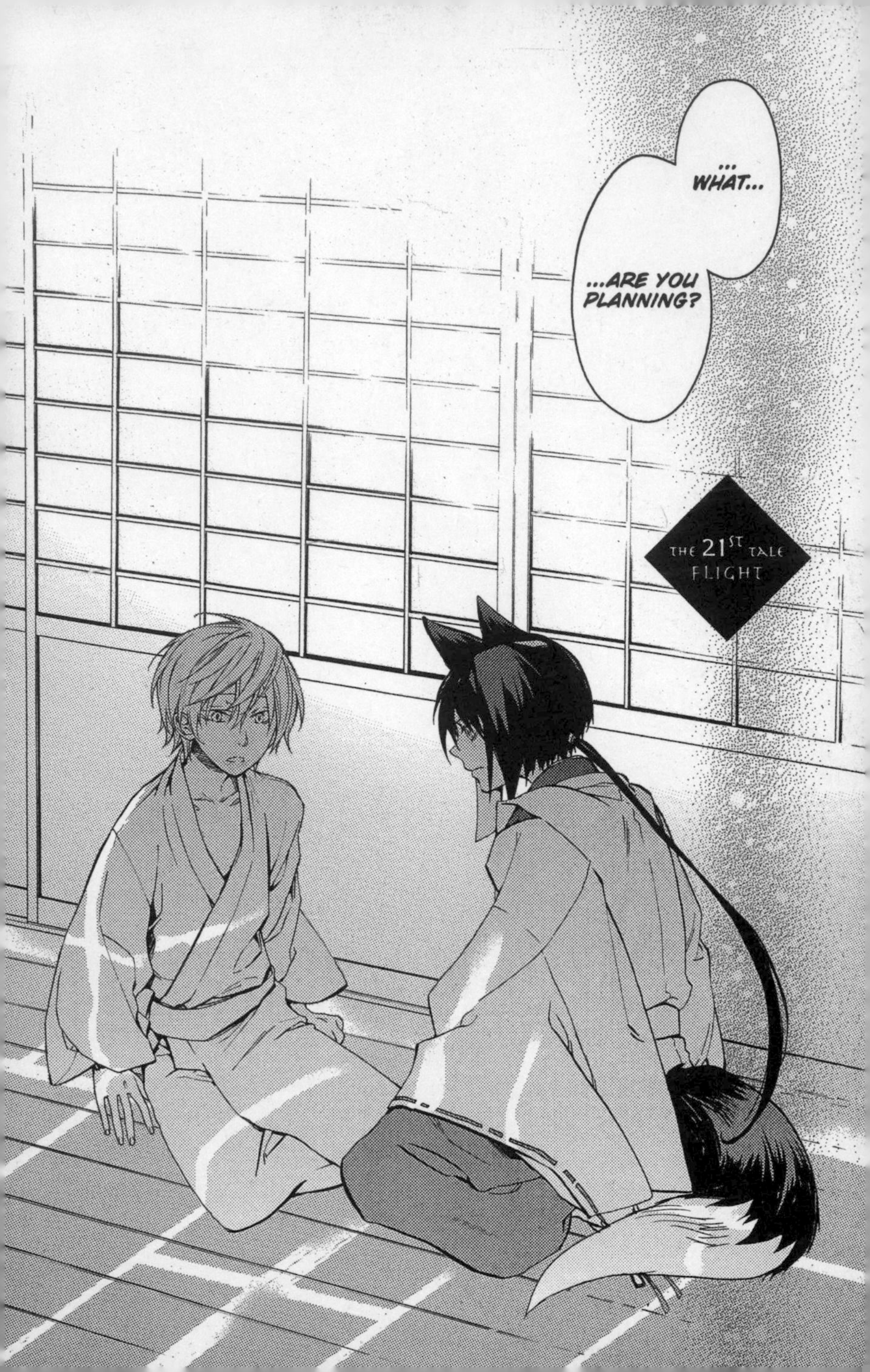
... WHAT...
...ARE YOU PLANNING?
THE 21ST TALE FLIGHT

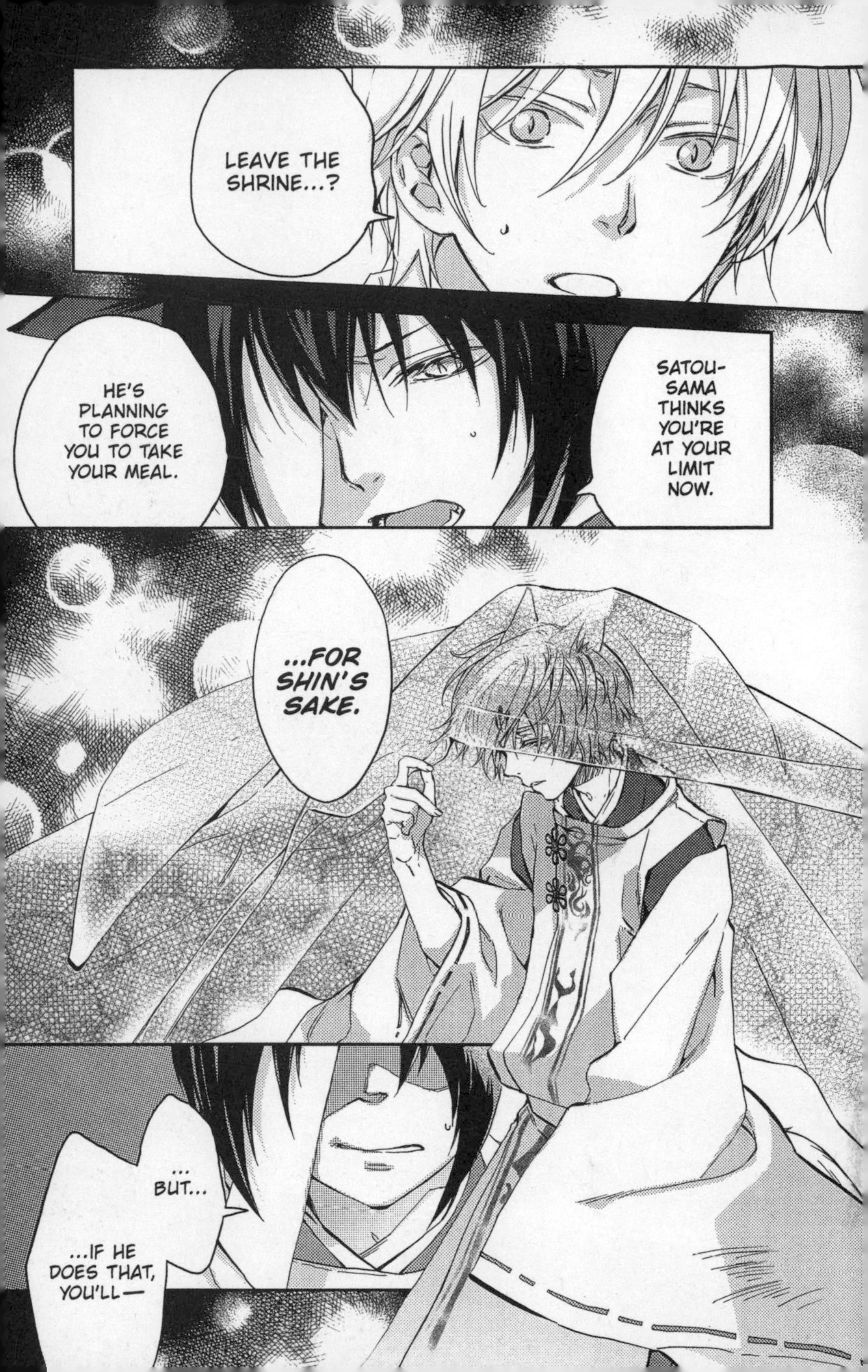
LEAVE THE SHRINE...?
SATOU-SAMA THINKS YOU'RE AT YOUR LIMIT NOW.
HE'S PLANNING TO FORCE YOU TO TAKE YOUR MEAL.
...FOR SHIN'S SAKE.
... BUT...
...IF HE DOES THAT, YOU'LL—

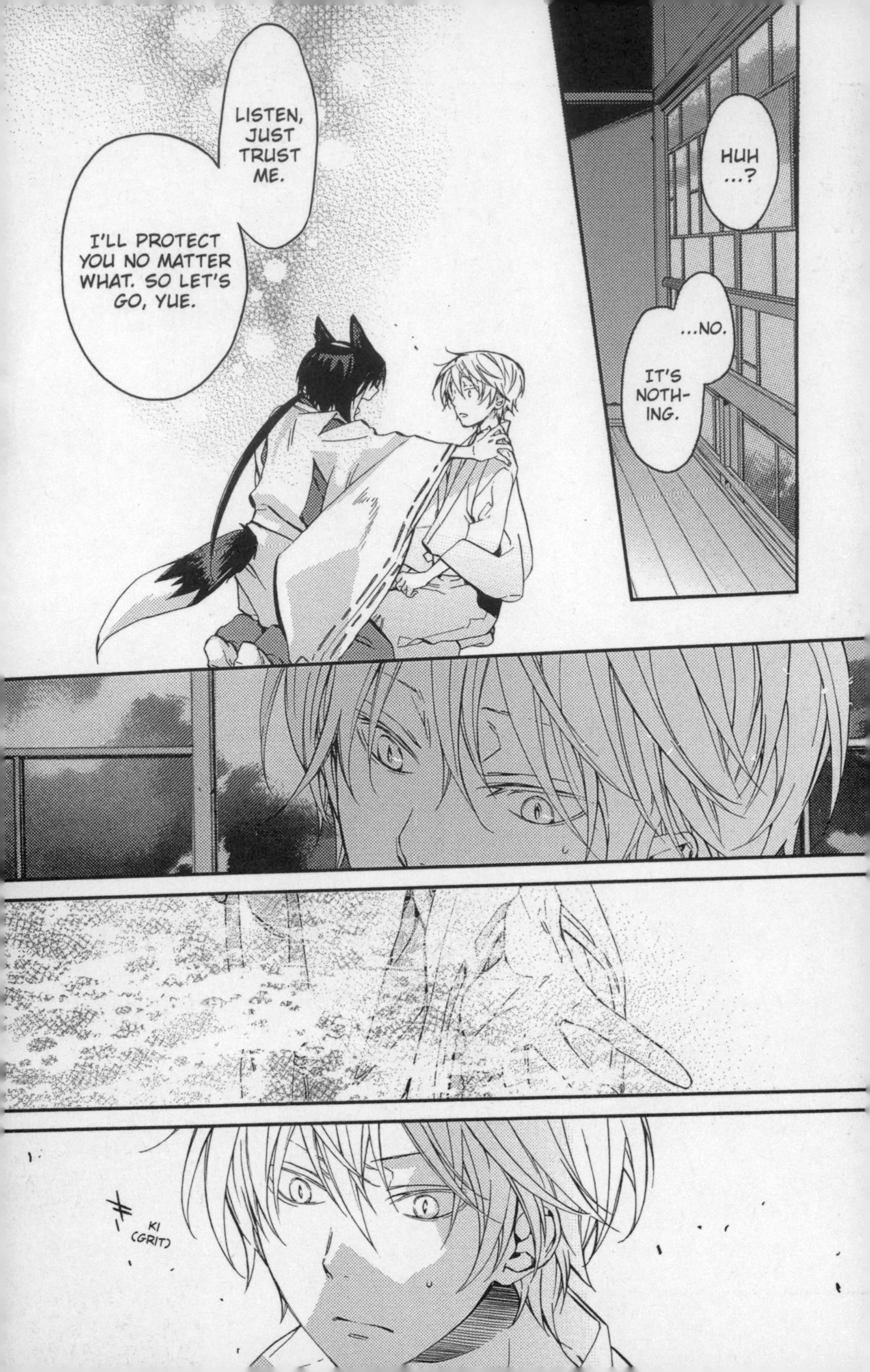
HUH ...?
...NO.
IT'S NOTHING.
LISTEN, JUST TRUST ME.
I'LL PROTECT YOU NO MATTER WHAT. SO LET'S GO, YUE.
KI (GRIT)

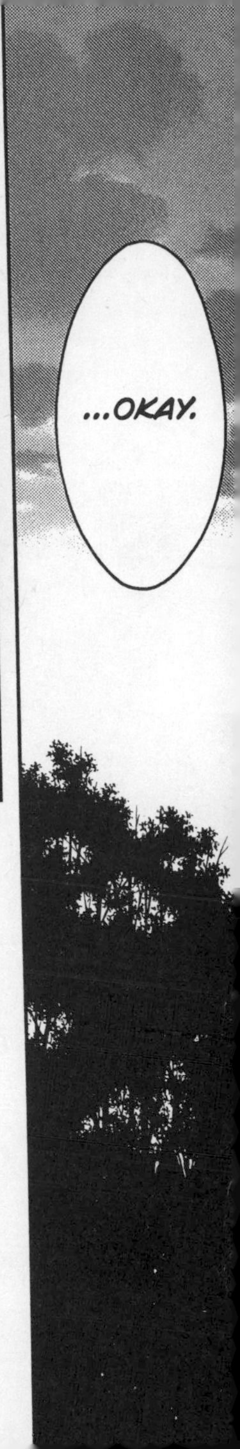
...OKAY.
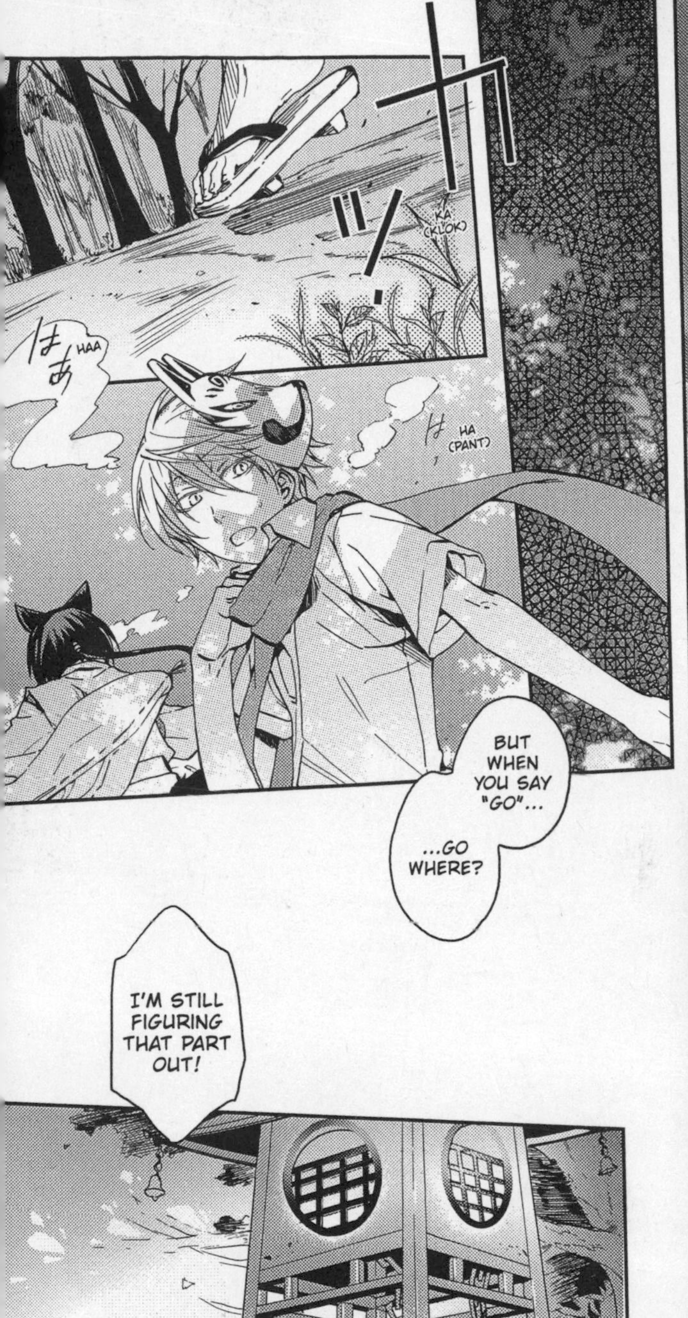
KA (KLOK)
はあ HAA
は HA (PANT)
BUT WHEN YOU SAY "GO"...
...GO WHERE?
I'M STILL FIGURING THAT PART OUT!

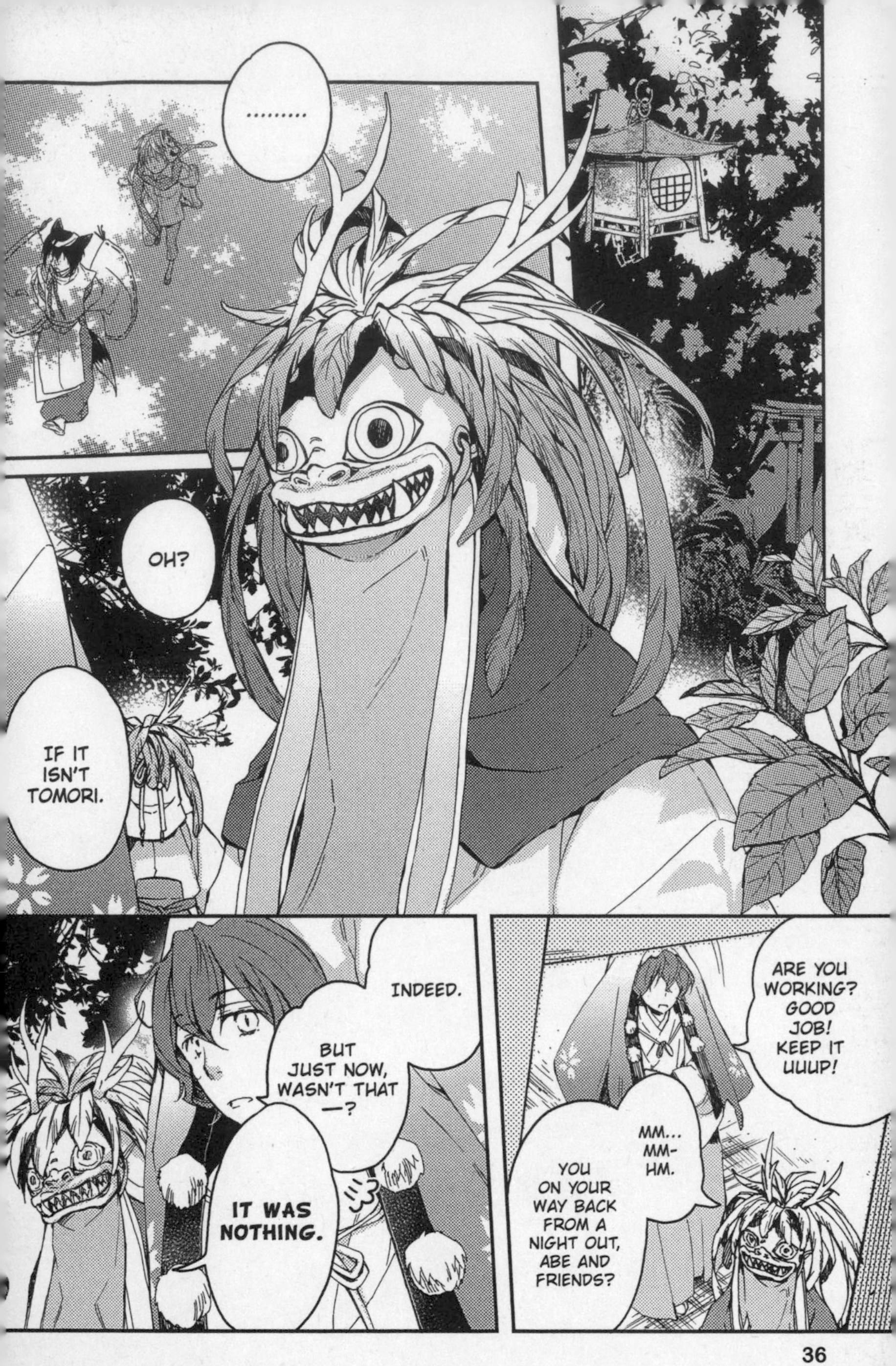
....
OH?
IF IT ISN'T TOMORI.
ARE YOU WORKING? GOOD JOB! KEEP IT UUUP!
MM... MM-HM.
YOU ON YOUR WAY BACK FROM A NIGHT OUT, ABE AND FRIENDS?
INDEED.
BUT JUST NOW, WASN'T THAT —?
IT WAS NOTHING.

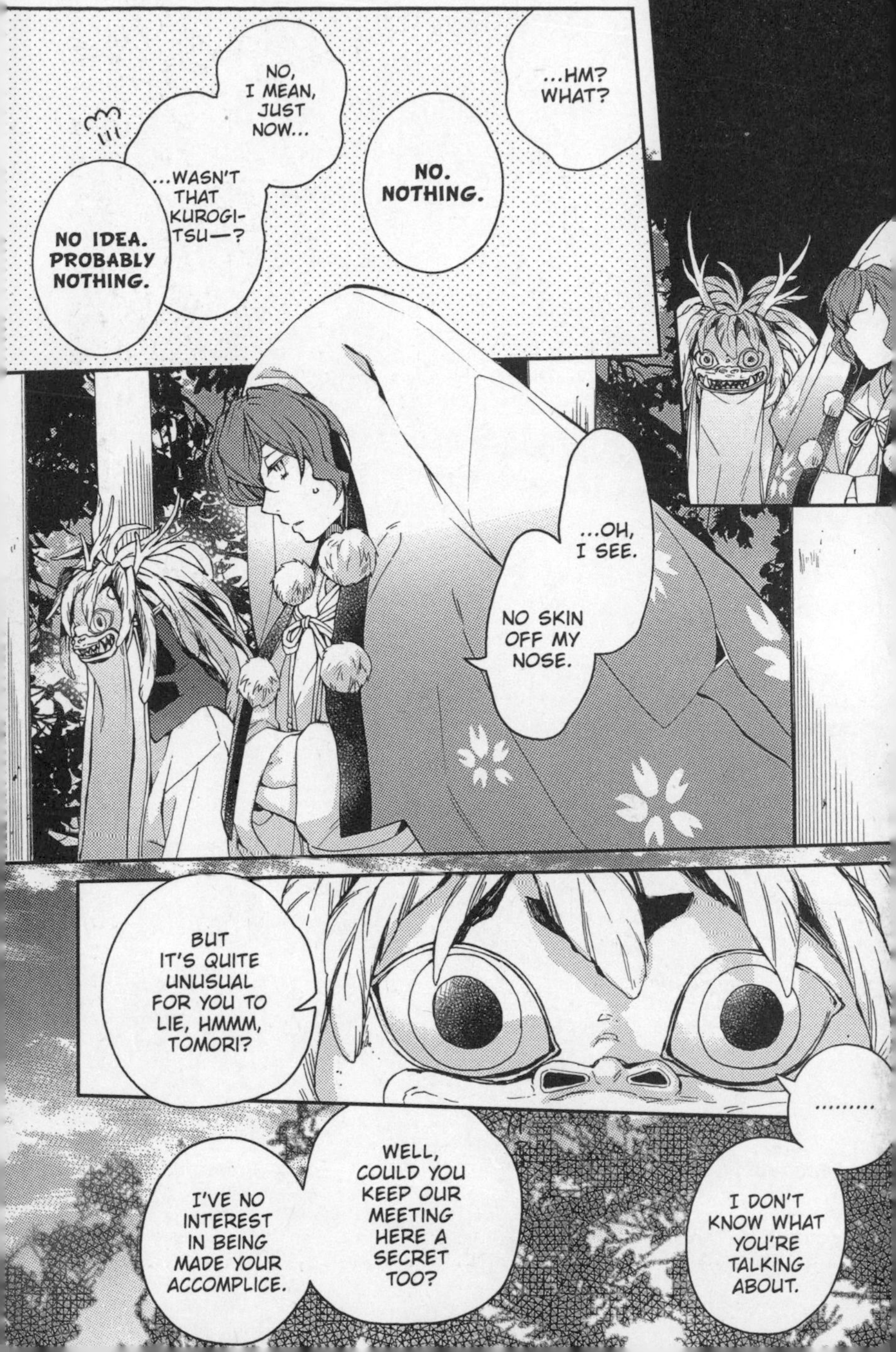
...HM? WHAT?
NO. NOTHING.
NO, I MEAN, JUST NOW...
...WASN'T THAT KUROGI-TSU—?
NO IDEA. PROBABLY NOTHING.
...OH, I SEE.
NO SKIN OFF MY NOSE.
BUT IT'S QUITE UNUSUAL FOR YOU TO LIE, HMMM, TOMORI?
....
I DON'T KNOW WHAT YOU'RE TALKING ABOUT.
WELL, COULD YOU KEEP OUR MEETING HERE A SECRET TOO?
I'VE NO INTEREST IN BEING MADE YOUR ACCOMPLICE.

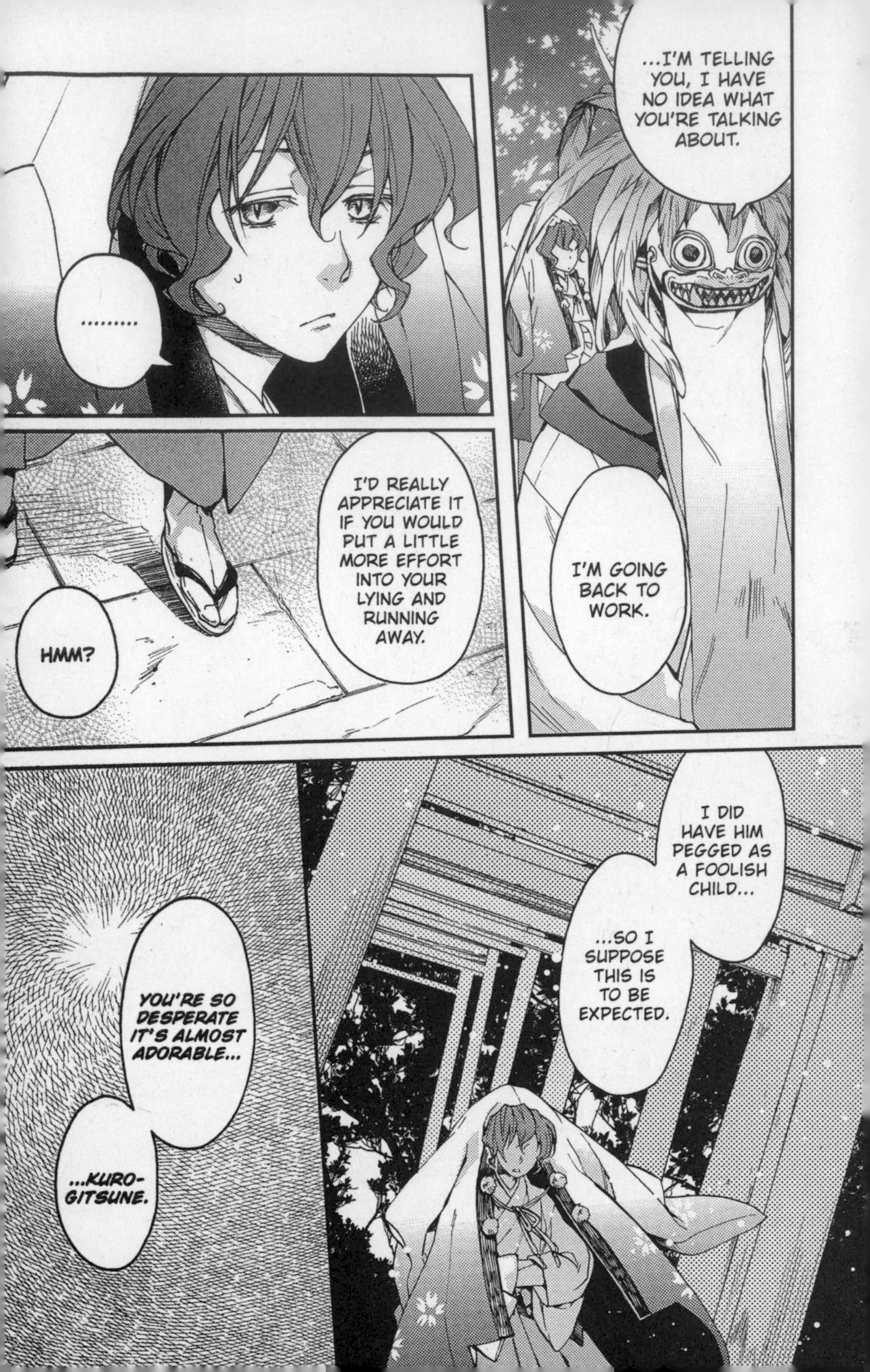
...I'M TELLING YOU, I HAVE NO IDEA WHAT YOU'RE TALKING ABOUT.
I'M GOING BACK TO WORK.
....
I'D REALLY APPRECIATE IT IF YOU WOULD PUT A LITTLE MORE EFFORT INTO YOUR LYING AND RUNNING AWAY.
HMM?
I DID HAVE HIM PEGGED AS A FOOLISH CHILD...
...SO I SUPPOSE THIS IS TO BE EXPECTED.
YOU'RE SO DESPERATE IT'S ALMOST ADORABLE...
...KURO-GITSUNE.

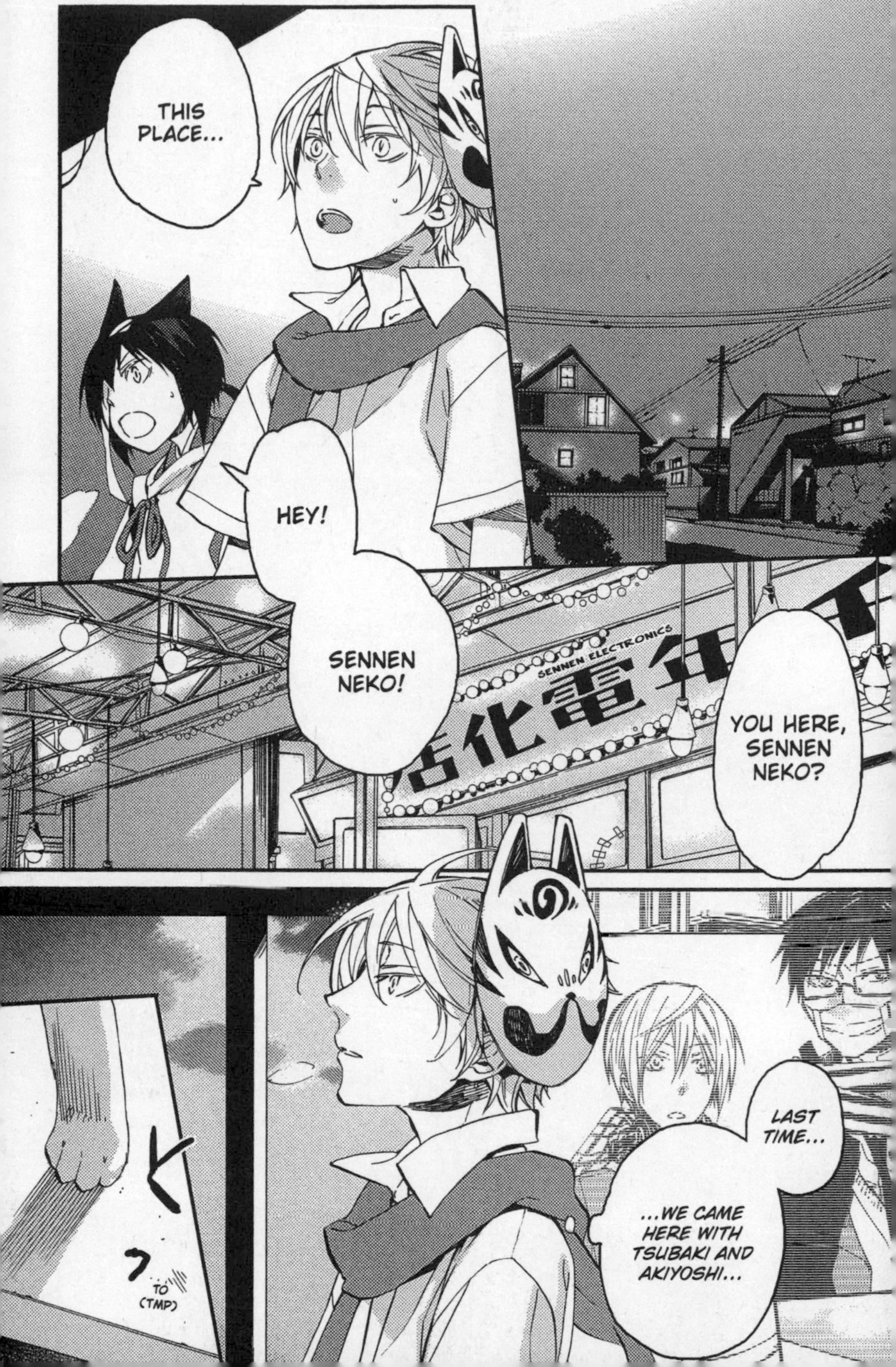
THIS PLACE...
HEY!
SENNEN NEKO!
SENNEN ELECTRONICS
YOU HERE, SENNEN NEKO?
LAST TIME...
...WE CAME HERE WITH TSUBAKI AND AKIYOSHI...
TO (TMP)

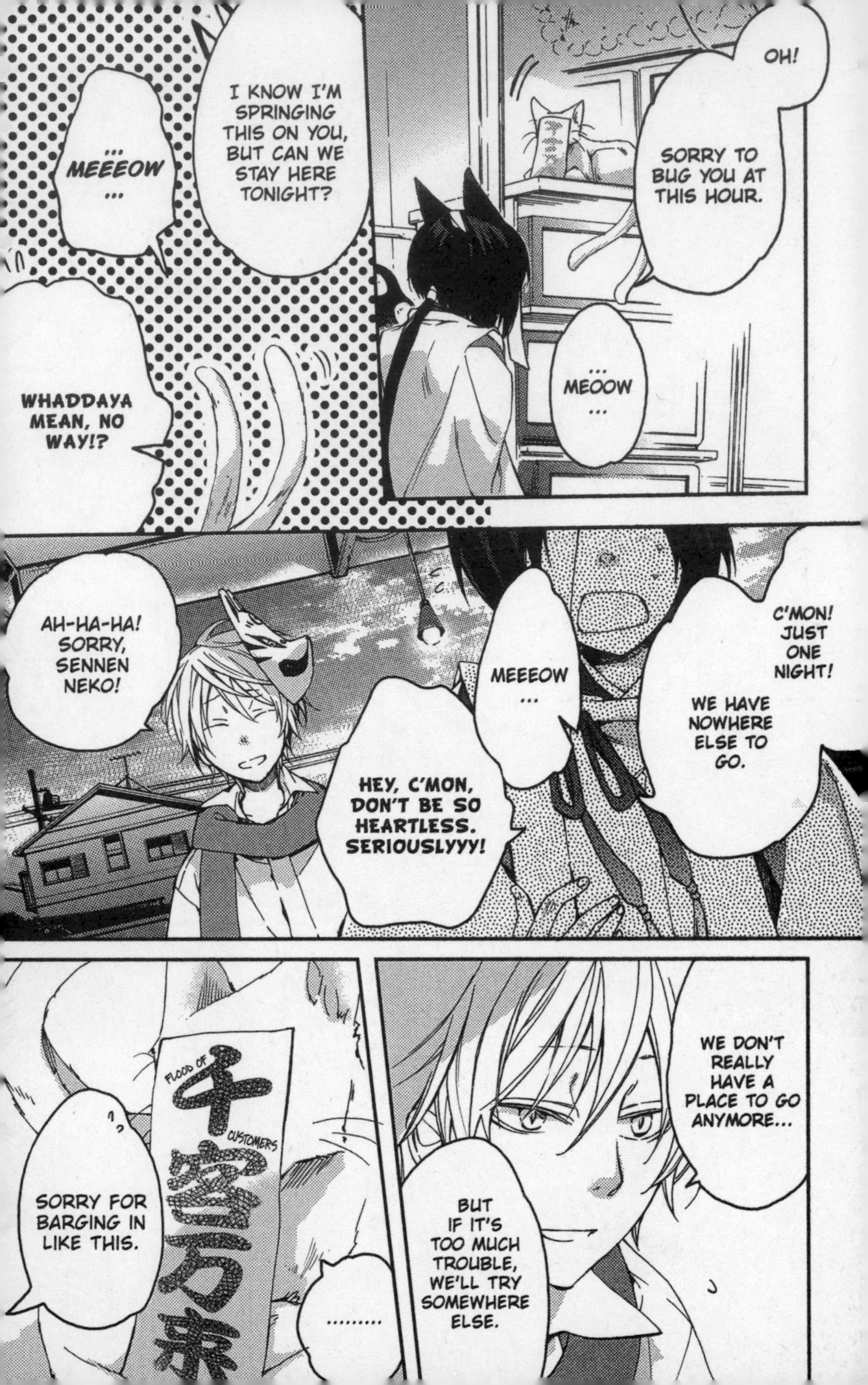
OH!
SORRY TO BUG YOU AT THIS HOUR.
... MEOOW ...
I KNOW I'M SPRINGING THIS ON YOU, BUT CAN WE STAY HERE TONIGHT?
... MEEEOW ...
WHADDAYA MEAN, NO WAY!?
C'MON! JUST ONE NIGHT!
WE HAVE NOWHERE ELSE TO GO.
MEEEOW ...
HEY, C'MON, DON'T BE SO HEARTLESS. SERIOUSLYYY!
AH-HA-HA! SORRY, SENNEN NEKO!
WE DON'T REALLY HAVE A PLACE TO GO ANYMORE...
BUT IF IT'S TOO MUCH TROUBLE, WE'LL TRY SOMEWHERE ELSE.
FLOOD OF
CUSTOMERS
....
SORRY FOR BARGING IN LIKE THIS.

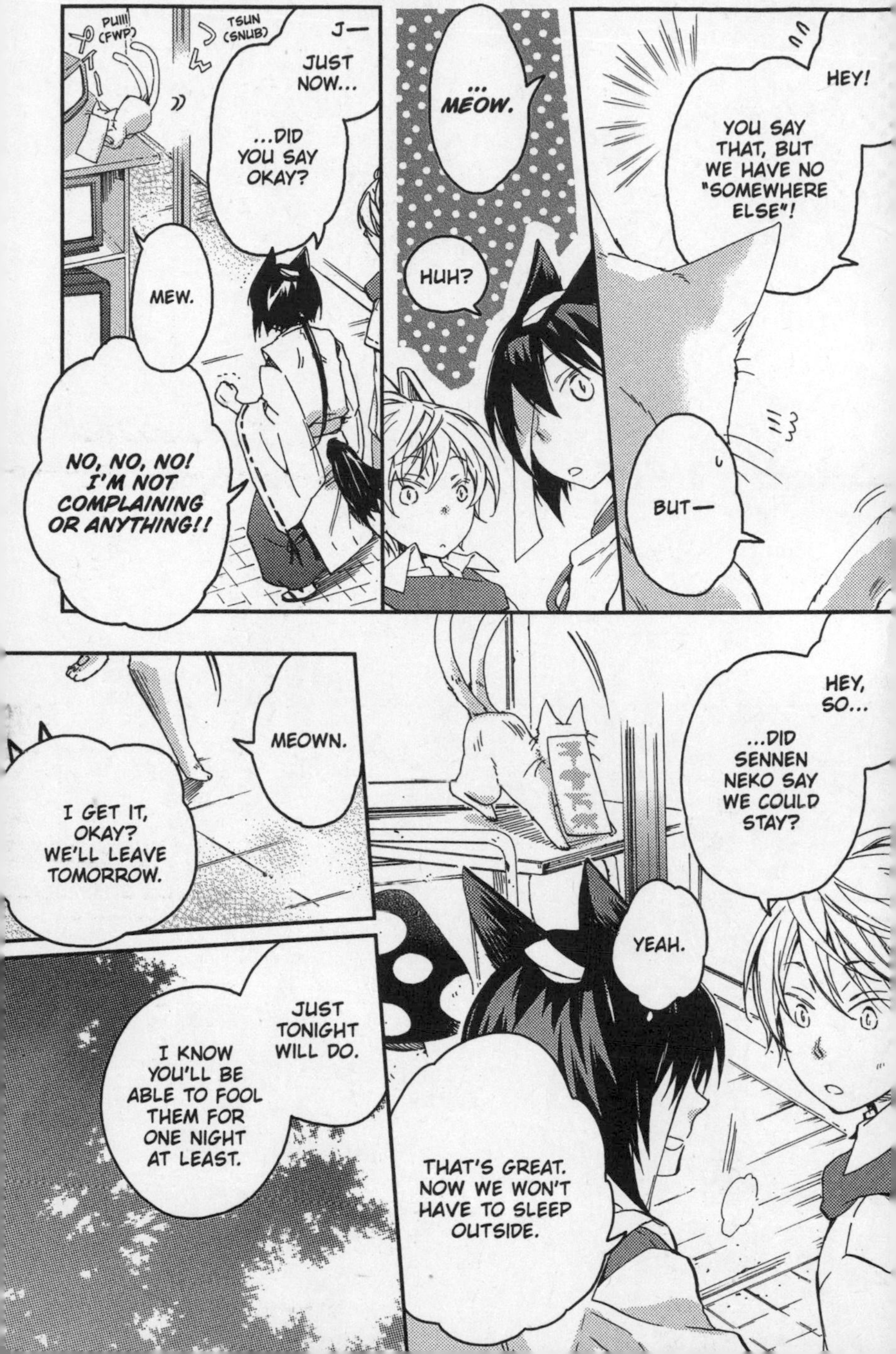
HEY!
YOU SAY THAT, BUT WE HAVE NO "SOMEWHERE ELSE"!
BUT—
...MEOW.
HUH?
J— JUST NOW...
...DID YOU SAY OKAY?
TSUN (SNUB)
PUIII (FWP)
MEW.
NO, NO, NO! I'M NOT COMPLAINING OR ANYTHING!!
HEY, SO...
...DID SENNEN NEKO SAY WE COULD STAY?
YEAH.
THAT'S GREAT. NOW WE WON'T HAVE TO SLEEP OUTSIDE.
MEOWN.
I GET IT, OKAY? WE'LL LEAVE TOMORROW.
JUST TONIGHT WILL DO.
I KNOW YOU'LL BE ABLE TO FOOL THEM FOR ONE NIGHT AT LEAST.

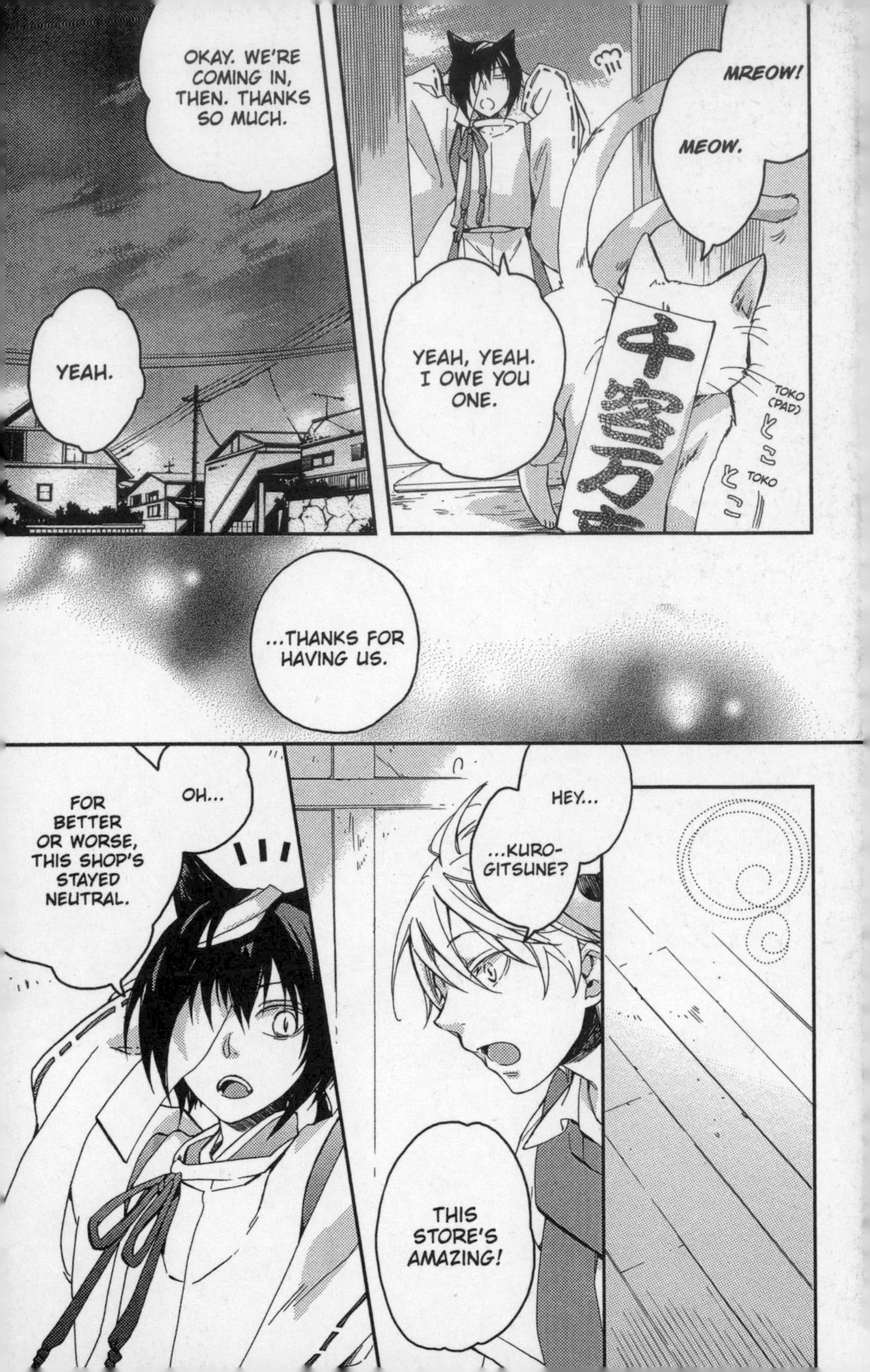
MREOW!
MEOW.
YEAH, YEAH. I OWE YOU ONE.
TOKO (PAD)
とこ
TOKO
とこ
OKAY. WE'RE COMING IN, THEN. THANKS SO MUCH.
YEAH.
...THANKS FOR HAVING US.
HEY...
...KURO-GITSUNE?
THIS STORE'S AMAZING!
OH...
FOR BETTER OR WORSE, THIS SHOP'S STAYED NEUTRAL.

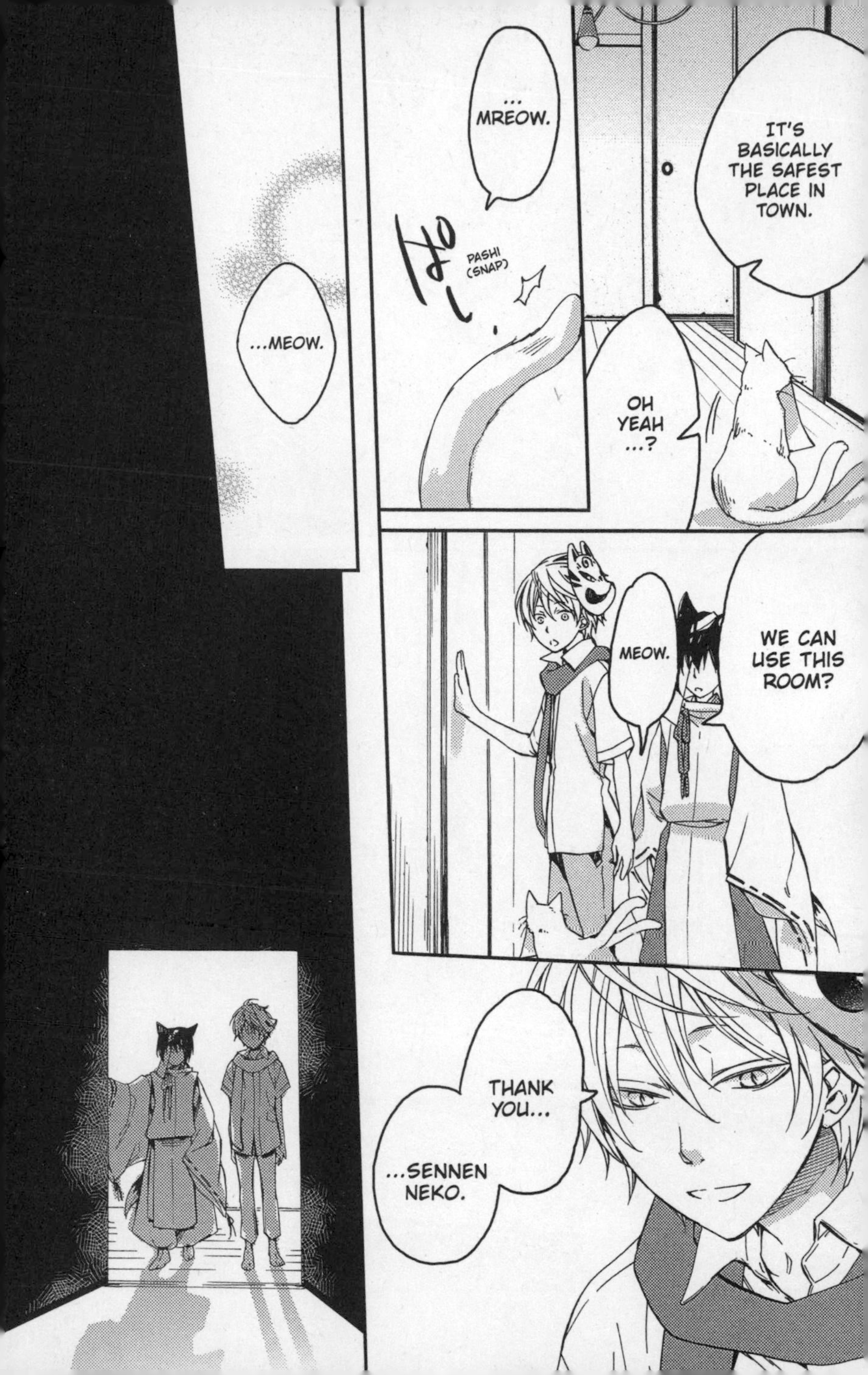
IT'S BASICALLY THE SAFEST PLACE IN TOWN.
OH YEAH ...?
... MREOW.
PASHI (SNAP)
WE CAN USE THIS ROOM?
MEOW.
THANK YOU...
...SENNEN NEKO.
...MEOW.

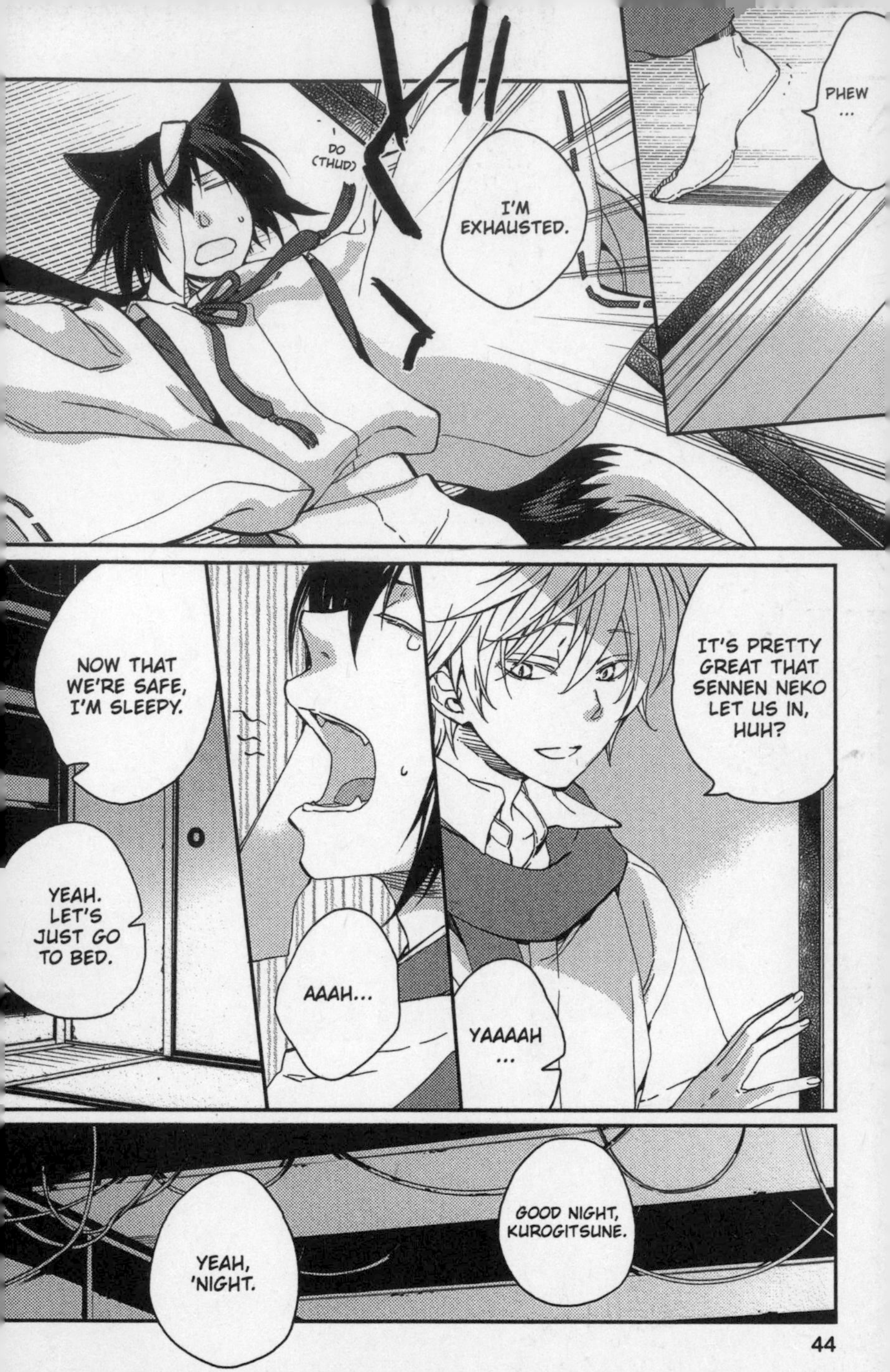
PHEW ...
I'M EXHAUSTED.
DO (THUD)
IT'S PRETTY GREAT THAT SENNEN NEKO LET US IN, HUH?
YAAAAH ...
AAAH...
NOW THAT WE'RE SAFE, I'M SLEEPY.
YEAH. LET'S JUST GO TO BED.
GOOD NIGHT, KUROGITSUNE.
YEAH, 'NIGHT.

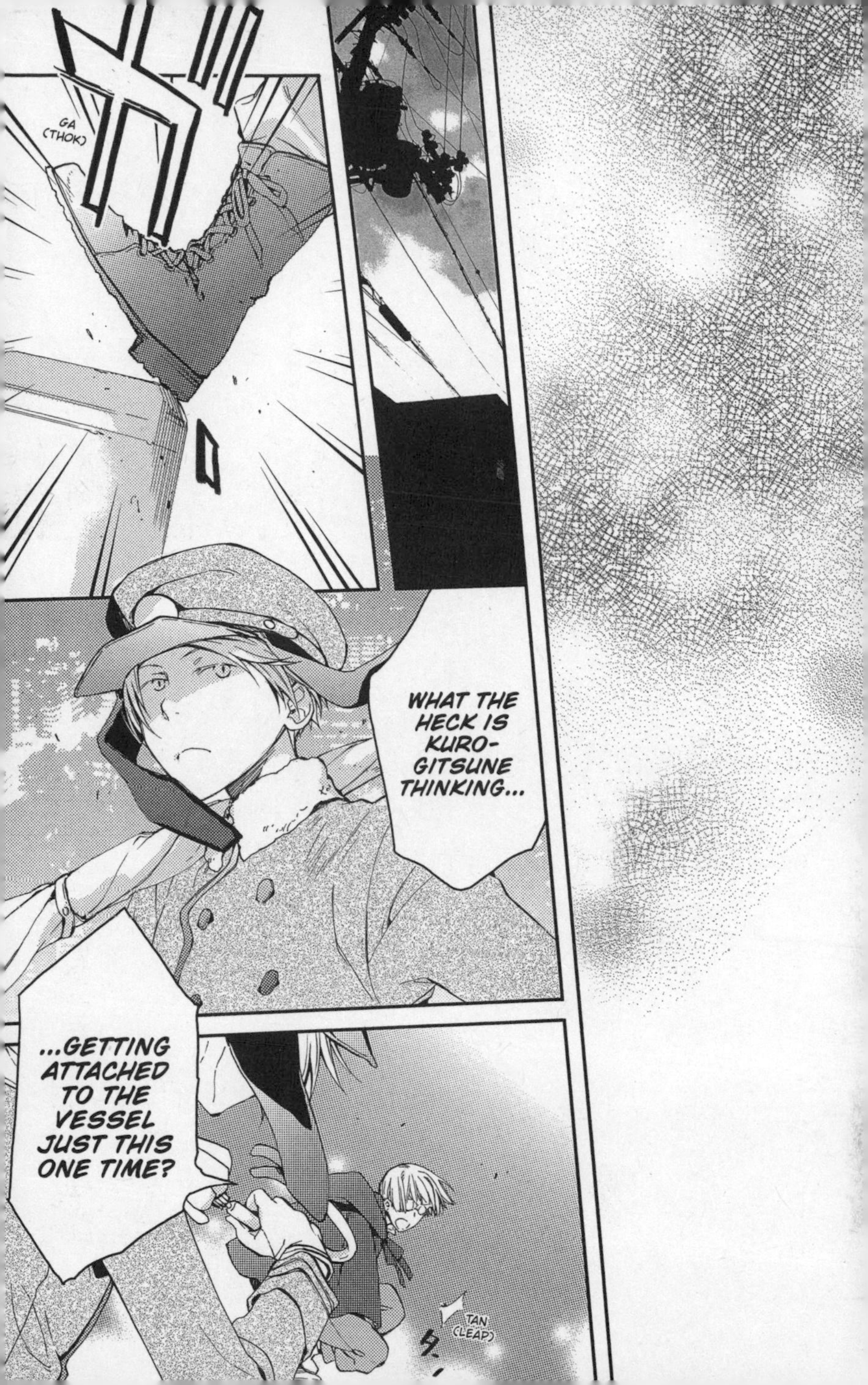
GA (THOK)
WHAT THE HECK IS KURO-GITSUNE THINKING...
...GETTING ATTACHED TO THE VESSEL JUST THIS ONE TIME?
TAN (LEAP)

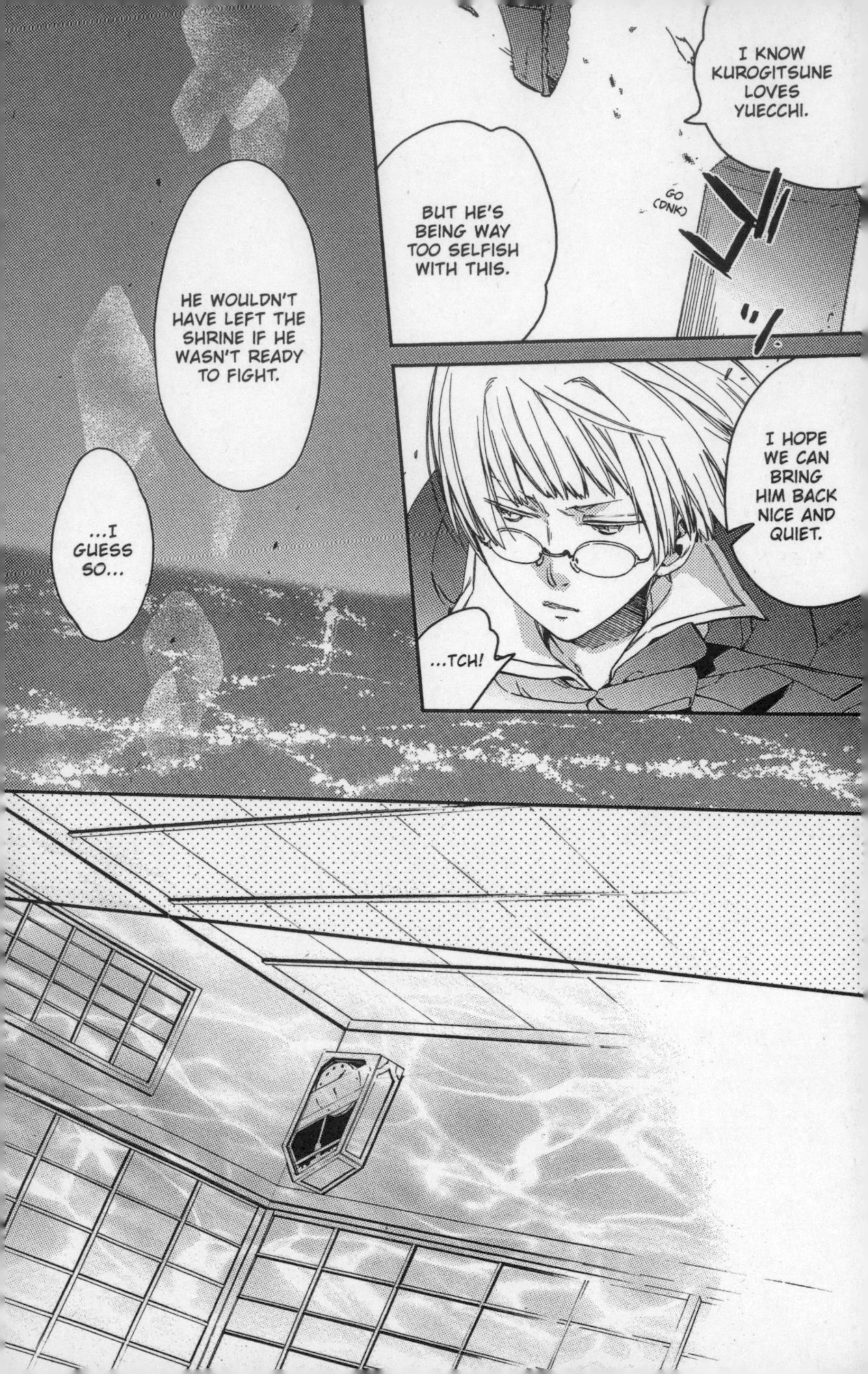
I KNOW KUROGITSUNE LOVES YUECCHI.
GO (DNK)
BUT HE'S BEING WAY TOO SELFISH WITH THIS.
I HOPE WE CAN BRING HIM BACK NICE AND QUIET.
...TCH!
HE WOULDN'T HAVE LEFT THE SHRINE IF HE WASN'T READY TO FIGHT.
...I GUESS SO...

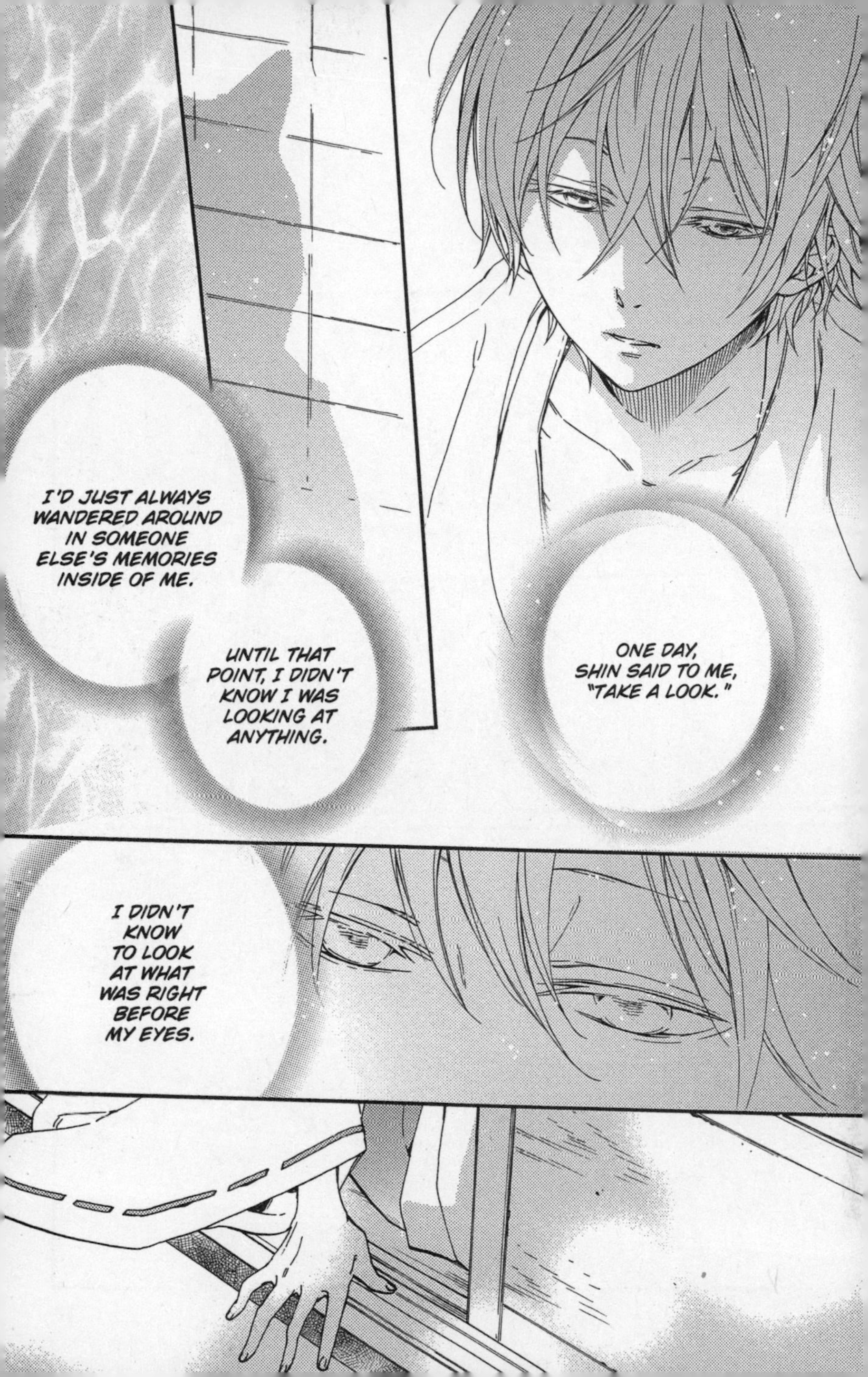
ONE DAY, SHIN SAID TO ME, "TAKE A LOOK."
UNTIL THAT POINT, I DIDN'T KNOW I WAS LOOKING AT ANYTHING.
I'D JUST ALWAYS WANDERED AROUND IN SOMEONE ELSE'S MEMORIES INSIDE OF ME.
I DIDN'T KNOW TO LOOK AT WHAT WAS RIGHT BEFORE MY EYES.

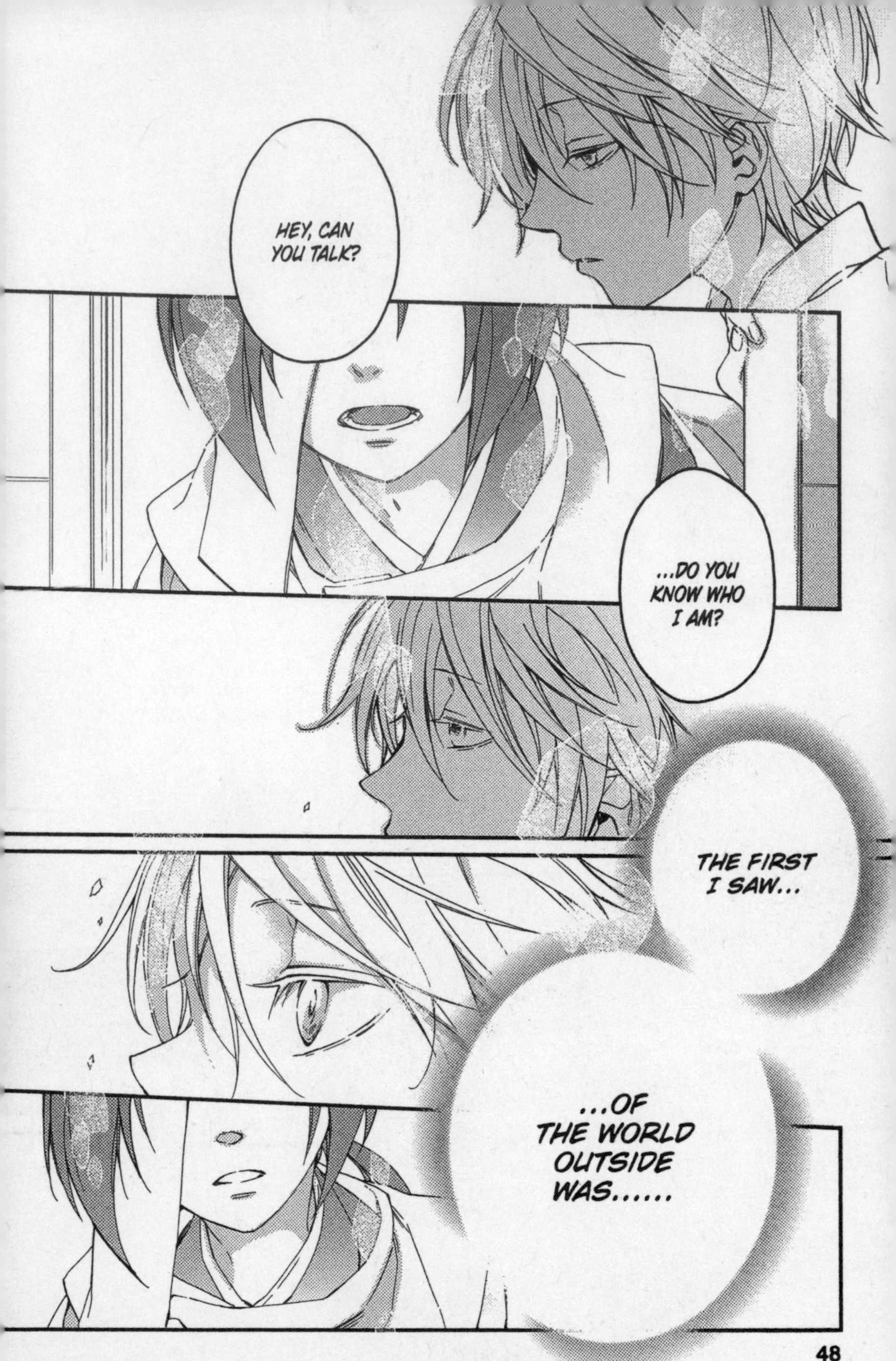
HEY, CAN YOU TALK?
...DO YOU KNOW WHO I AM?
THE FIRST I SAW...
...OF THE WORLD OUTSIDE WAS......

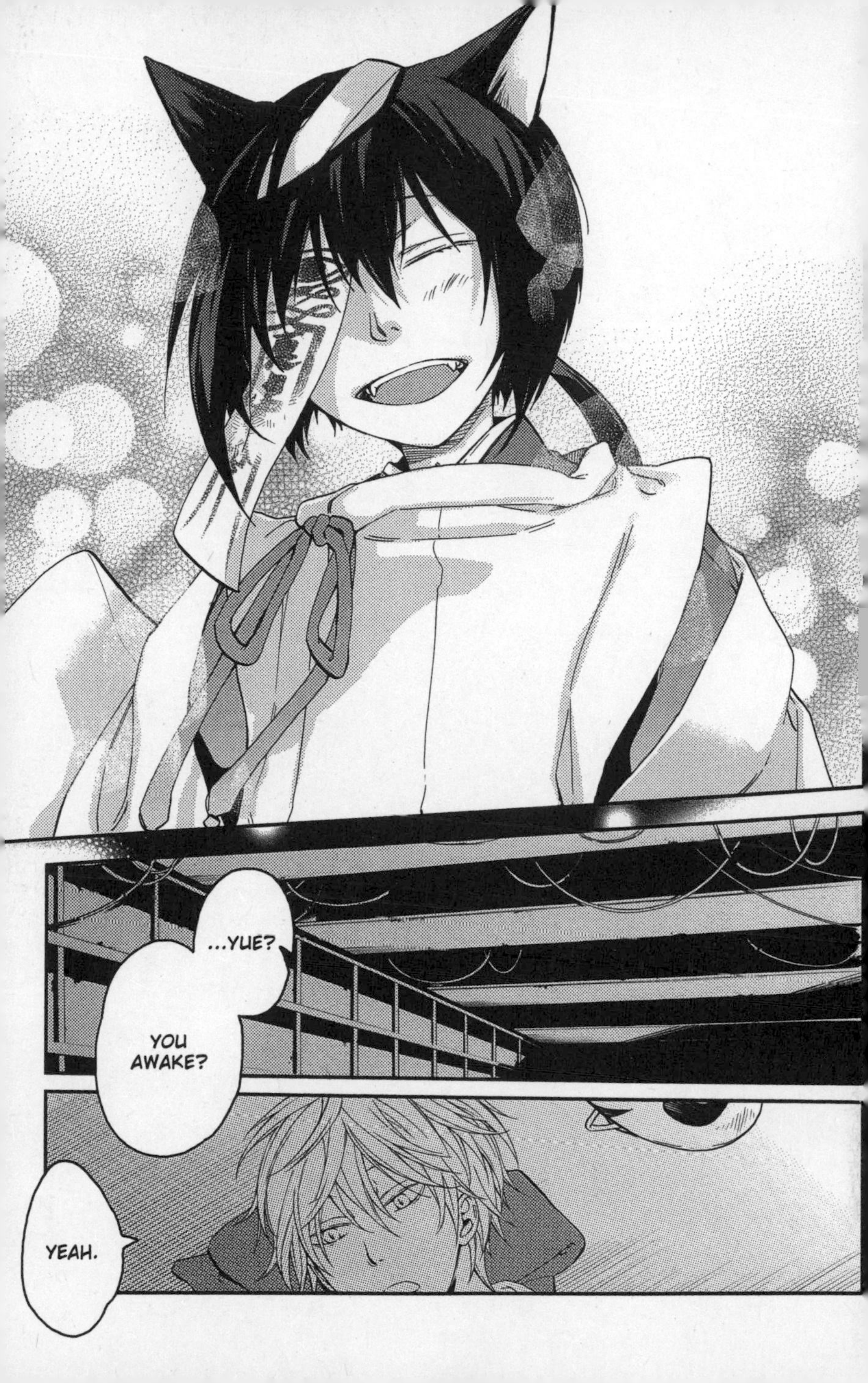
...YUE?
YOU AWAKE?
YEAH.

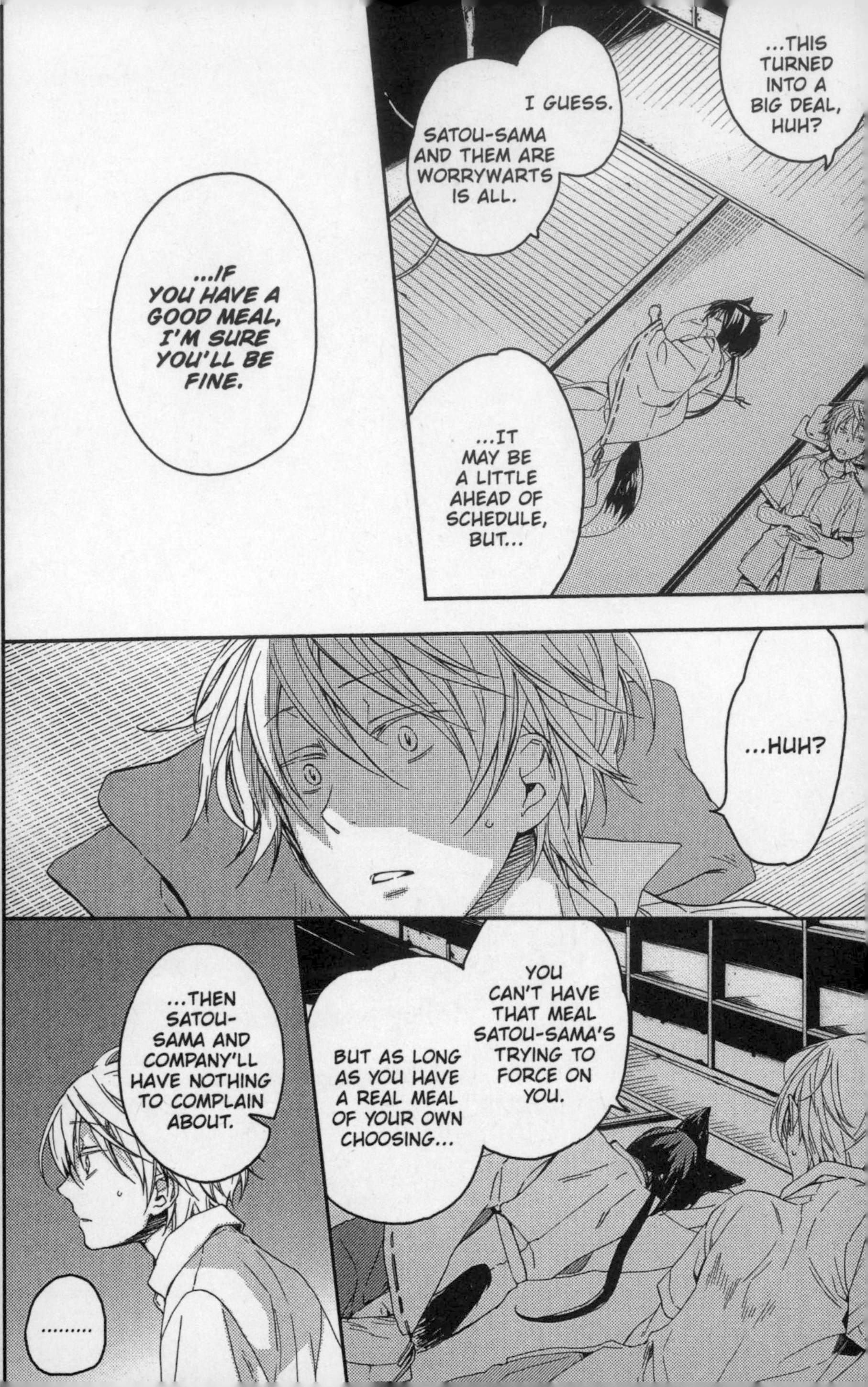
...THIS TURNED INTO A BIG DEAL, HUH?
I GUESS. SATOU-SAMA AND THEM ARE WORRYWARTS IS ALL.
...IT MAY BE A LITTLE AHEAD OF SCHEDULE, BUT...
...IF YOU HAVE A GOOD MEAL, I'M SURE YOU'LL BE FINE.
...HUH?
YOU CAN'T HAVE THAT MEAL SATOU-SAMA'S TRYING TO FORCE ON YOU.
BUT AS LONG AS YOU HAVE A REAL MEAL OF YOUR OWN CHOOSING...
...THEN SATOU-SAMA AND COMPANY'LL HAVE NOTHING TO COMPLAIN ABOUT.
....

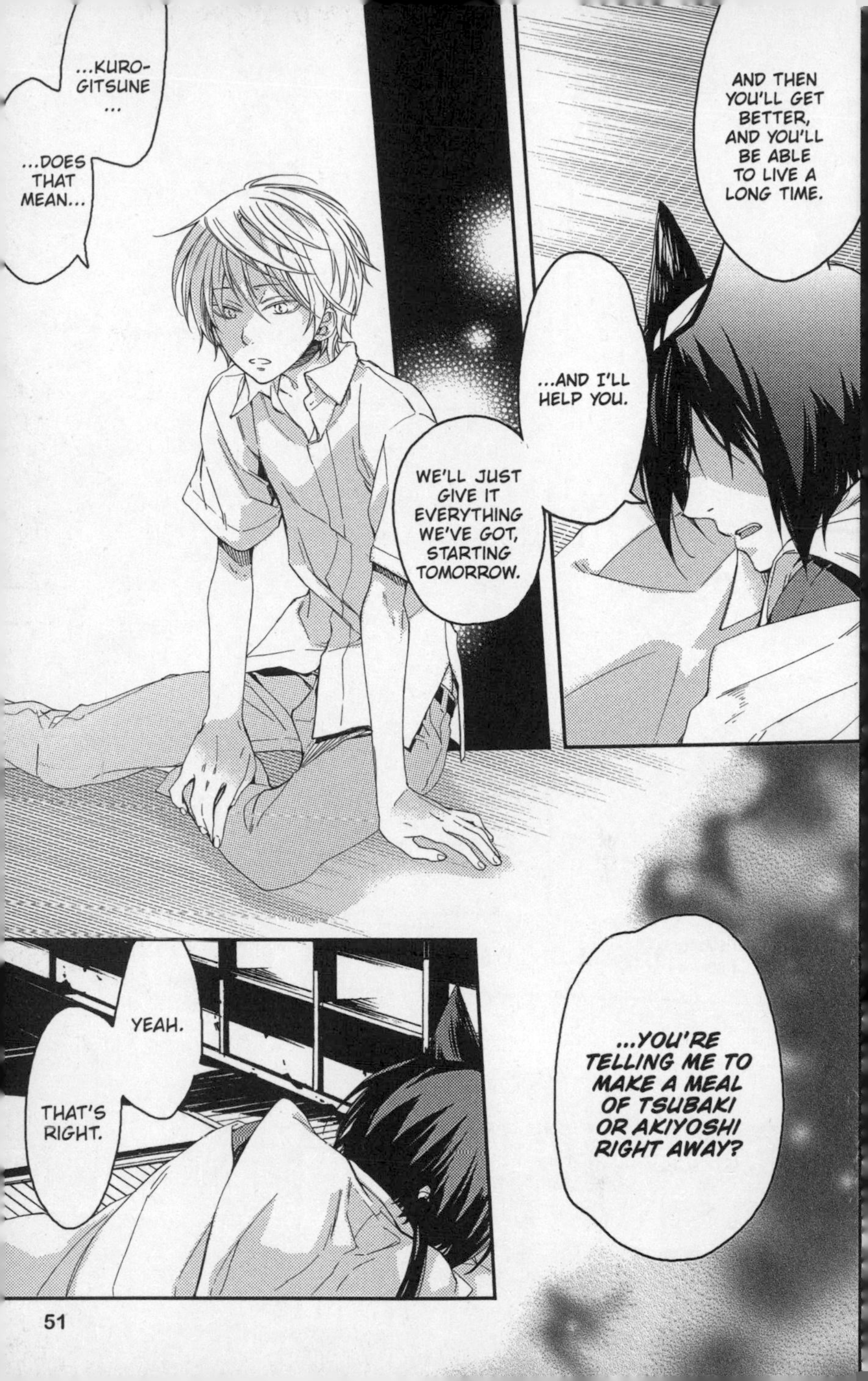
AND THEN YOU'LL GET BETTER, AND YOU'LL BE ABLE TO LIVE A LONG TIME.
...AND I'LL HELP YOU.
...KURO-GITSUNE...
...DOES THAT MEAN...
WE'LL JUST GIVE IT EVERYTHING WE'VE GOT, STARTING TOMORROW.
...YOU'RE TELLING ME TO MAKE A MEAL OF TSUBAKI OR AKIYOSHI RIGHT AWAY?
YEAH.
THAT'S RIGHT.

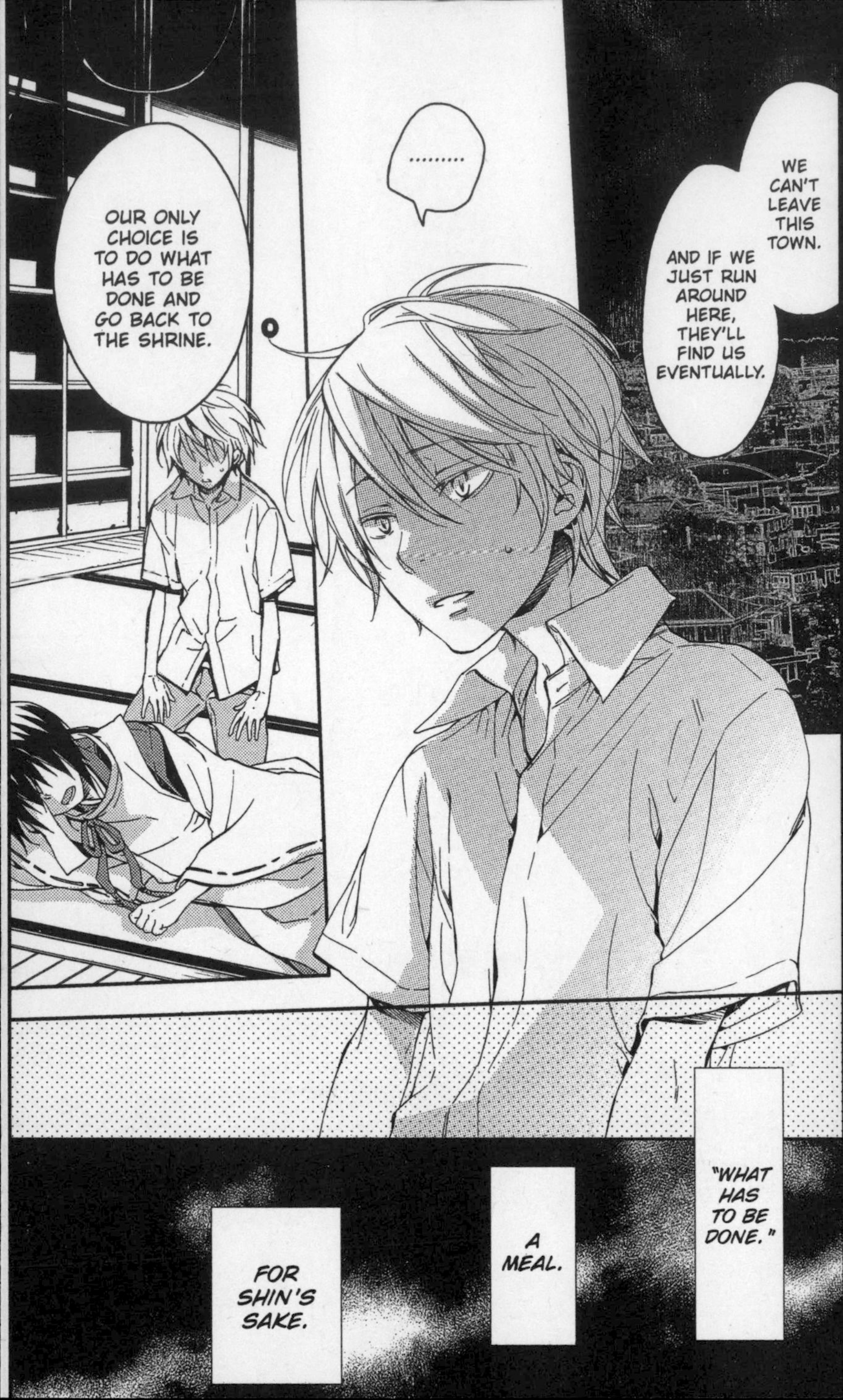
WE CAN'T LEAVE THIS TOWN.
AND IF WE JUST RUN AROUND HERE, THEY'LL FIND US EVENTUALLY.
....
OUR ONLY CHOICE IS TO DO WHAT HAS TO BE DONE AND GO BACK TO THE SHRINE.
"WHAT HAS TO BE DONE."
A MEAL.
FOR SHIN'S SAKE.

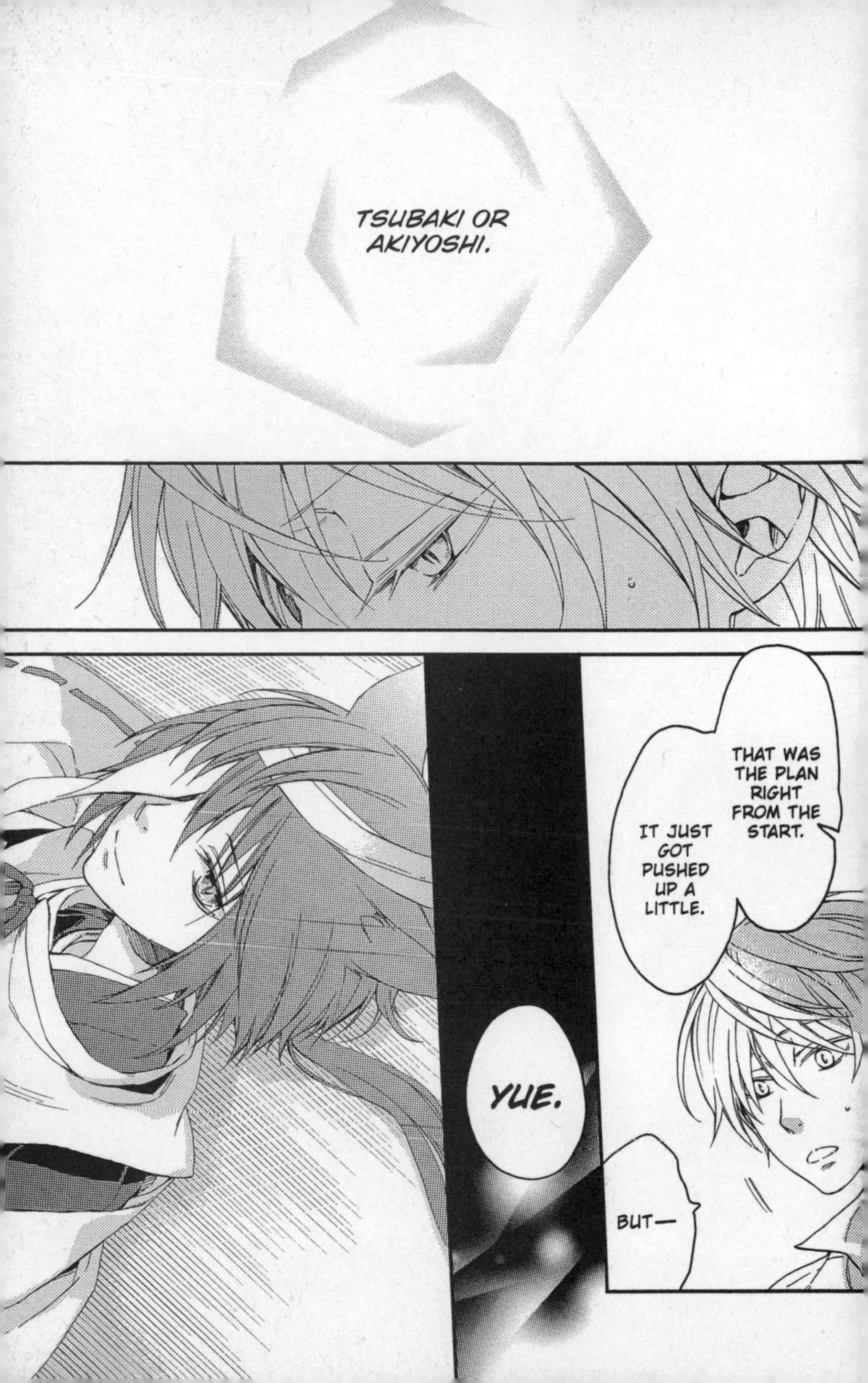
TSUBAKI OR AKIYOSHI.
THAT WAS THE PLAN RIGHT FROM THE START.
IT JUST GOT PUSHED UP A LITTLE.
BUT—
YUE.

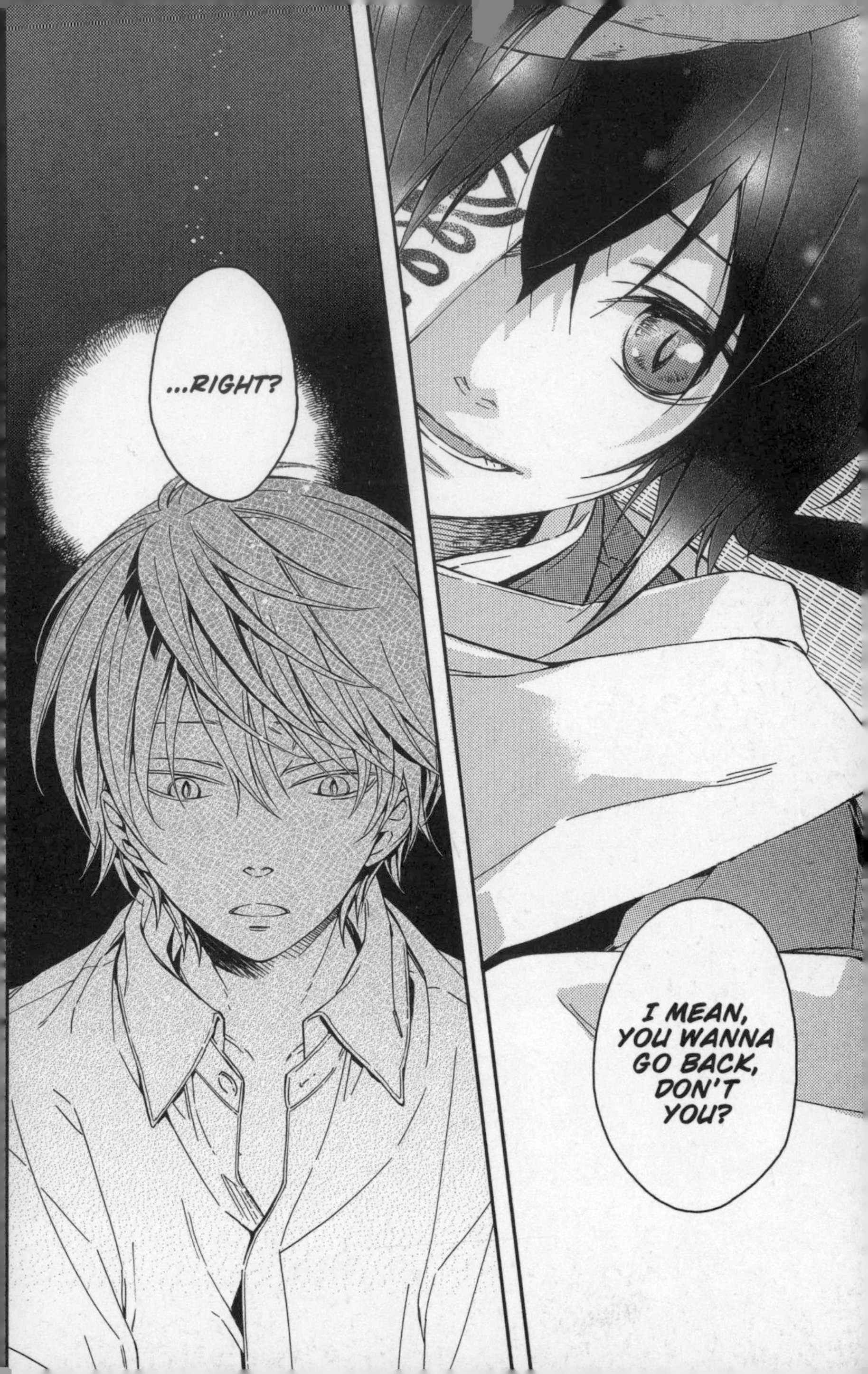
I MEAN, YOU WANNA GO BACK, DON'T YOU?
...RIGHT?

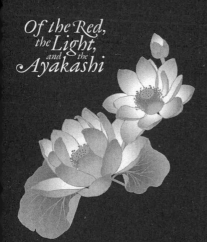

Of the Red,
the Light,
and the
Ayakashi

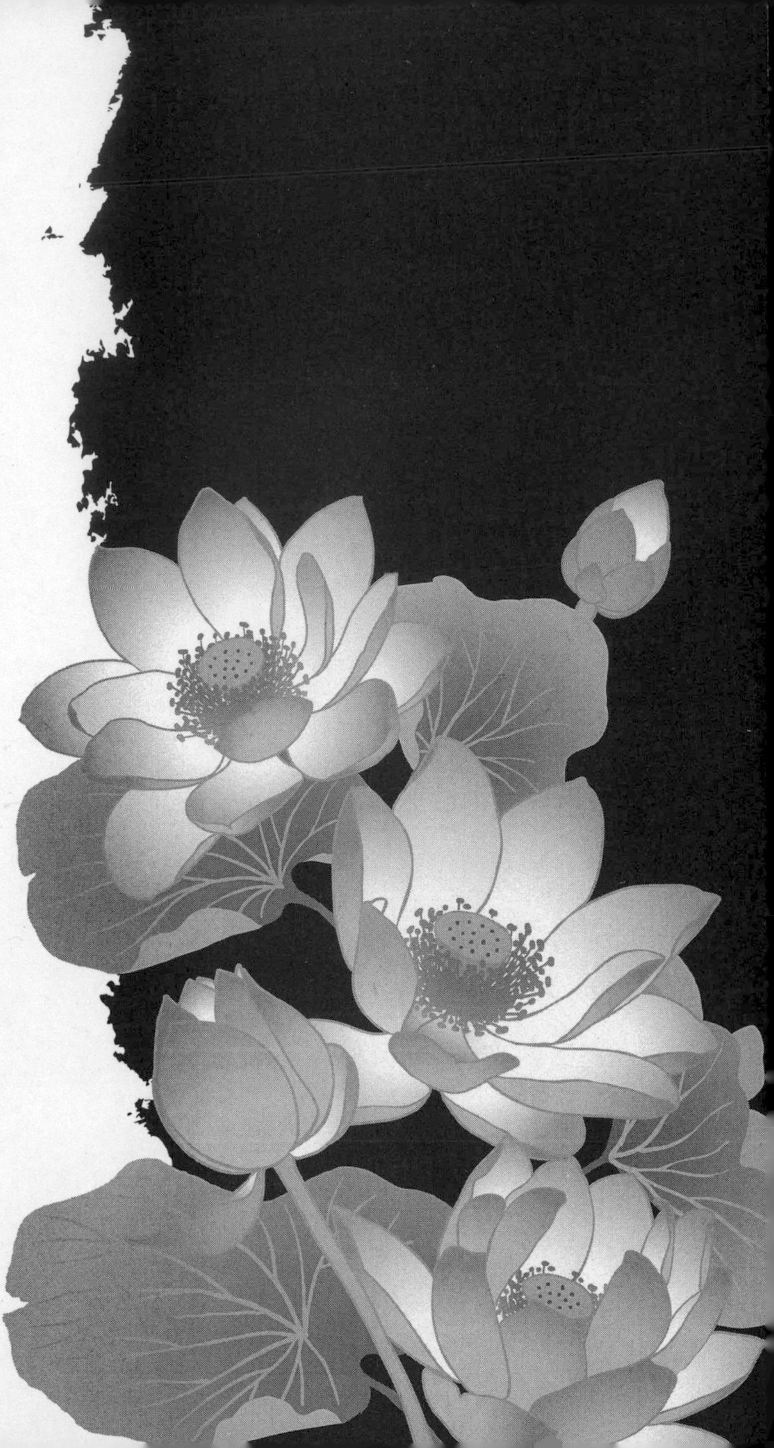

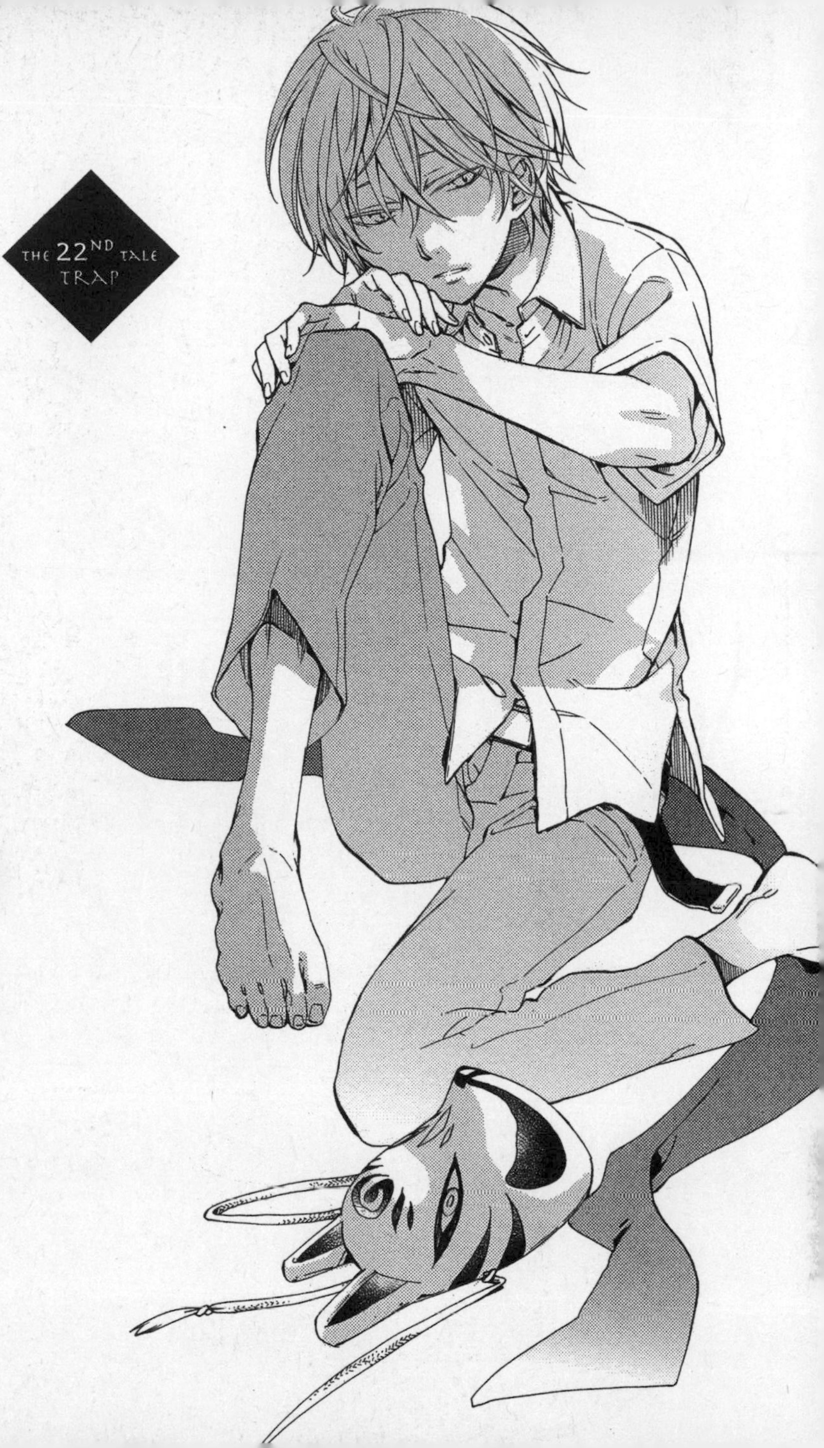
THE 22ND TALE
TRAP

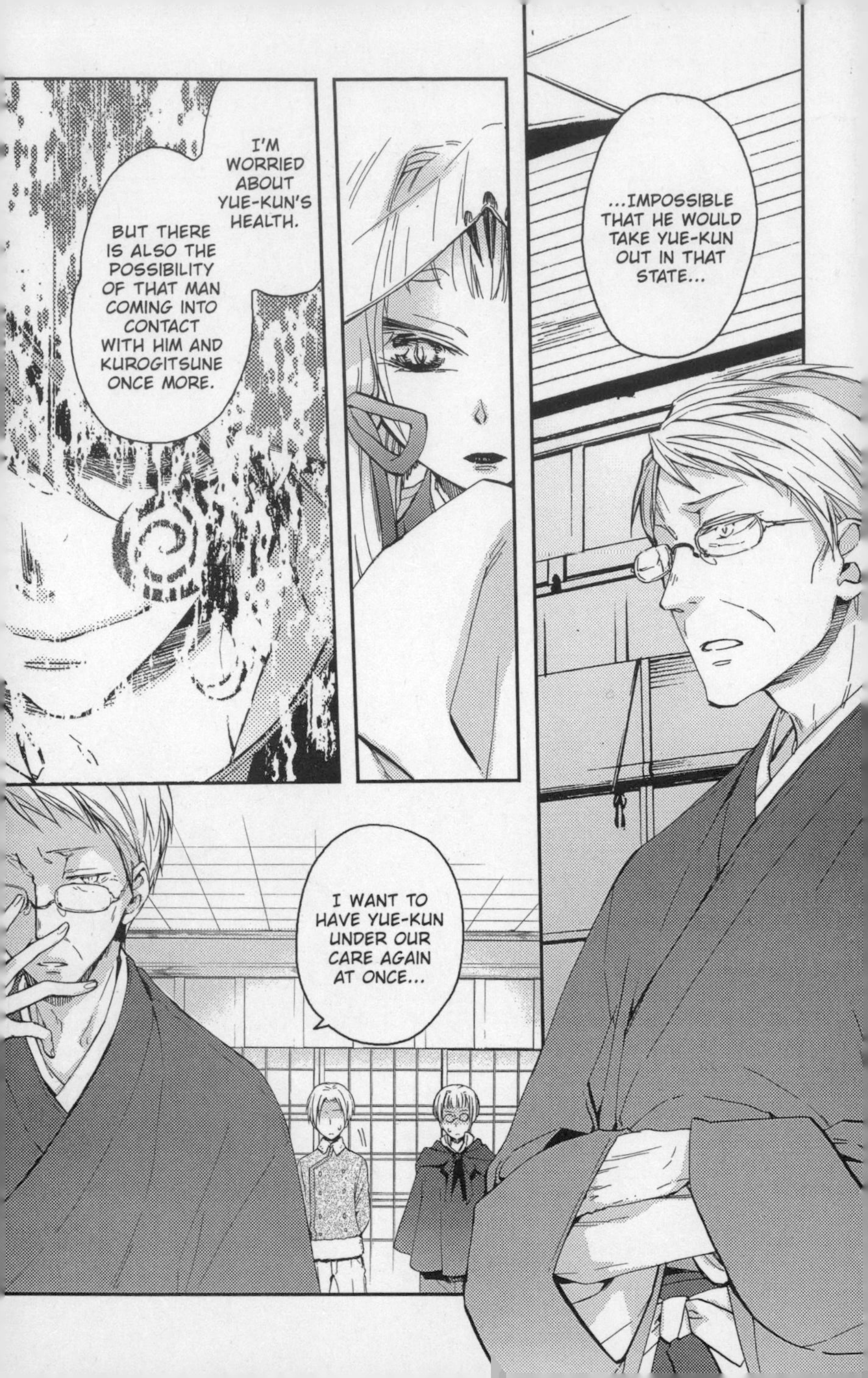
...IMPOSSIBLE THAT HE WOULD TAKE YUE-KUN OUT IN THAT STATE...
I'M WORRIED ABOUT YUE-KUN'S HEALTH.
BUT THERE IS ALSO THE POSSIBILITY OF THAT MAN COMING INTO CONTACT WITH HIM AND KUROGITSUNE ONCE MORE.
I WANT TO HAVE YUE-KUN UNDER OUR CARE AGAIN AT ONCE...

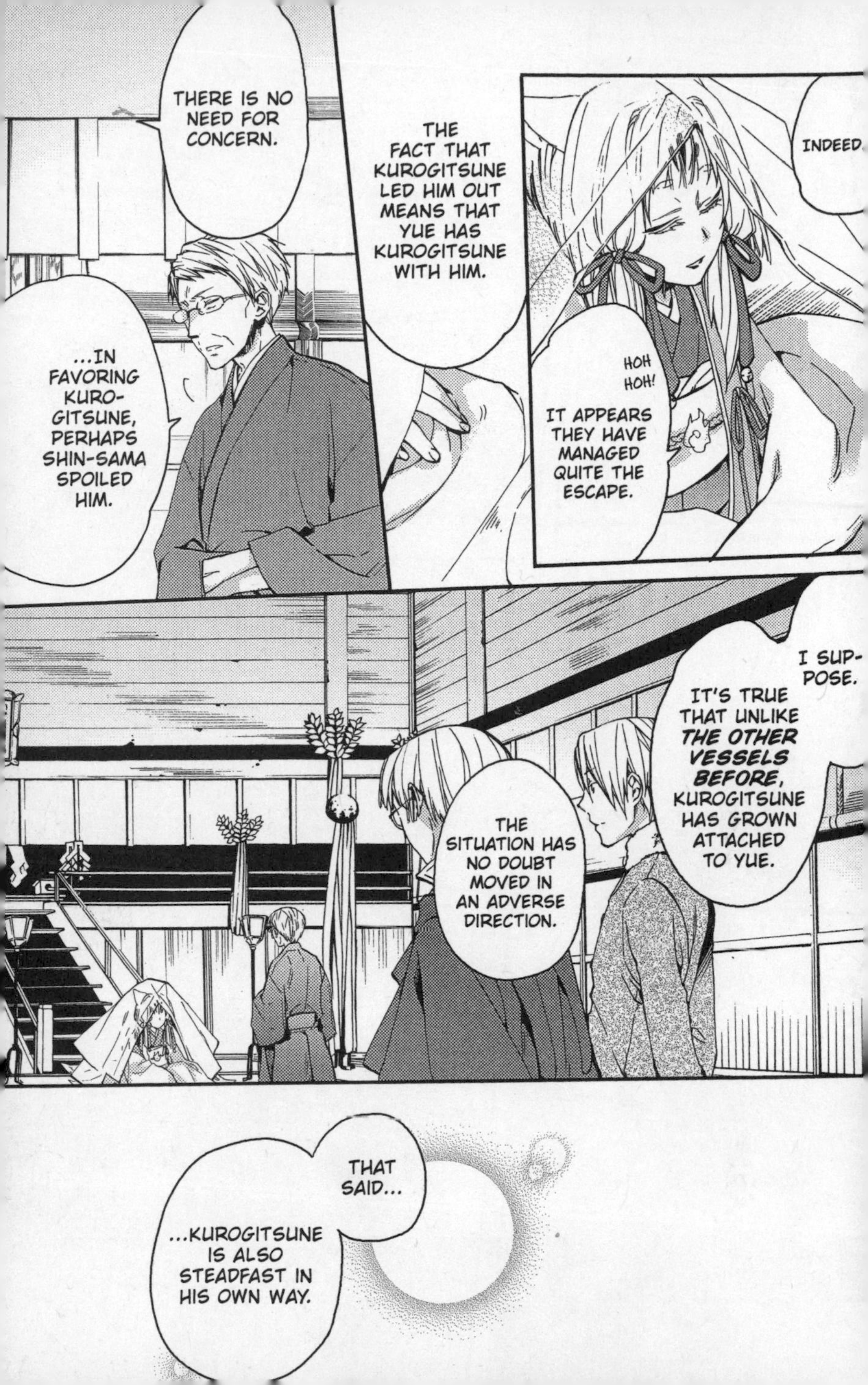
INDEED.
HOH HOH!
IT APPEARS THEY HAVE MANAGED QUITE THE ESCAPE.
THERE IS NO NEED FOR CONCERN.
THE FACT THAT KUROGITSUNE LED HIM OUT MEANS THAT YUE HAS KUROGITSUNE WITH HIM.
...IN FAVORING KURO-GITSUNE, PERHAPS SHIN-SAMA SPOILED HIM.
I SUP-POSE.
IT'S TRUE THAT UNLIKE ***THE OTHER VESSELS BEFORE***, KUROGITSUNE HAS GROWN ATTACHED TO YUE.
THE SITUATION HAS NO DOUBT MOVED IN AN ADVERSE DIRECTION.
THAT SAID...
...KUROGITSUNE IS ALSO STEADFAST IN HIS OWN WAY.

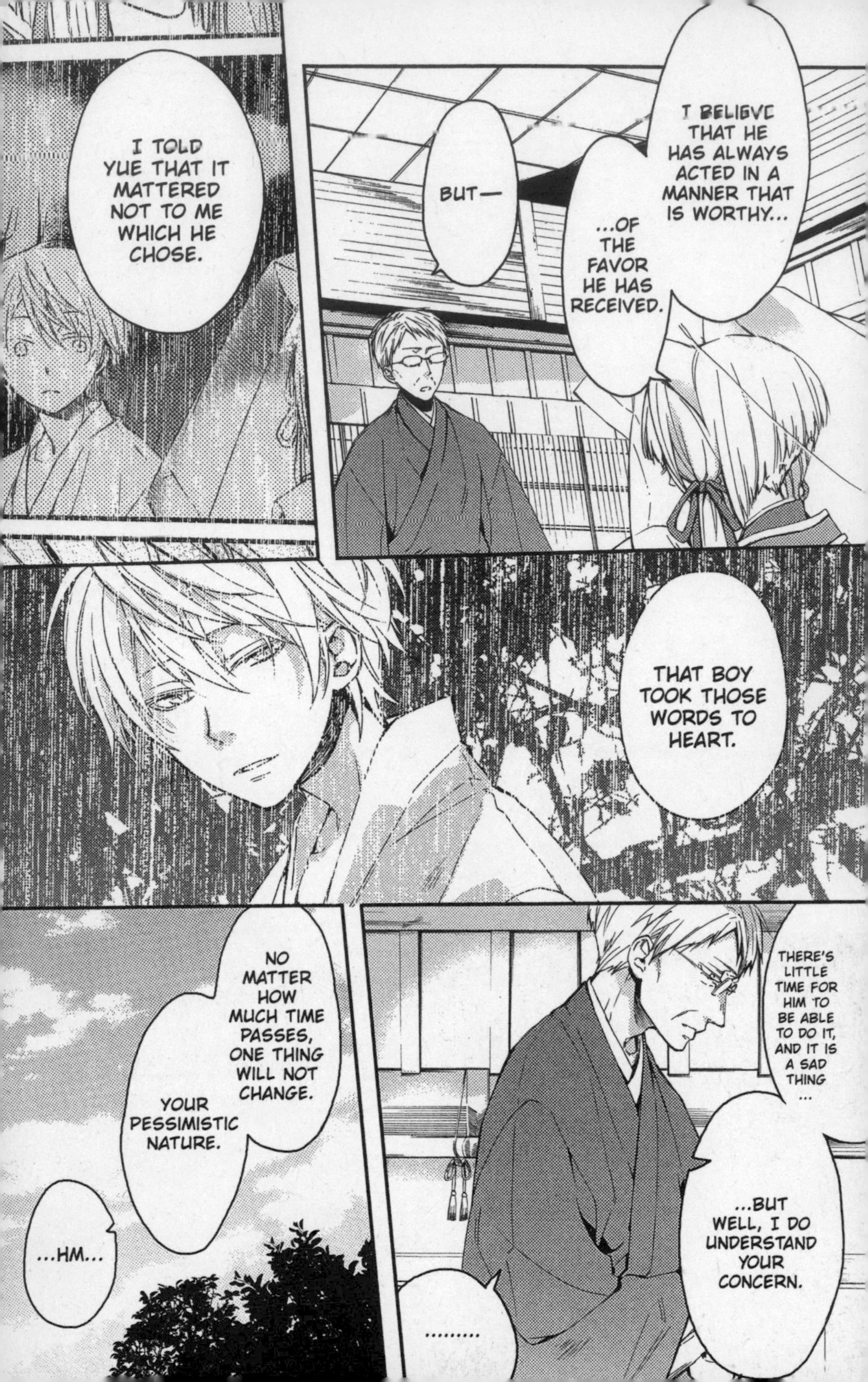
I BELIEVE THAT HE HAS ALWAYS ACTED IN A MANNER THAT IS WORTHY...
...OF THE FAVOR HE HAS RECEIVED.
BUT—
I TOLD YUE THAT IT MATTERED NOT TO ME WHICH HE CHOSE.
THAT BOY TOOK THOSE WORDS TO HEART.
THERE'S LITTLE TIME FOR HIM TO BE ABLE TO DO IT, AND IT IS A SAD THING ...
...BUT WELL, I DO UNDERSTAND YOUR CONCERN.
....
NO MATTER HOW MUCH TIME PASSES, ONE THING WILL NOT CHANGE.
YOUR PESSIMISTIC NATURE.
...HM...

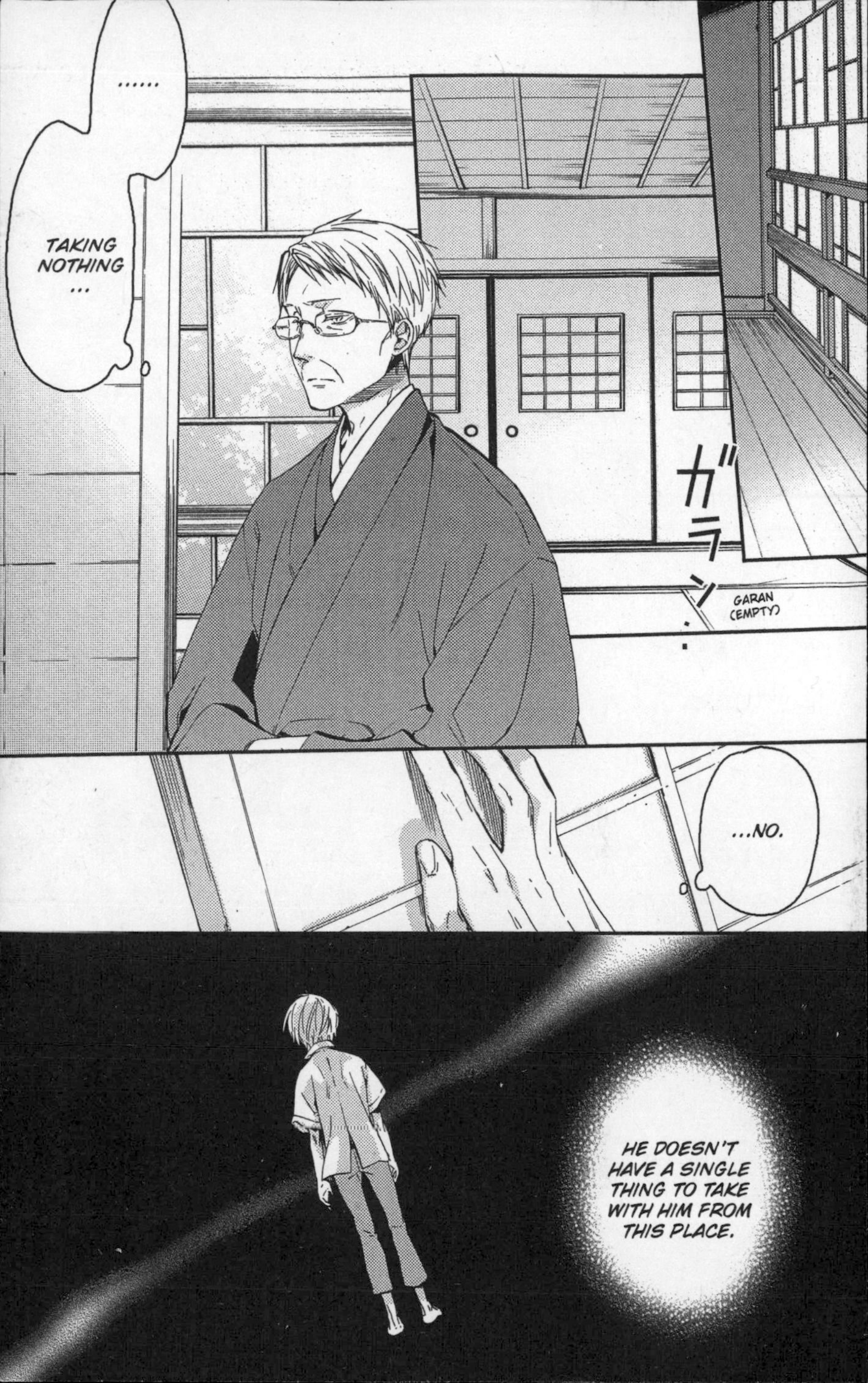
......
TAKING NOTHING ...
ガラン
GARAN (EMPTY)
...NO.
HE DOESN'T HAVE A SINGLE THING TO TAKE WITH HIM FROM THIS PLACE.

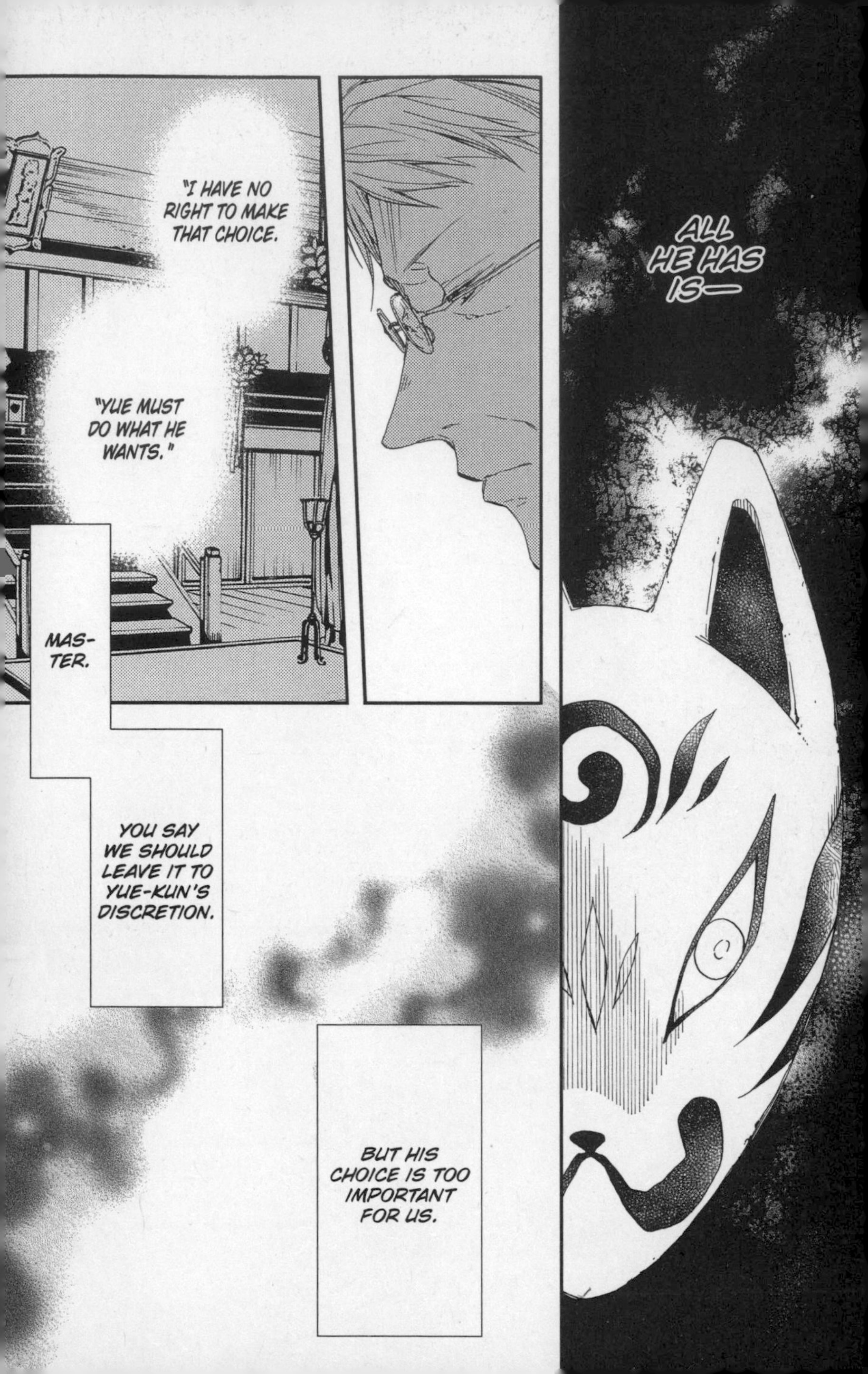
ALL HE HAS IS—
"I HAVE NO RIGHT TO MAKE THAT CHOICE.
"YUE MUST DO WHAT HE WANTS."
MASTER.
YOU SAY WE SHOULD LEAVE IT TO YUE-KUN'S DISCRETION.
BUT HIS CHOICE IS TOO IMPORTANT FOR US.

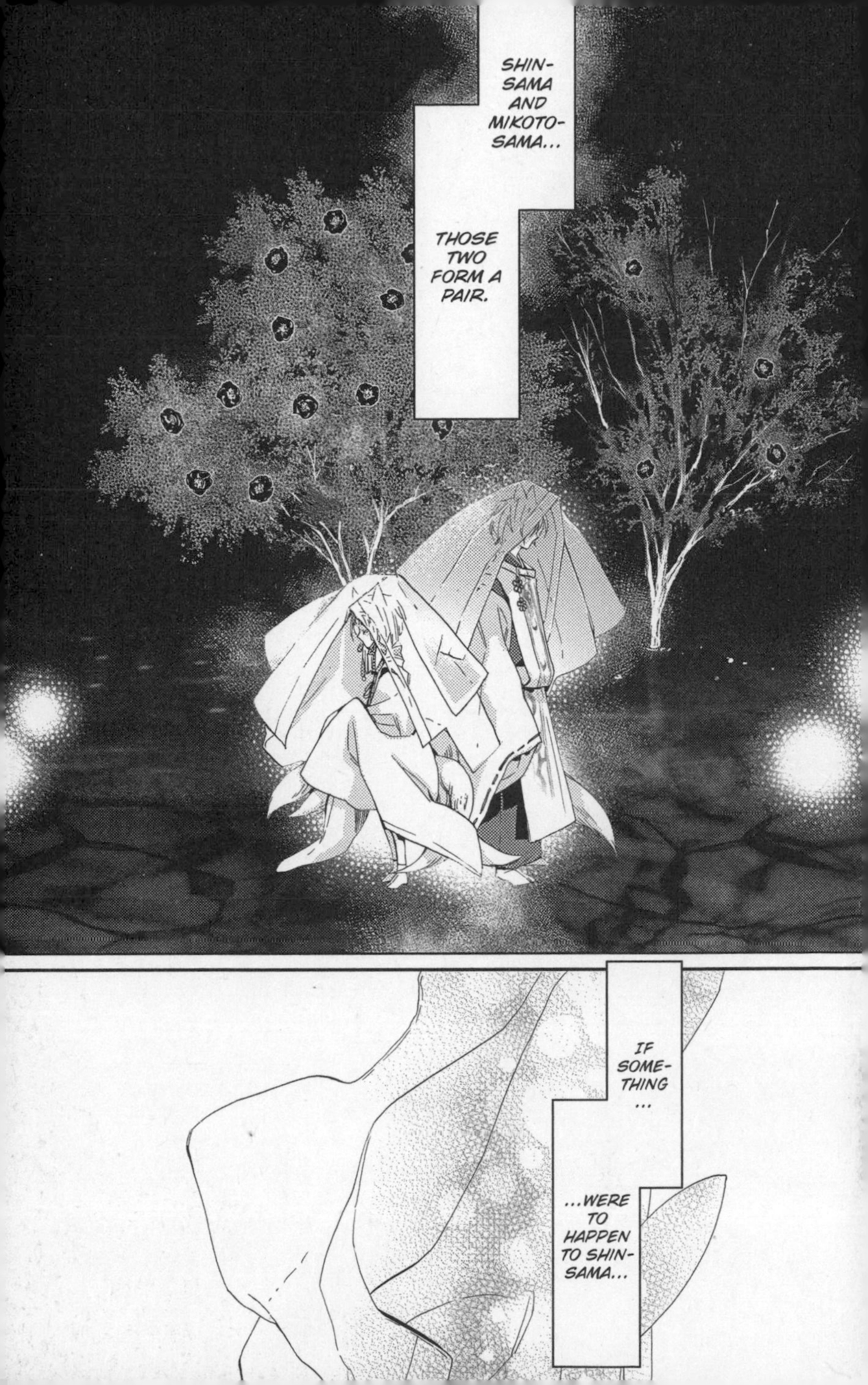
SHIN-SAMA AND MIKOTO-SAMA...
THOSE TWO FORM A PAIR.
IF SOME-THING...
...WERE TO HAPPEN TO SHIN-SAMA...

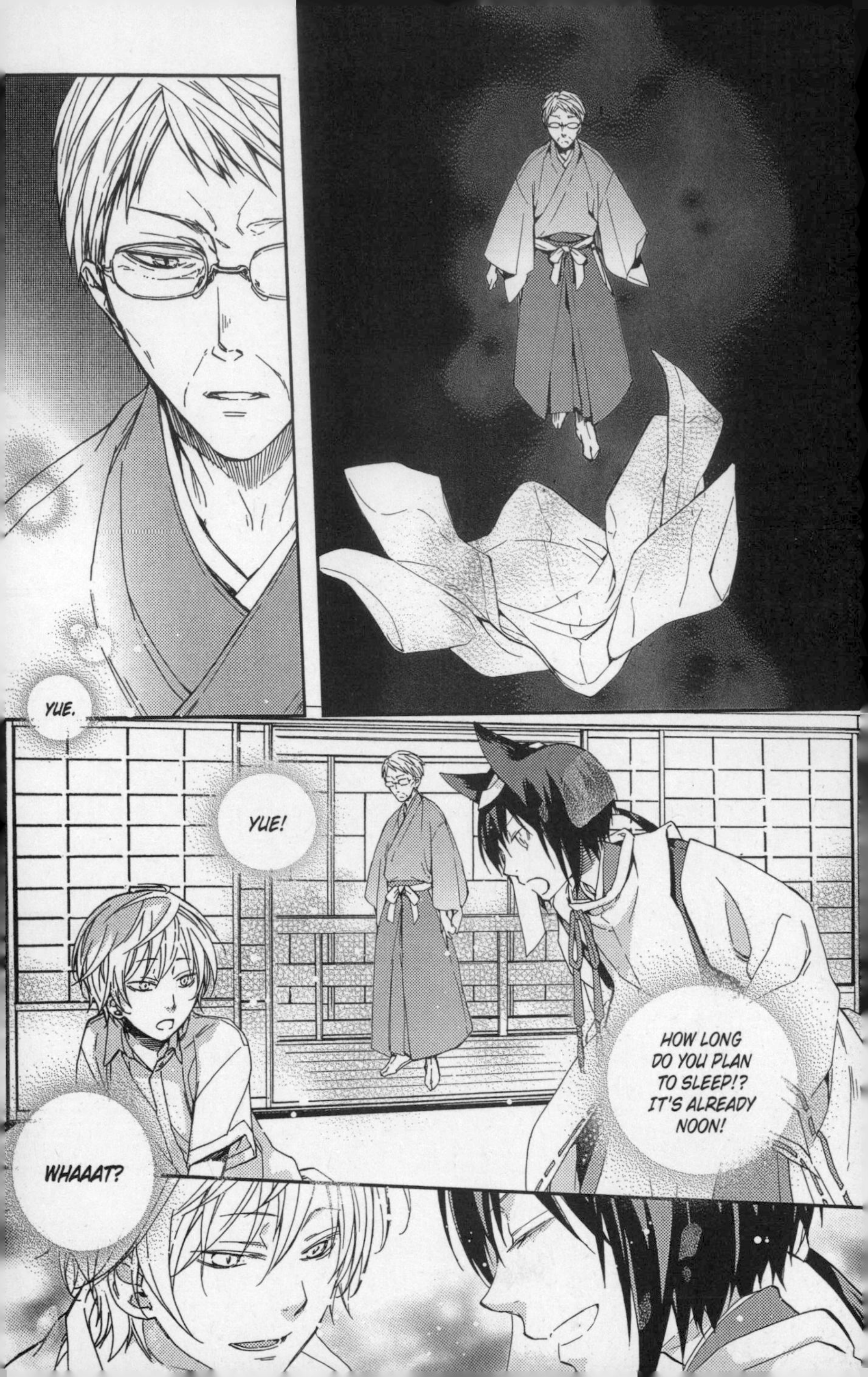
YUE.
YUE!
HOW LONG DO YOU PLAN TO SLEEP!? IT'S ALREADY NOON!
WHAAAT?

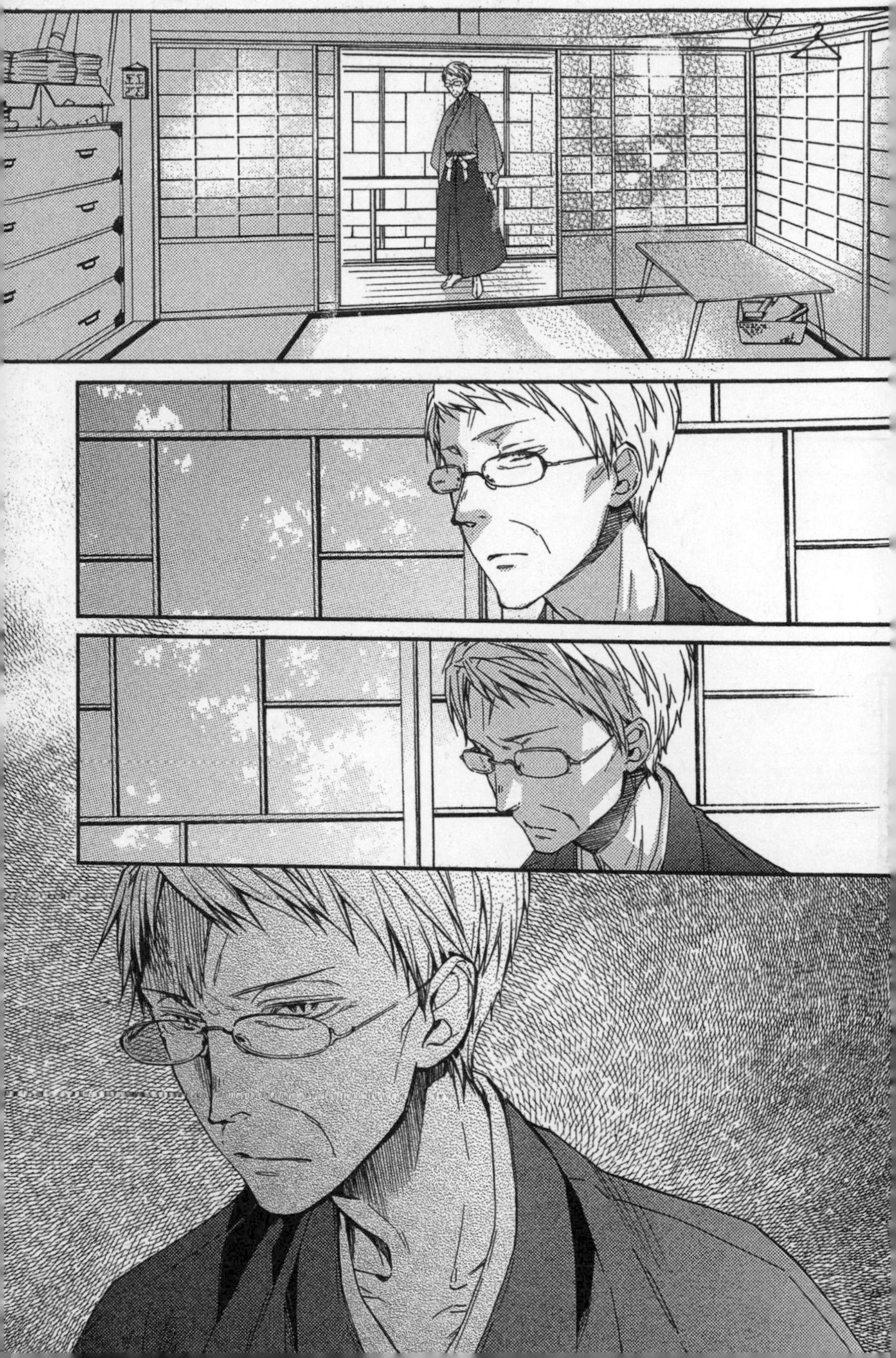

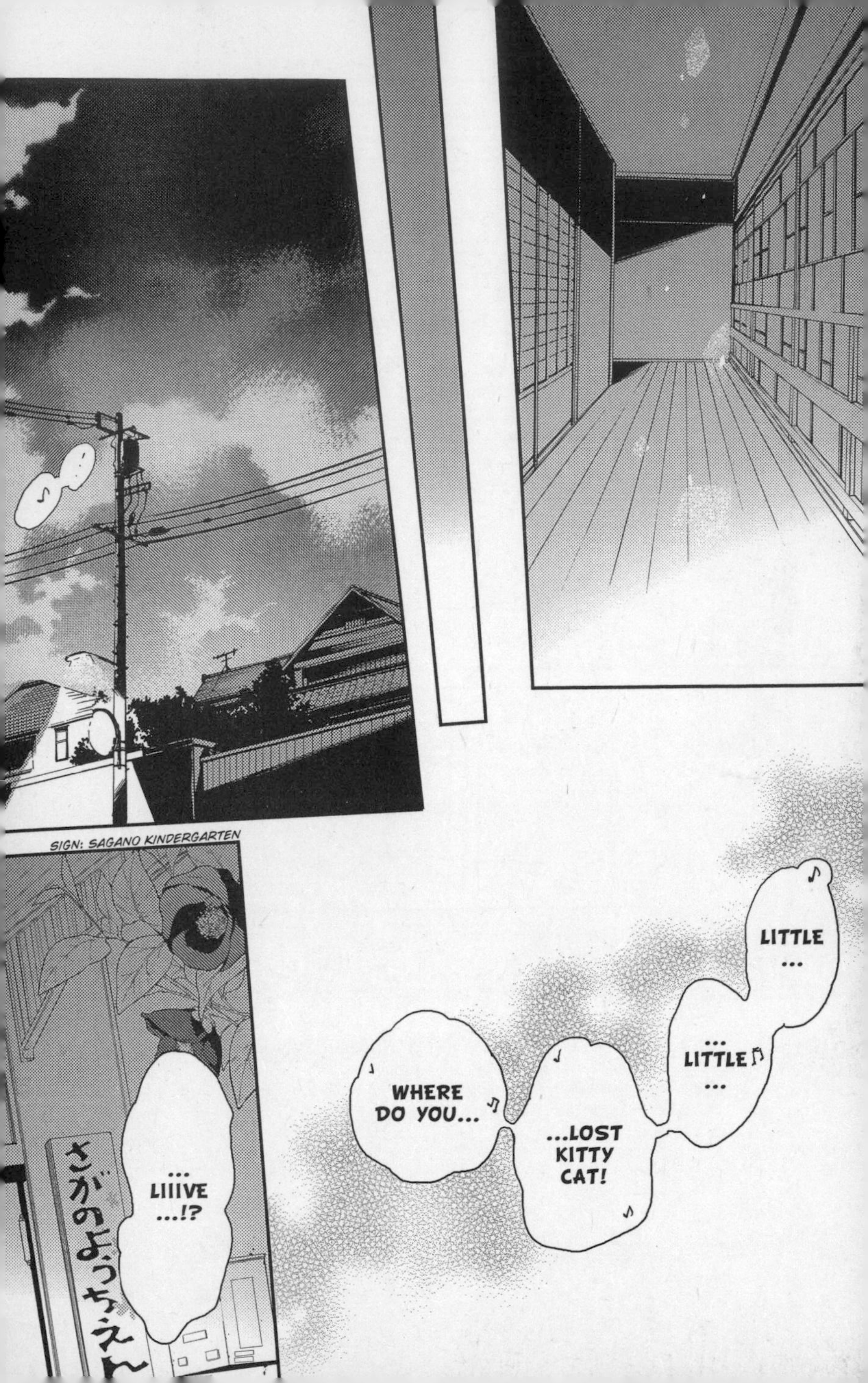
LITTLE ...
... LITTLE♪ ...
...LOST KITTY CAT!
WHERE DO YOU...
... LIIIVE ...!?
SIGN: SAGANO KINDERGARTEN
さがのようちえん

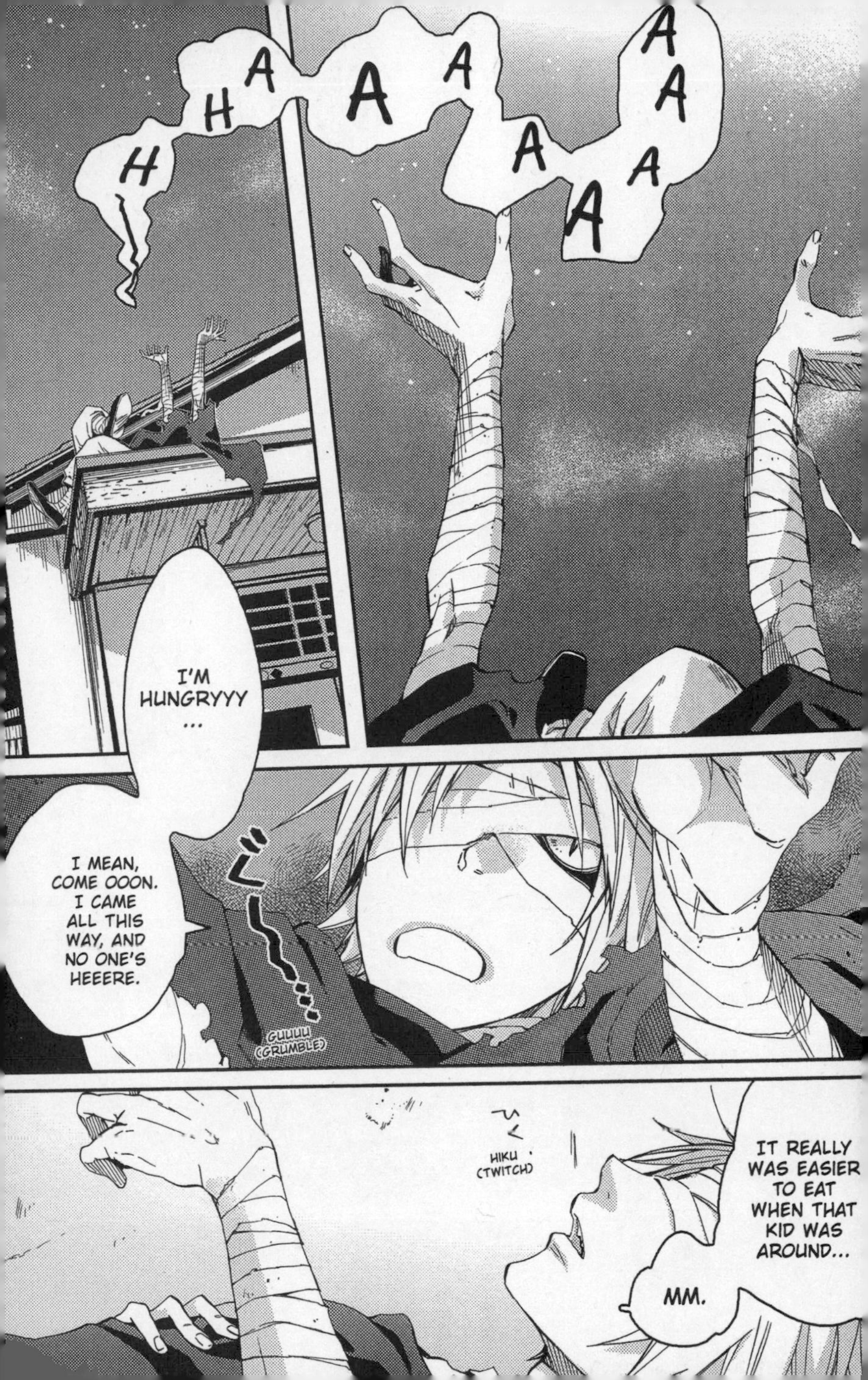
HHAAAAAAAA
I'M HUNGRYYY...
I MEAN, COME OOON. I CAME ALL THIS WAY, AND NO ONE'S HEEERE.
GUUUU (GRUMBLE)
IT REALLY WAS EASIER TO EAT WHEN THAT KID WAS AROUND...
MM.
HIKU (TWITCH)

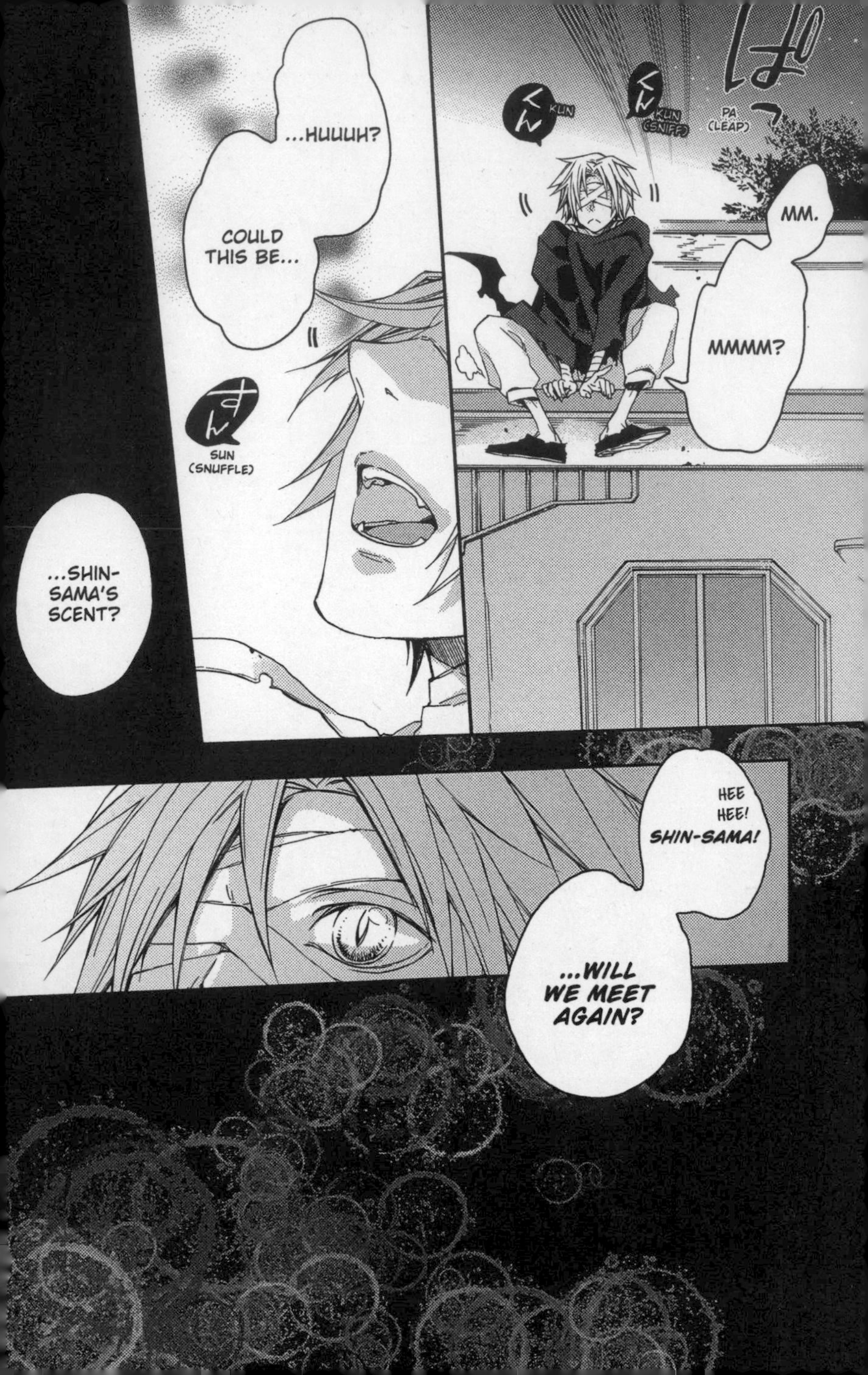
ぱっ
PA (LEAP)
くん
KUN (SNIFF)
くん
KUN
MM.
MMMM?
...HUUUH?
COULD THIS BE...
すん
SUN (SNUFFLE)
...SHIN-SAMA'S SCENT?
HEE HEE! SHIN-SAMA!
...WILL WE MEET AGAIN?

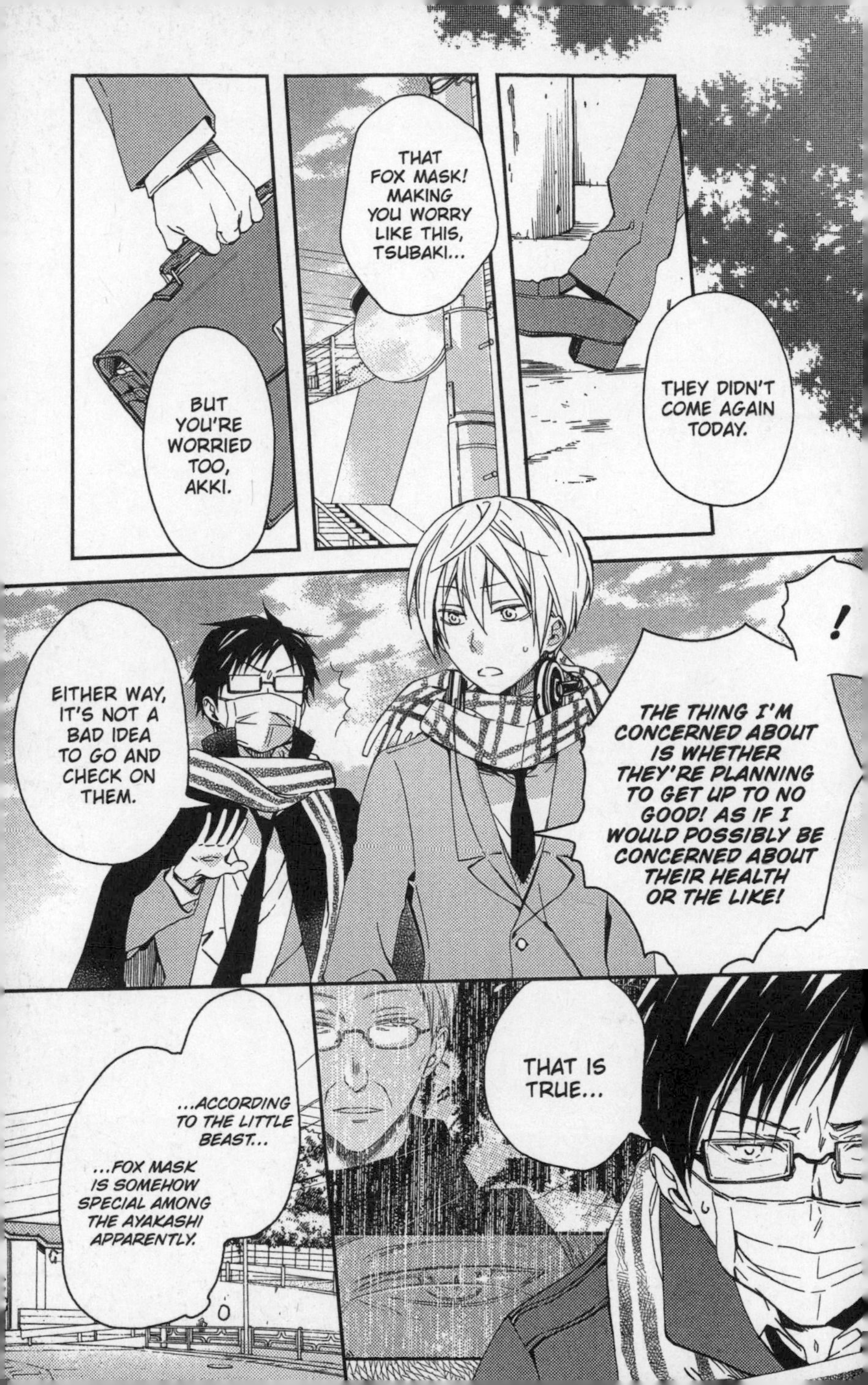
THEY DIDN'T COME AGAIN TODAY.
THAT FOX MASK! MAKING YOU WORRY LIKE THIS, TSUBAKI...
BUT YOU'RE WORRIED TOO, AKKI.
!
THE THING I'M CONCERNED ABOUT IS WHETHER THEY'RE PLANNING TO GET UP TO NO GOOD! AS IF I WOULD POSSIBLY BE CONCERNED ABOUT THEIR HEALTH OR THE LIKE!
EITHER WAY, IT'S NOT A BAD IDEA TO GO AND CHECK ON THEM.
THAT IS TRUE...
...ACCORDING TO THE LITTLE BEAST...
...FOX MASK IS SOMEHOW SPECIAL AMONG THE AYAKASHI APPARENTLY.

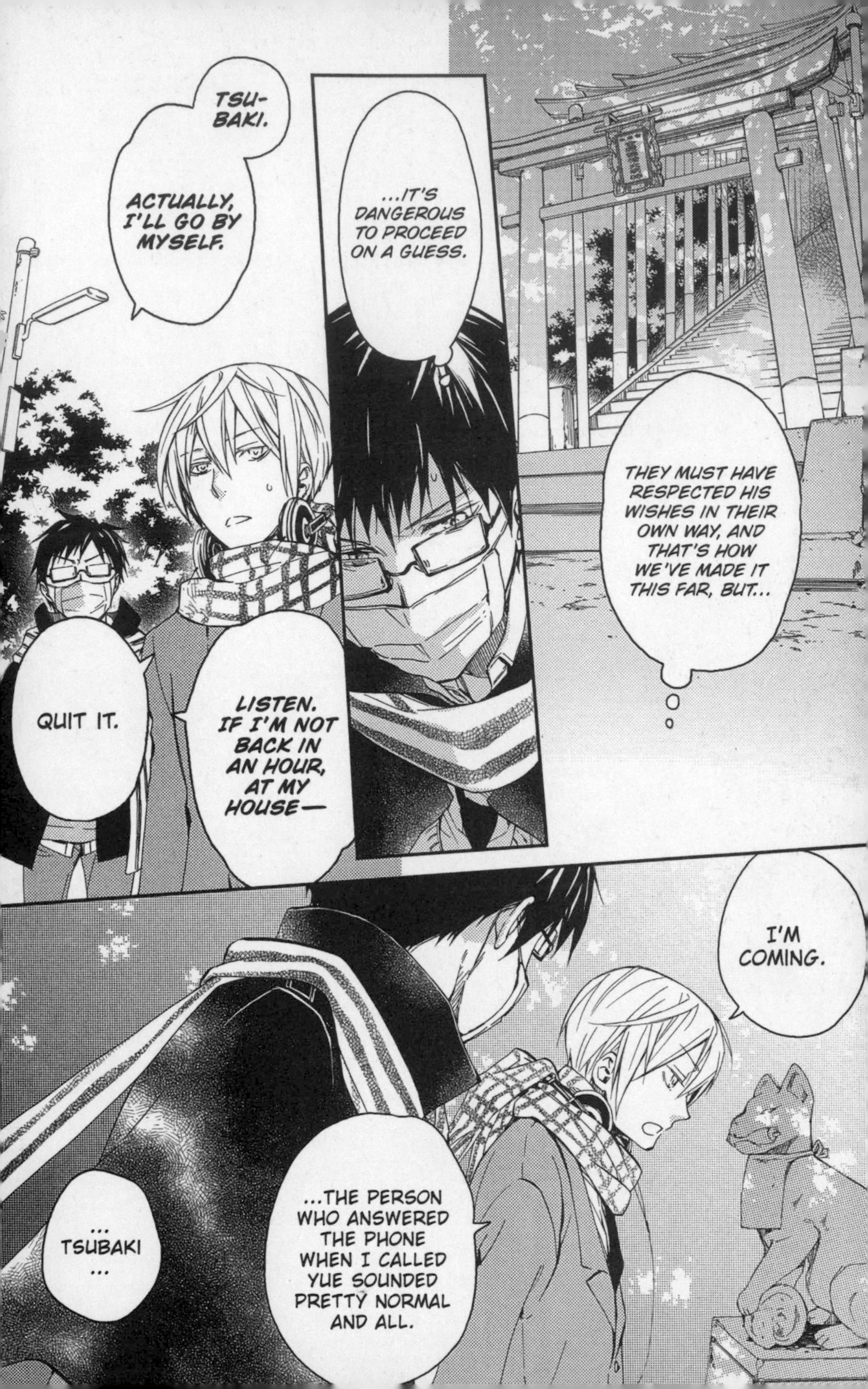
THEY MUST HAVE RESPECTED HIS WISHES IN THEIR OWN WAY, AND THAT'S HOW WE'VE MADE IT THIS FAR, BUT...
...IT'S DANGEROUS TO PROCEED ON A GUESS.
TSUBAKI.
ACTUALLY, I'LL GO BY MYSELF.
LISTEN. IF I'M NOT BACK IN AN HOUR, AT MY HOUSE—
QUIT IT.
I'M COMING.
...THE PERSON WHO ANSWERED THE PHONE WHEN I CALLED YUE SOUNDED PRETTY NORMAL AND ALL.
... TSUBAKI ...

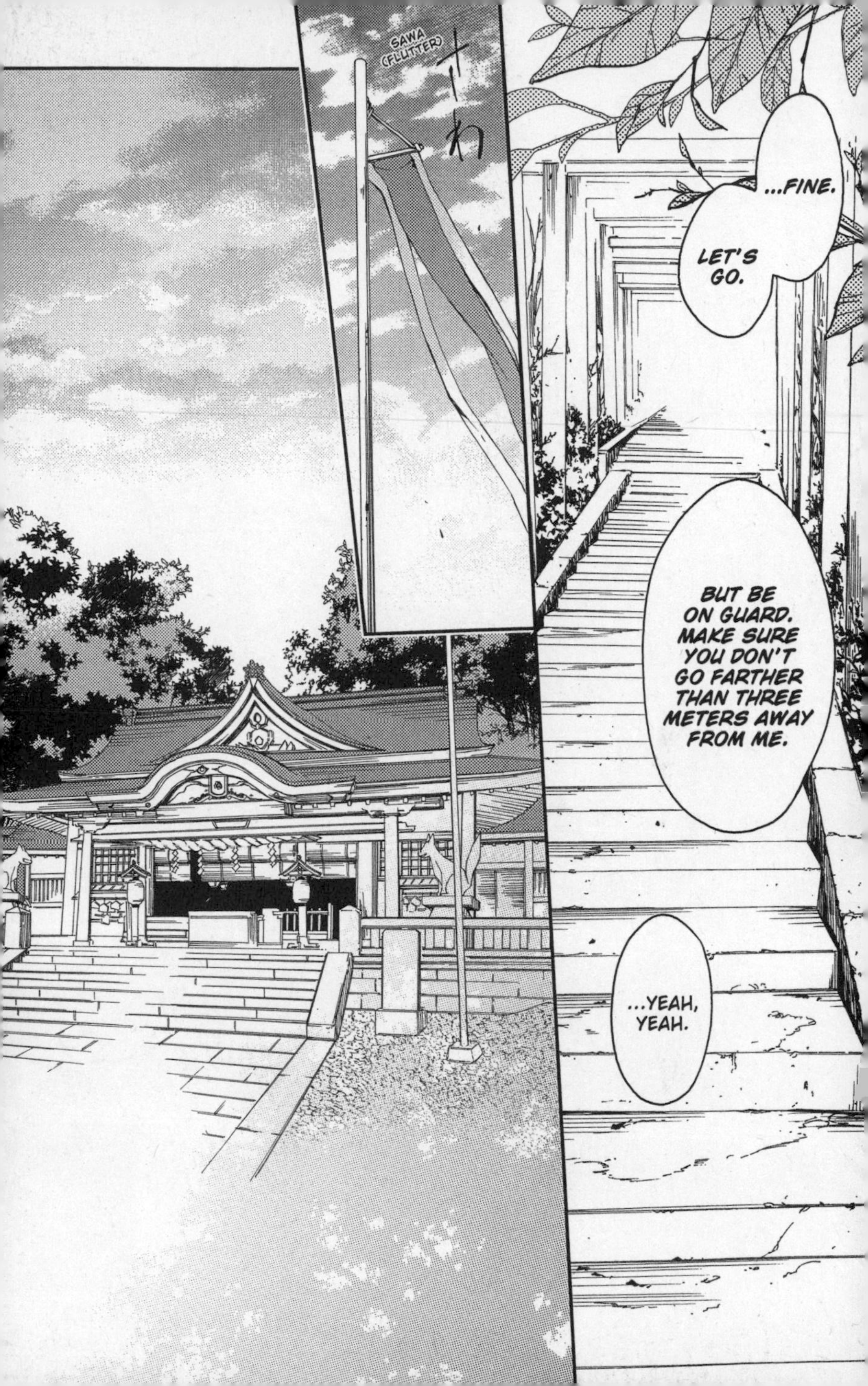
...FINE.
LET'S GO.
BUT BE ON GUARD. MAKE SURE YOU DON'T GO FARTHER THAN THREE METERS AWAY FROM ME.
...YEAH, YEAH.
SAWA (FLUTTER)

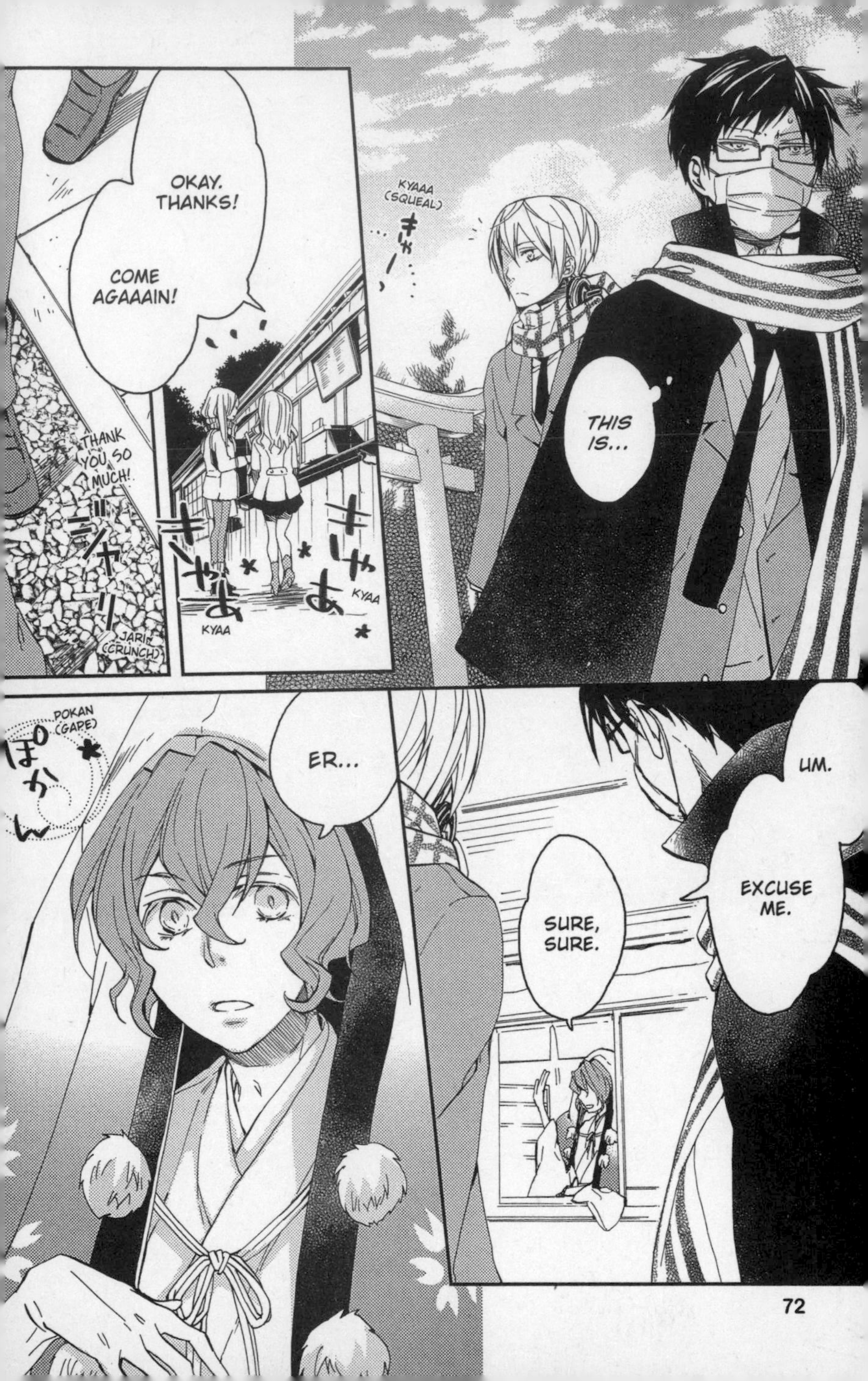

KYAAA (SQUEAL)
THIS IS...
OKAY. THANKS!
COME AGAAAIN!
THANK YOU SO MUCH!
KYAA
KYAA
JARI (CRUNCH)
UM.
EXCUSE ME.
SURE, SURE.
ER...
POKAN (GAPE)
ぽかん

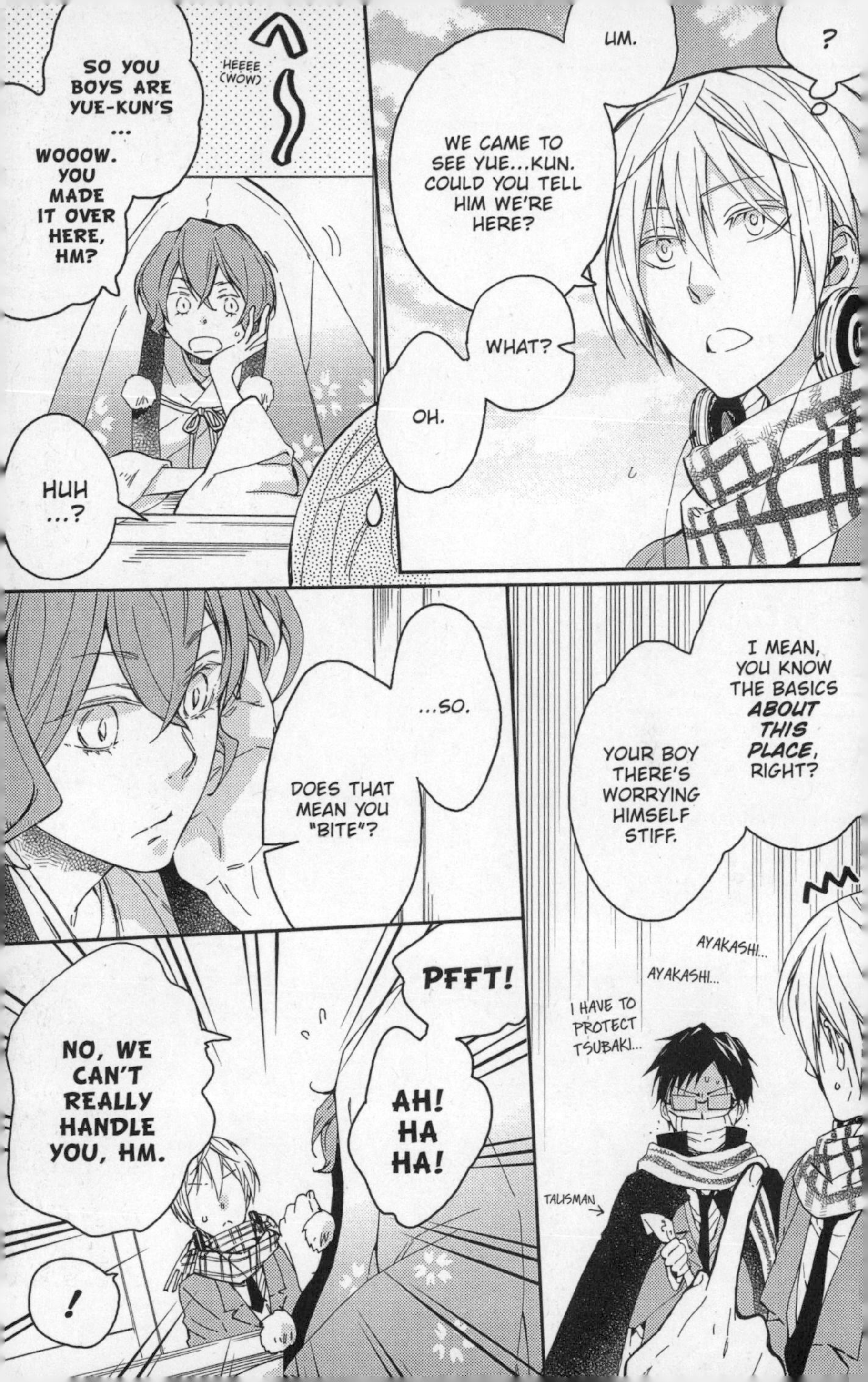
?
UM.
WE CAME TO SEE YUE...KUN. COULD YOU TELL HIM WE'RE HERE?
WHAT?
OH.
HEEEE (WOW)
SO YOU BOYS ARE YUE-KUN'S ...
WOOOW. YOU MADE IT OVER HERE, HM?
HUH ...?
I MEAN, YOU KNOW THE BASICS *ABOUT THIS PLACE*, RIGHT?
YOUR BOY THERE'S WORRYING HIMSELF STIFF.
...SO.
DOES THAT MEAN YOU "BITE"?
AYAKASHI...
AYAKASHI...
I HAVE TO PROTECT TSUBAKI...
TALISMAN
PFFT!
AH! HA HA!
NO, WE CAN'T REALLY HANDLE YOU, HM.
!

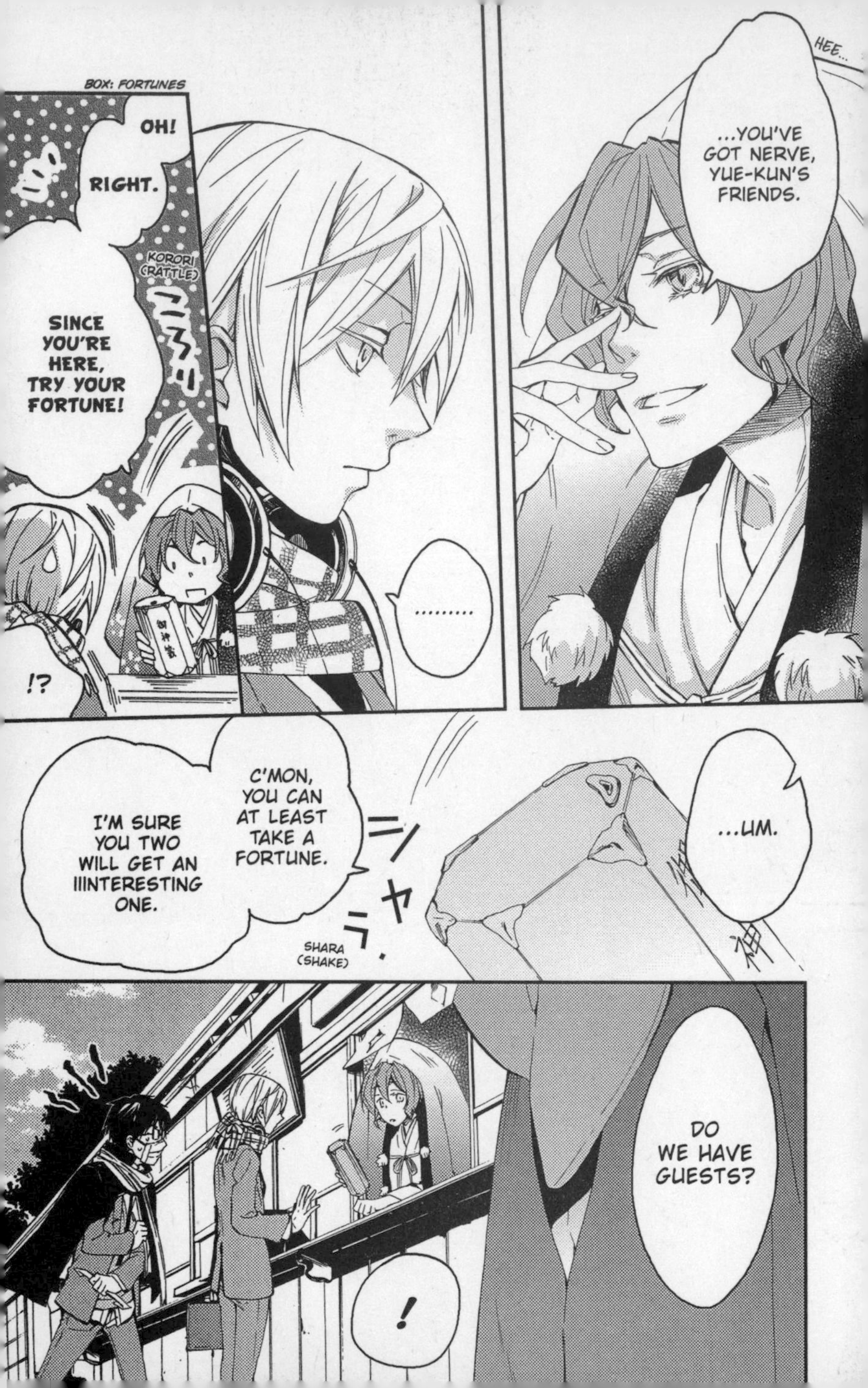
HEE...
...YOU'VE GOT NERVE, YUE-KUN'S FRIENDS.
....
BOX: FORTUNES
OH!
RIGHT.
KORORI (RATTLE)
SINCE YOU'RE HERE, TRY YOUR FORTUNE!
!?
...UM.
C'MON, YOU CAN AT LEAST TAKE A FORTUNE.
I'M SURE YOU TWO WILL GET AN IIINTERESTING ONE.
SHARA (SHAKE)
DO WE HAVE GUESTS?
!

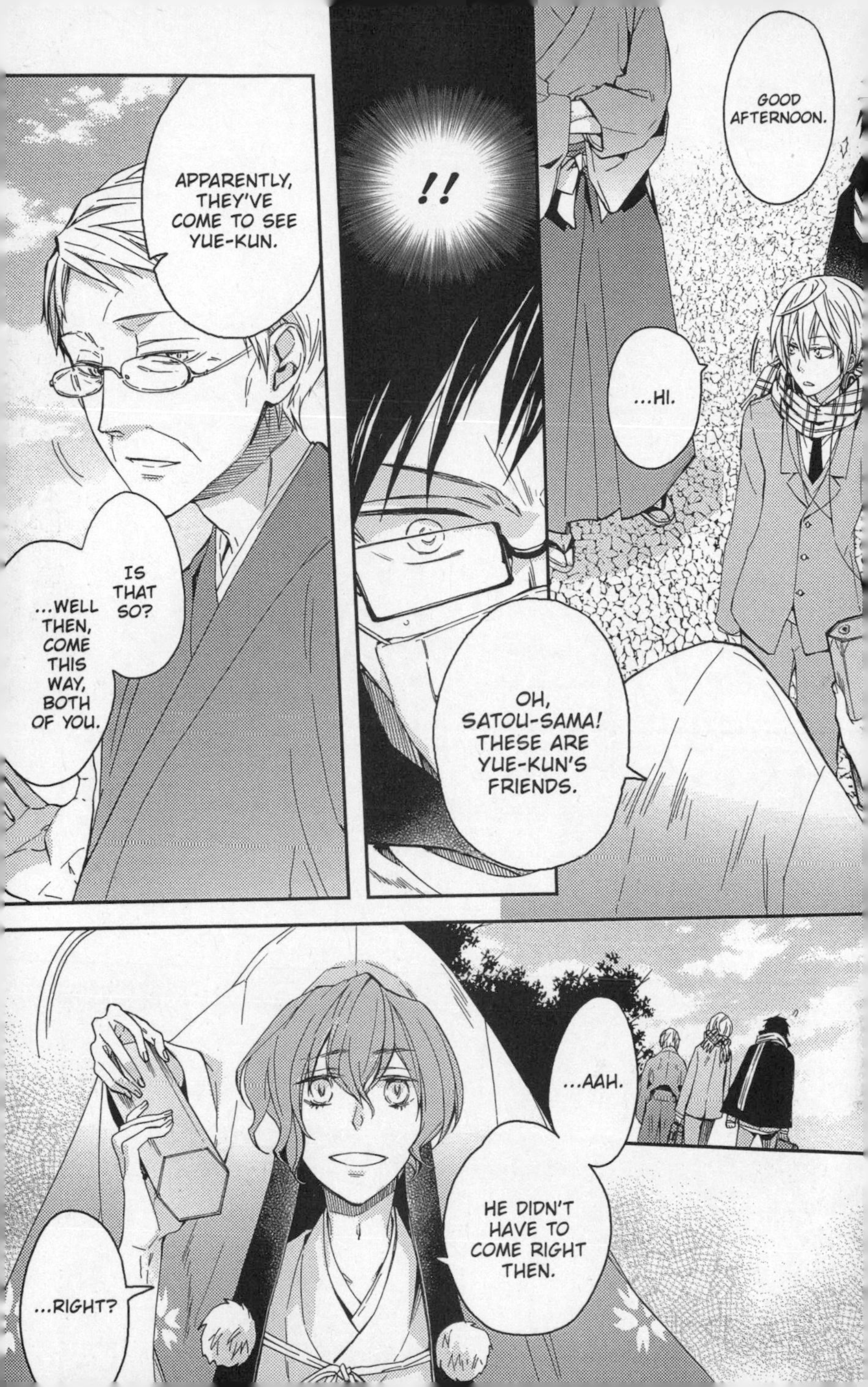
GOOD AFTERNOON.
...HI.
OH, SATOU-SAMA! THESE ARE YUE-KUN'S FRIENDS.
!!
APPARENTLY, THEY'VE COME TO SEE YUE-KUN.
IS THAT SO?
...WELL THEN, COME THIS WAY, BOTH OF YOU.
...AAH.
HE DIDN'T HAVE TO COME RIGHT THEN.
...RIGHT?

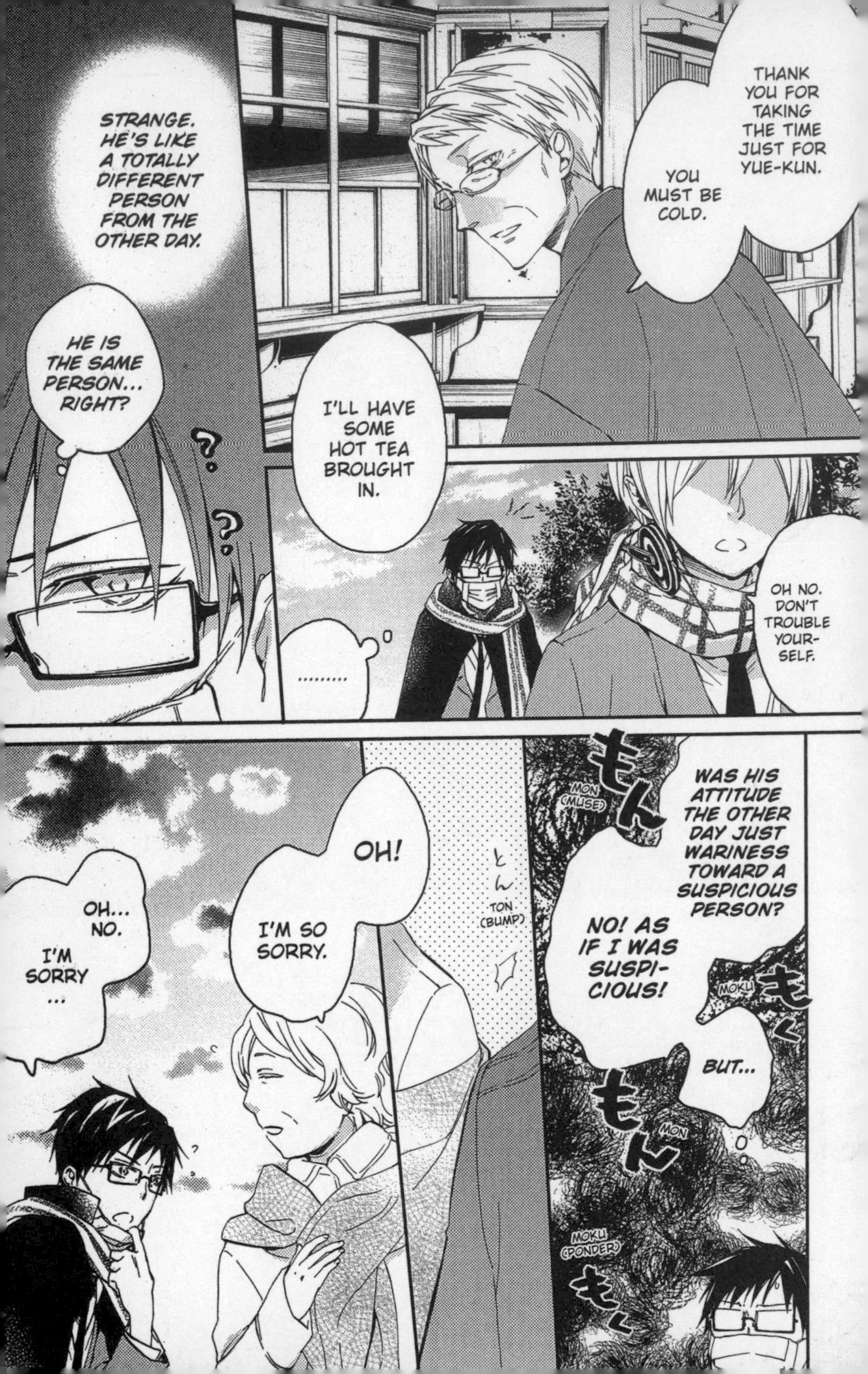
THANK YOU FOR TAKING THE TIME JUST FOR YUE-KUN.
YOU MUST BE COLD.
I'LL HAVE SOME HOT TEA BROUGHT IN.
OH NO. DON'T TROUBLE YOUR-SELF.
....
STRANGE. HE'S LIKE A TOTALLY DIFFERENT PERSON FROM THE OTHER DAY.
HE IS THE SAME PERSON... RIGHT?
もん MON (MUSE)
WAS HIS ATTITUDE THE OTHER DAY JUST WARINESS TOWARD A SUSPICIOUS PERSON?
NO! AS IF I WAS SUSPI-CIOUS!
もく MOKU
BUT...
もん MON
もく MOKU (PONDER)
とん TON (BUMP)
OH!
I'M SO SORRY.
OH... NO.
I'M SORRY ...

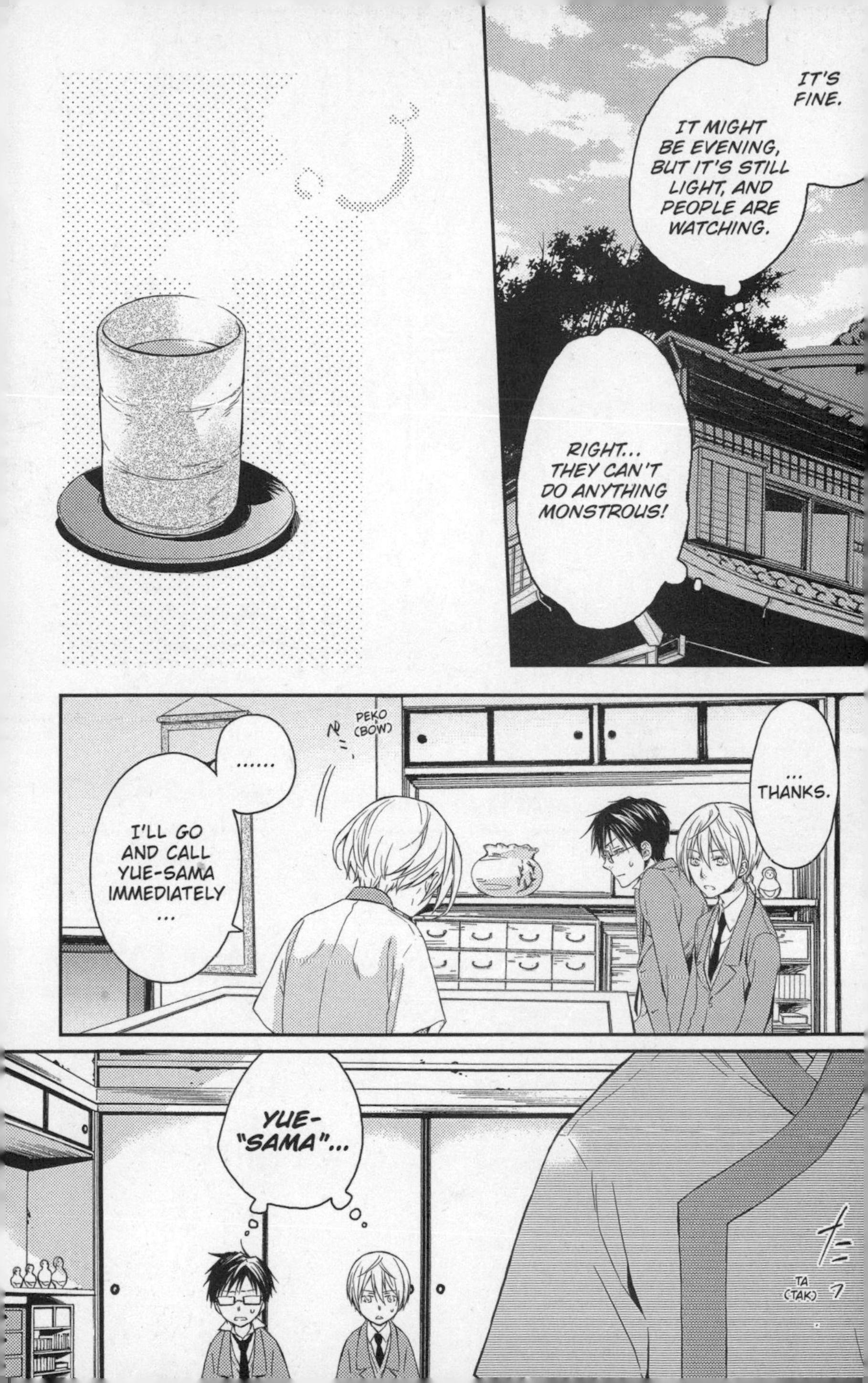
IT'S FINE.
IT MIGHT BE EVENING, BUT IT'S STILL LIGHT, AND PEOPLE ARE WATCHING.
RIGHT... THEY CAN'T DO ANYTHING MONSTROUS!
... THANKS.
PEKO (BOW)
......
I'LL GO AND CALL YUE-SAMA IMMEDIATELY ...
TA (TAK)
YUE- "SAMA"...

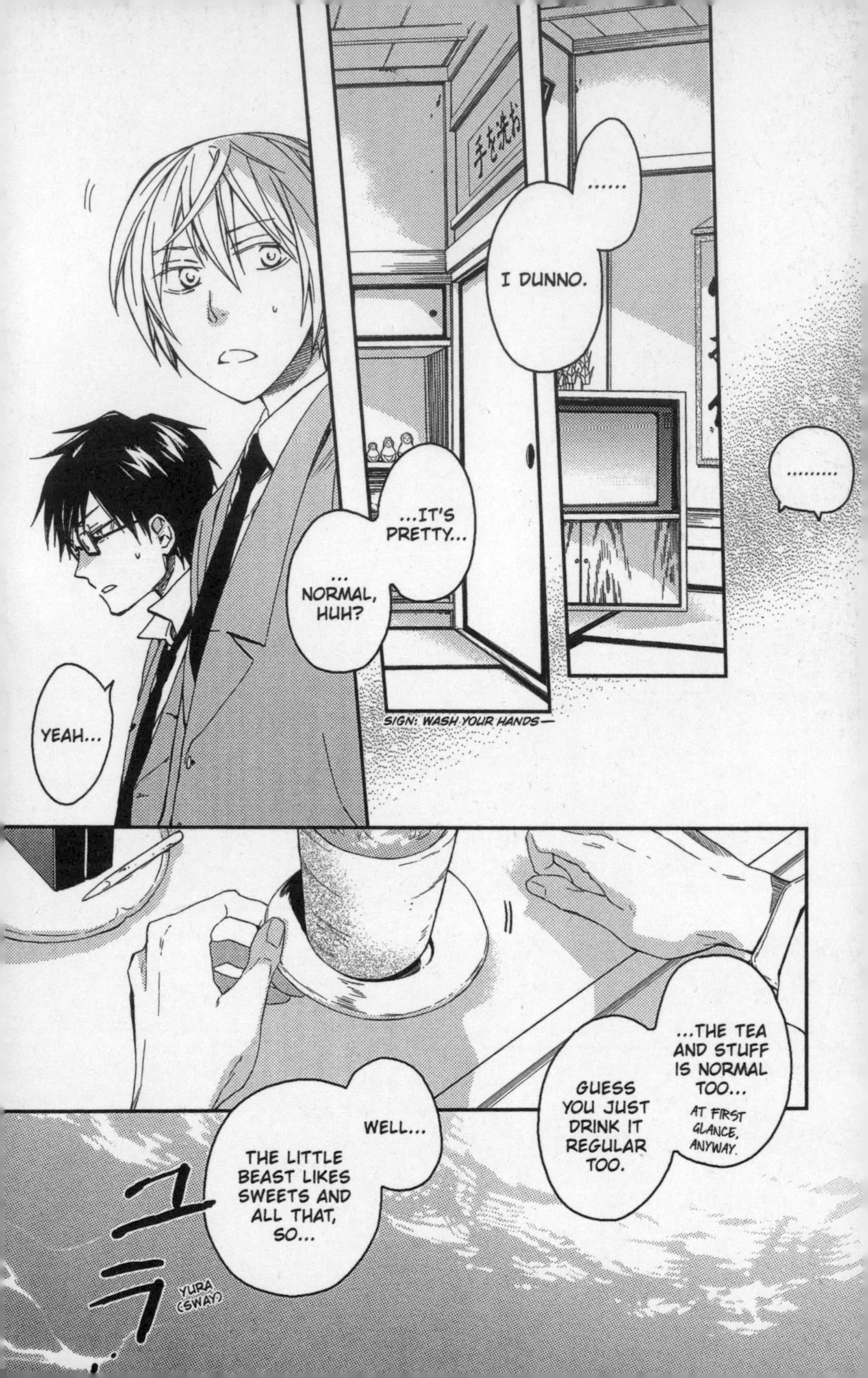
....
......
I DUNNO.
...IT'S PRETTY...
... NORMAL, HUH?
手を洗お
SIGN: WASH YOUR HANDS—
YEAH...
...THE TEA AND STUFF IS NORMAL TOO...
AT FIRST GLANCE, ANYWAY.
GUESS YOU JUST DRINK IT REGULAR TOO.
WELL...
THE LITTLE BEAST LIKES SWEETS AND ALL THAT, SO...
ユラ
YURA (SWAY)

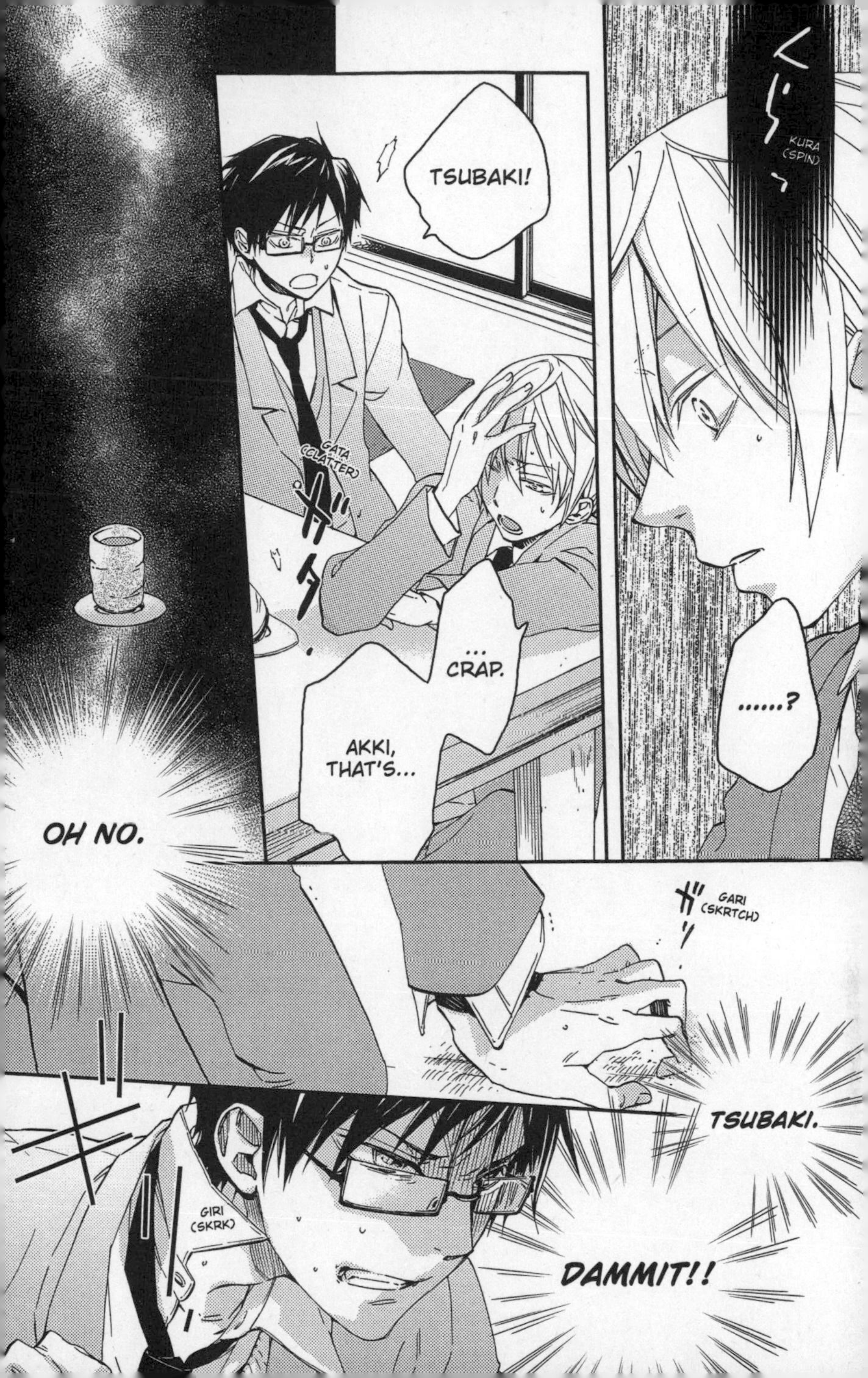
KURA (SPIN)
......?
TSUBAKI!
GATA (CLATTER)
... CRAP.
AKKI, THAT'S...
OH NO.
GARI (SKRTCH)
TSUBAKI.
GIRI (SKRK)
DAMMIT!!

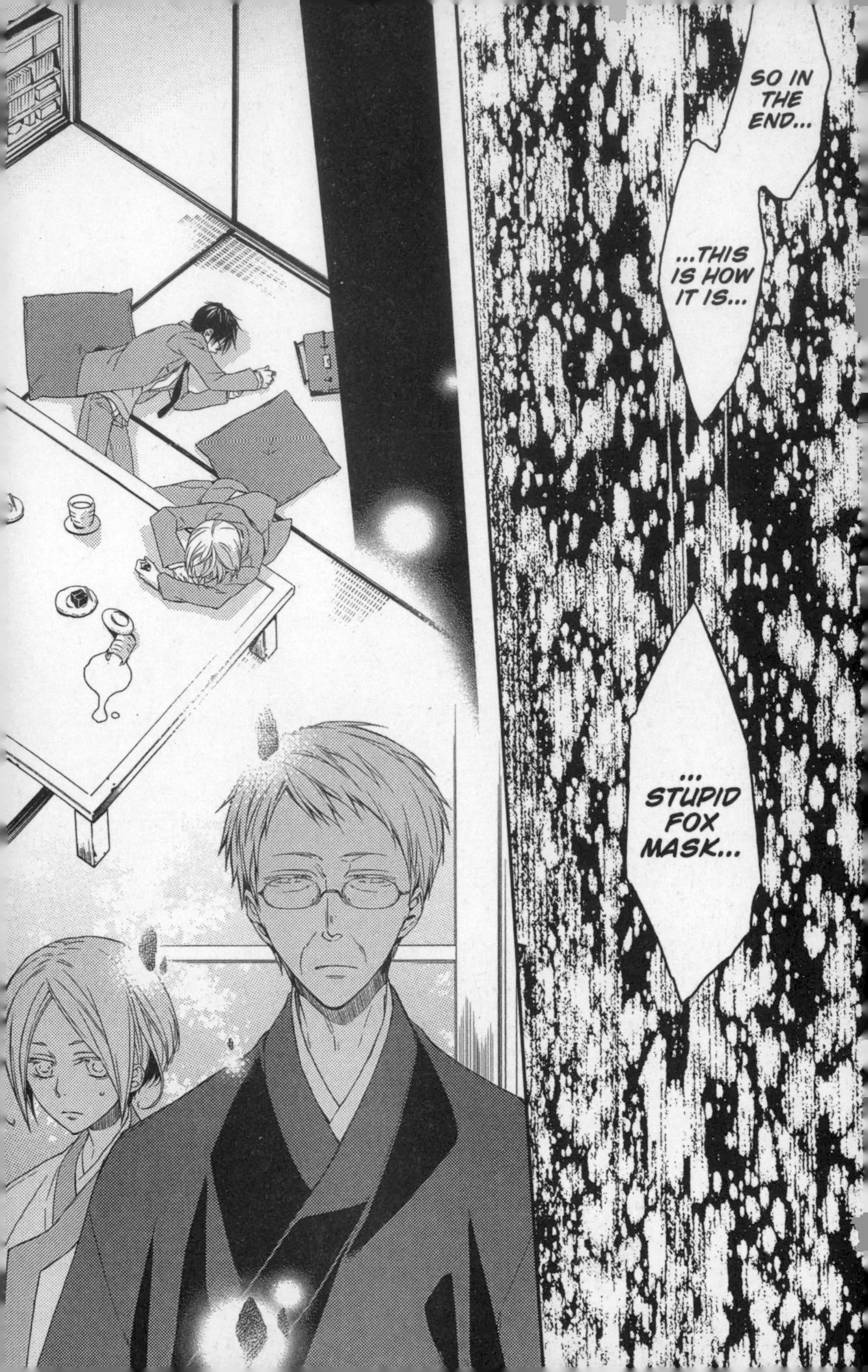
SO IN THE END...
...THIS IS HOW IT IS...
...STUPID FOX MASK...

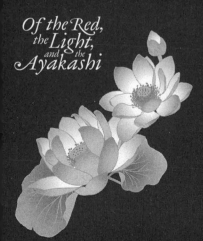

Of the Red,
the Light,
and the
Ayakashi

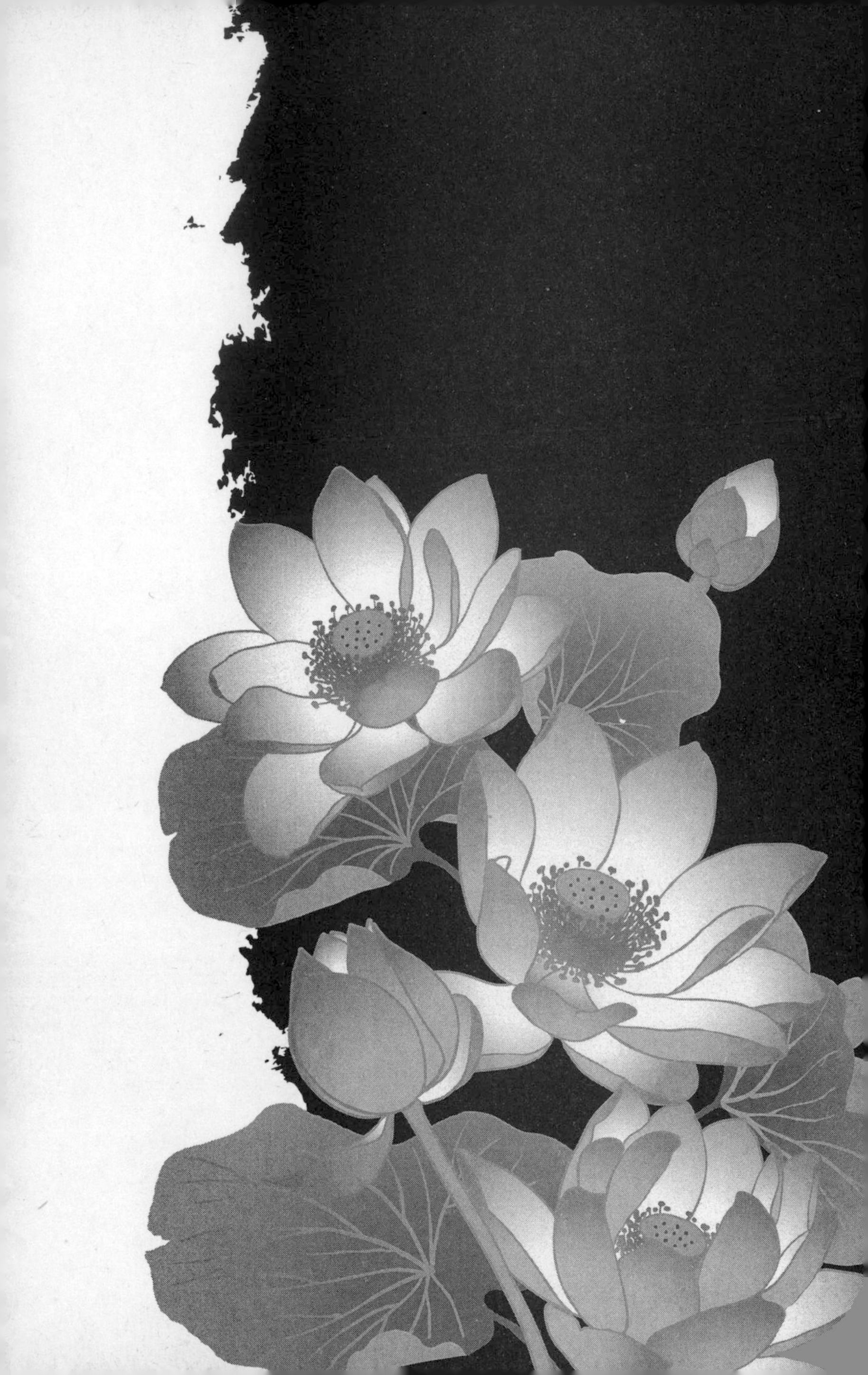

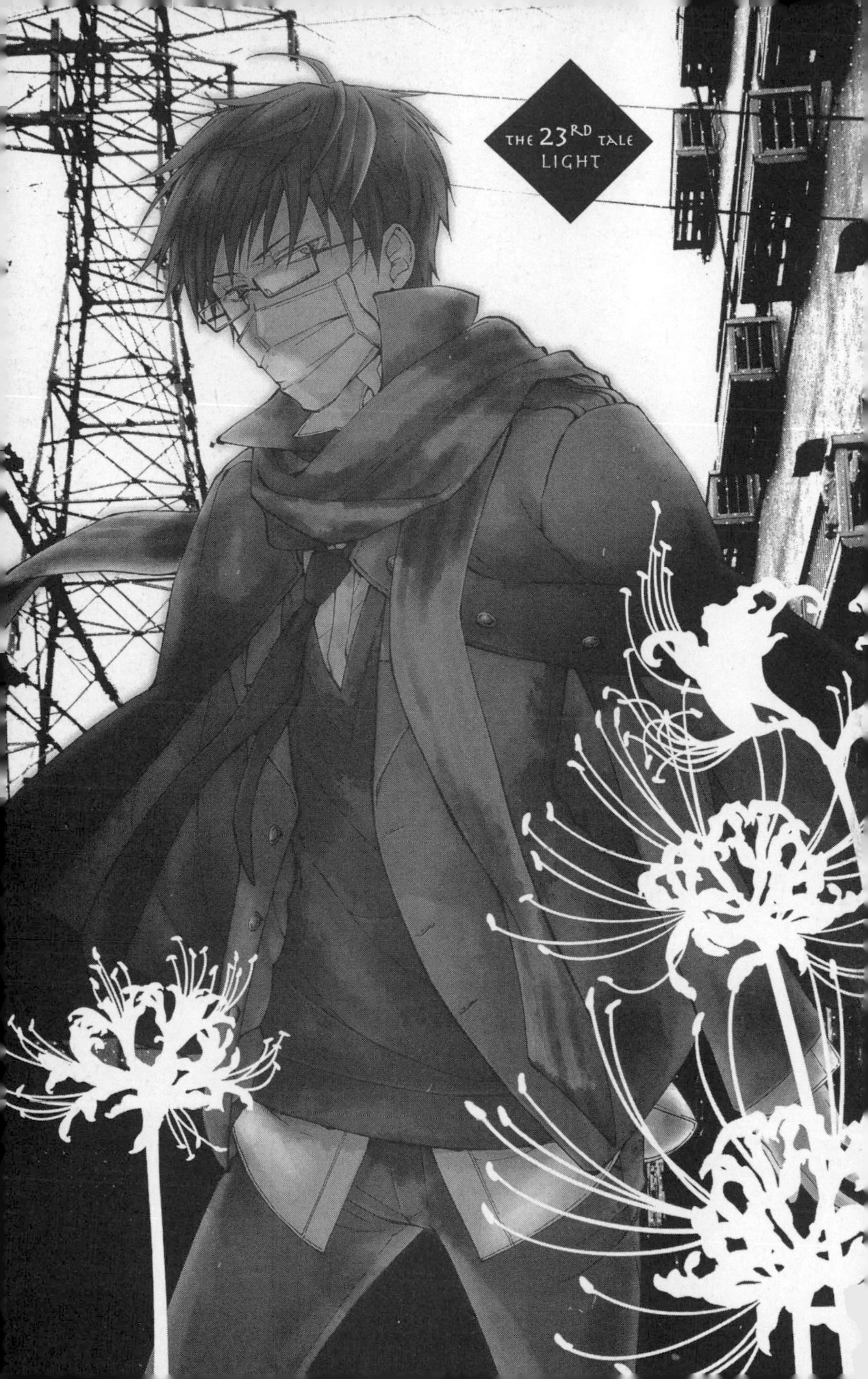
THE 23RD TALE
LIGHT

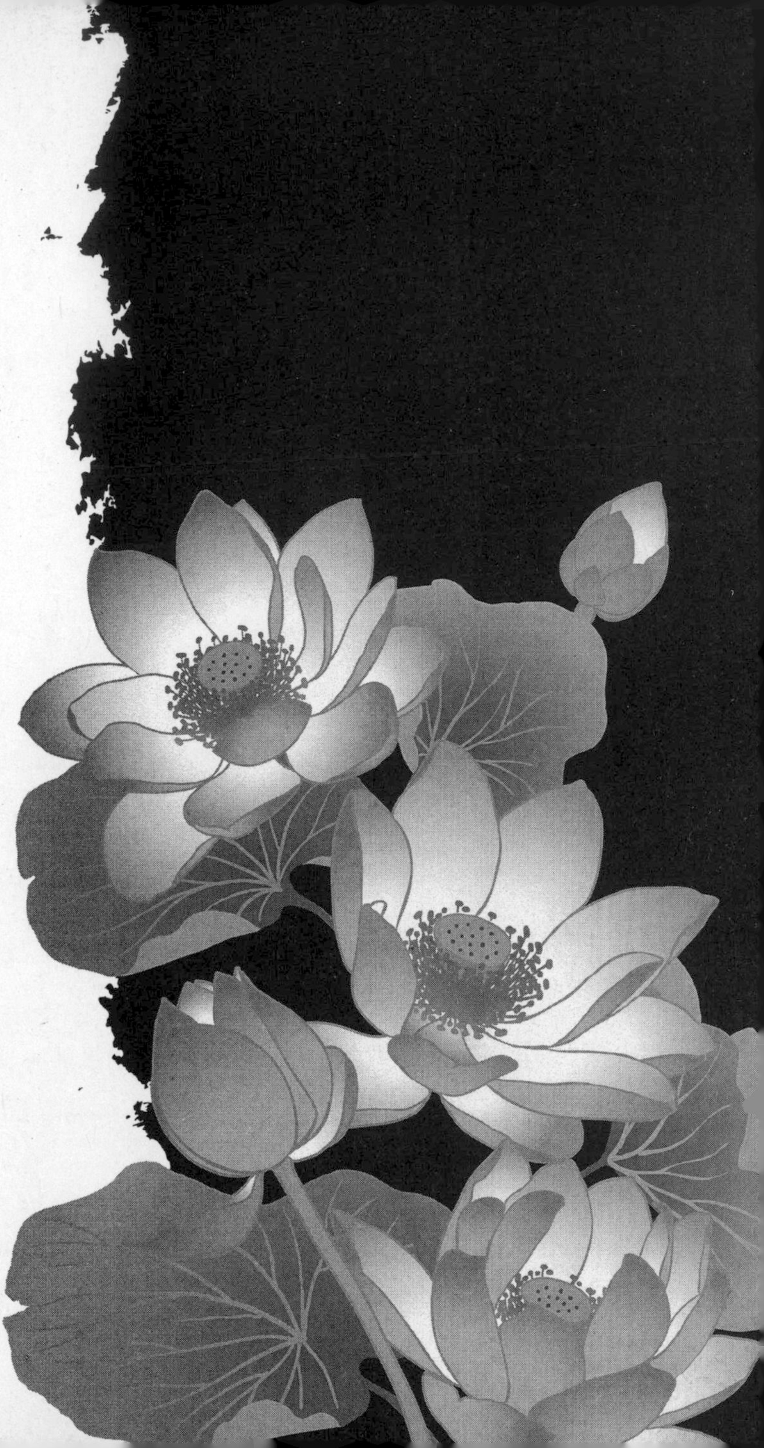

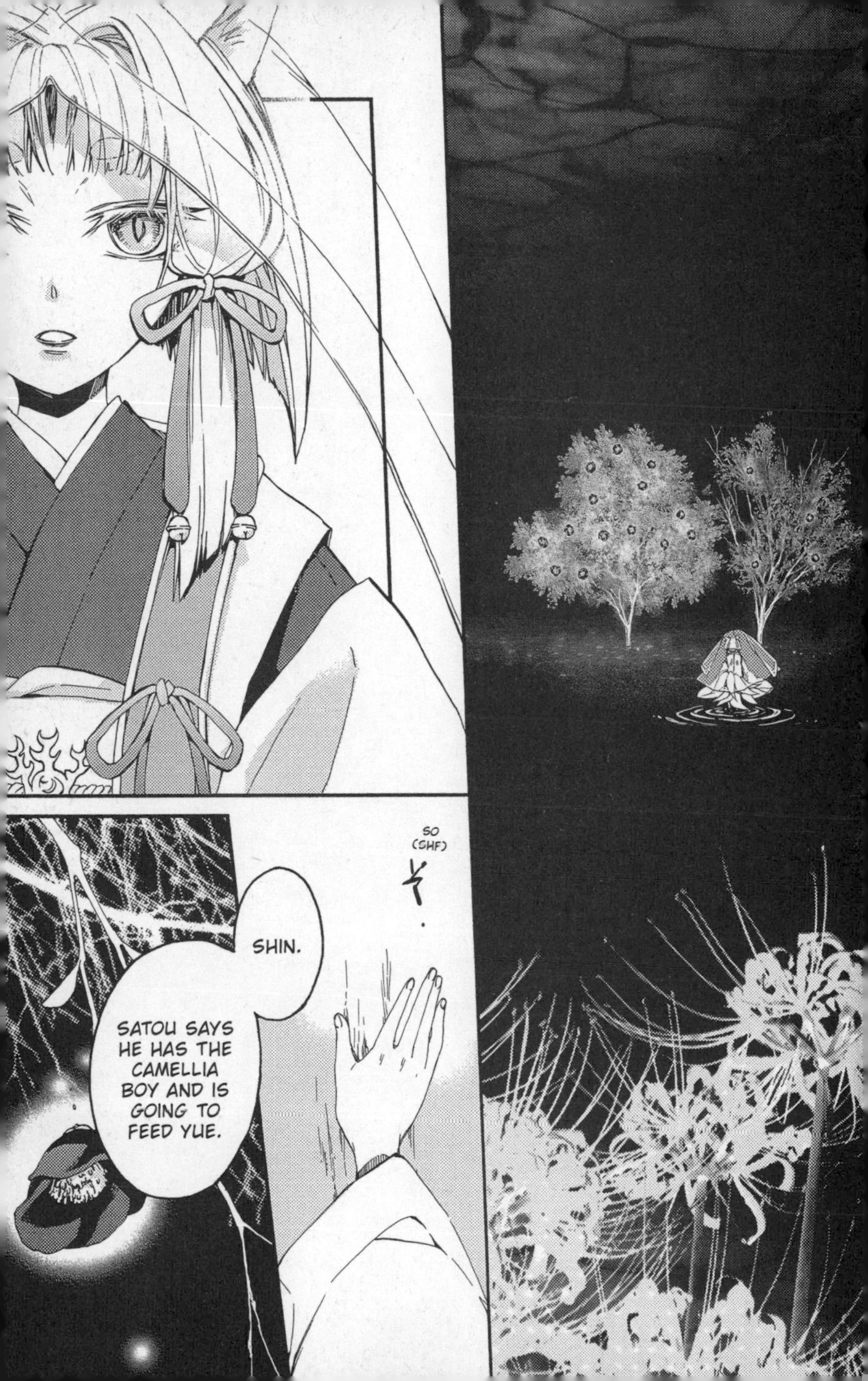
SO (SHF)
SHIN.
SATOU SAYS HE HAS THE CAMELLIA BOY AND IS GOING TO FEED YUE.

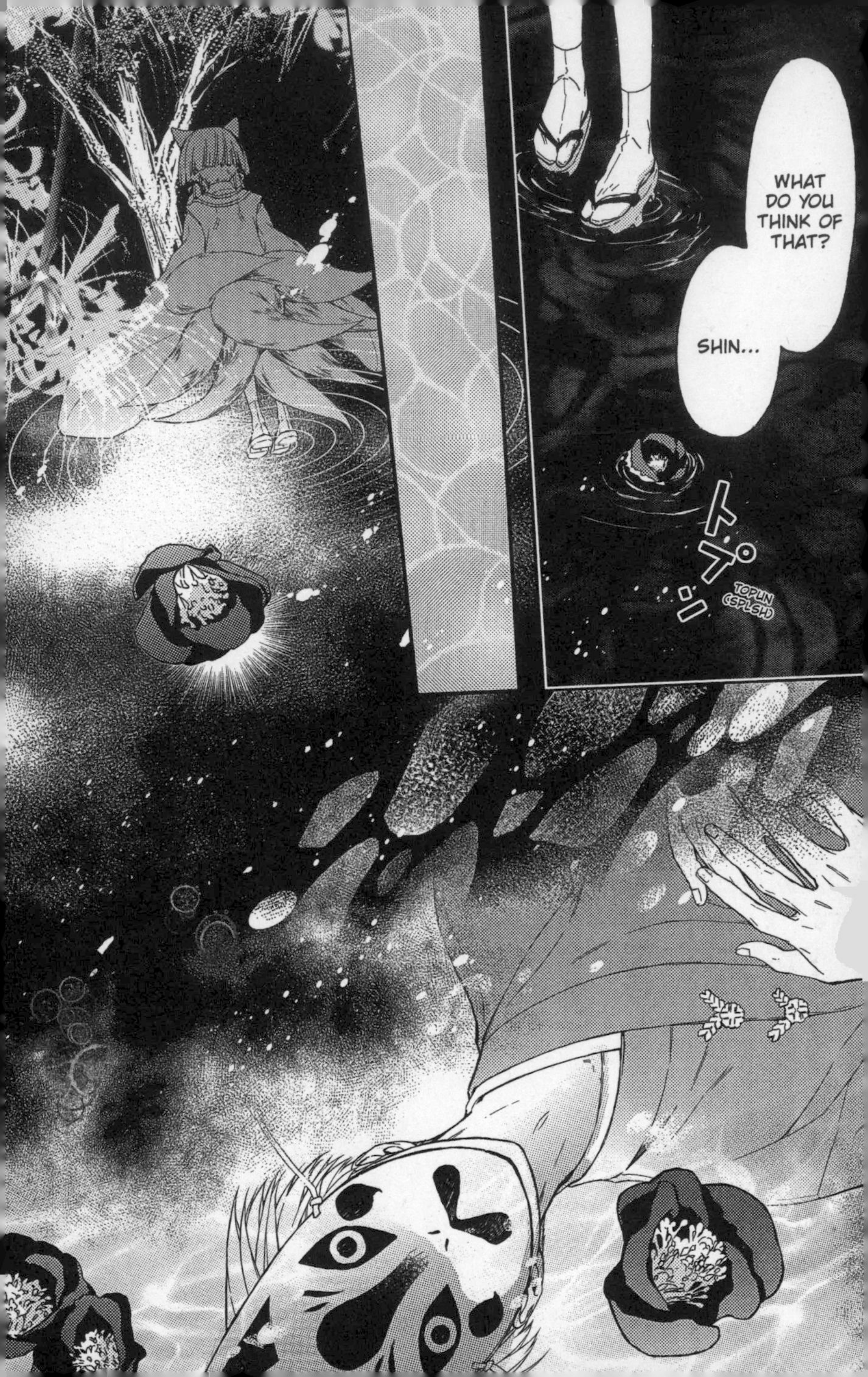

WHAT DO YOU THINK OF THAT?
SHIN...
トプッ
TOPUN (SPLSH)

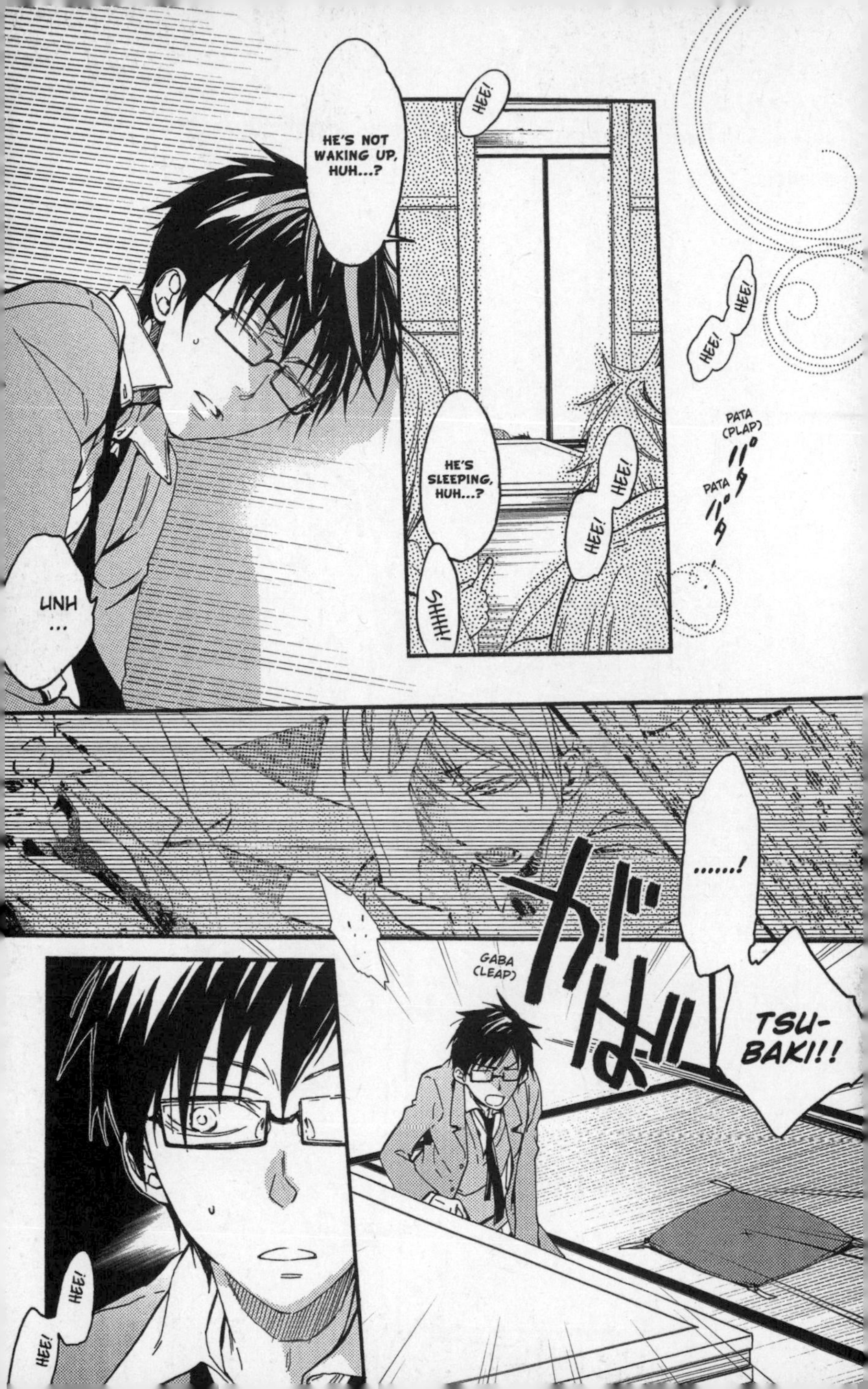
HEE! HEE! HEE!
PATA (PLAP)
PATA
HEE!
HE'S SLEEPING, HUH...?
HEE! HEE!
SHHH!
HE'S NOT WAKING UP, HUH...?
UNH ...
......!
TSU-BAKI!!
GABA (LEAP)
HEE! HEE! HEE!

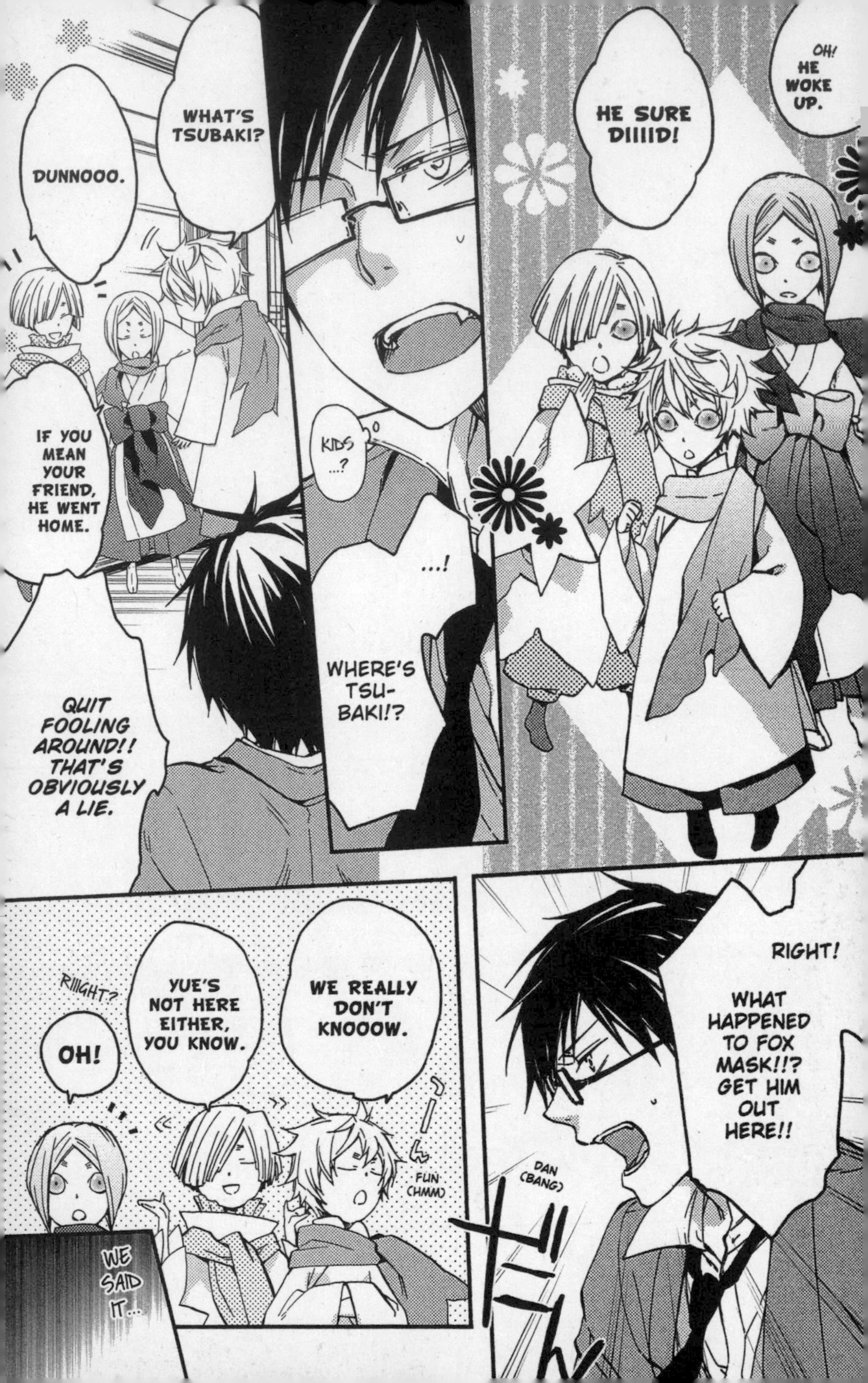
OH! HE WOKE UP.
HE SURE DIIIID!
KIDS ...?
...!
WHERE'S TSU-BAKI!?
WHAT'S TSUBAKI?
DUNNOOO.
IF YOU MEAN YOUR FRIEND, HE WENT HOME.
QUIT FOOLING AROUND!! THAT'S OBVIOUSLY A LIE.
RIGHT!
WHAT HAPPENED TO FOX MASK!!? GET HIM OUT HERE!!
DAN (BANG)
WE REALLY DON'T KNOOOW.
FUN (HMM)
YUE'S NOT HERE EITHER, YOU KNOW.
RIIIGHT?
OH!
WE SAID IT...

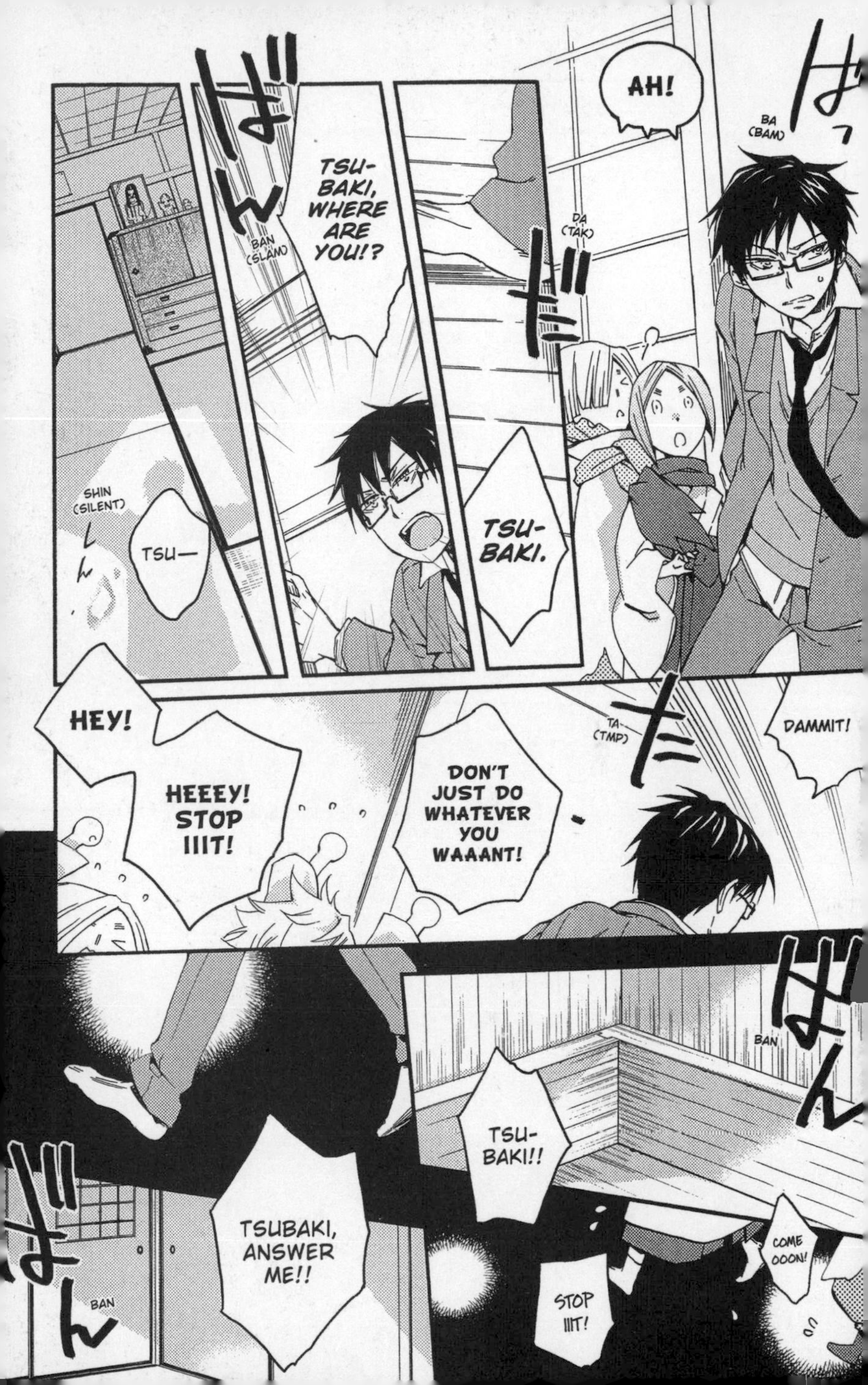

AH!
BA
(BAM)
DA
(TAK)
TSU-
BAKI.
TSU-
BAKI,
WHERE
ARE
YOU!?
BAN
(SLAM)
SHIN
(SILENT)
TSU—
DAMMIT!
TA
(TMP)
DON'T
JUST DO
WHATEVER
YOU
WAAANT!
HEEEY!
STOP
IIIT!
HEY!
BAN
TSU-
BAKI!!
COME
OOON!
STOP
IIIT!
TSUBAKI,
ANSWER
ME!!
BAN

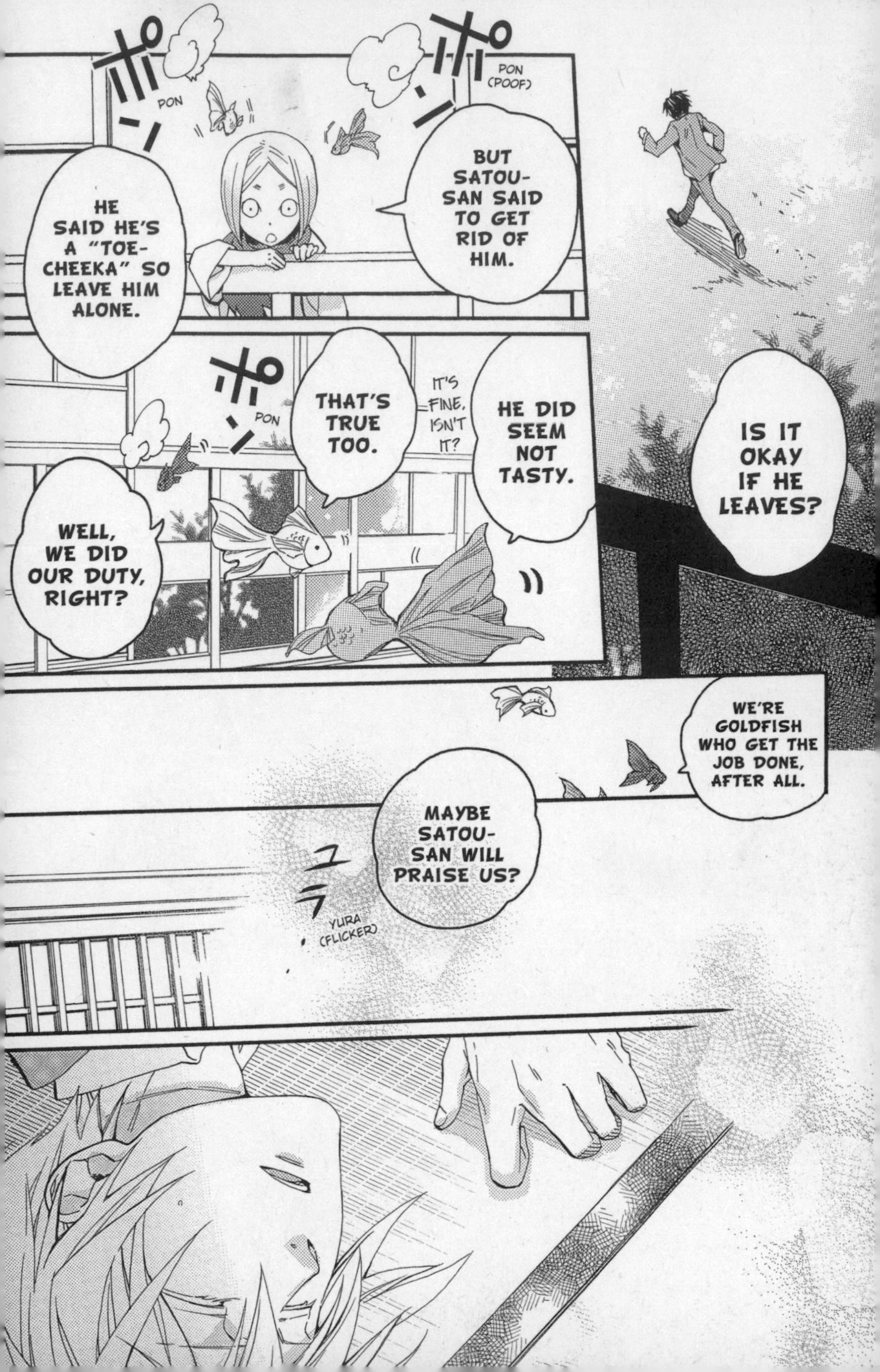
IS IT OKAY IF HE LEAVES?
PON (POOF)
BUT SATOU-SAN SAID TO GET RID OF HIM.
PON
HE SAID HE'S A "TOE-CHEEKA" SO LEAVE HIM ALONE.
HE DID SEEM NOT TASTY.
IT'S FINE, ISN'T IT?
THAT'S TRUE TOO.
PON
WELL, WE DID OUR DUTY, RIGHT?
WE'RE GOLDFISH WHO GET THE JOB DONE, AFTER ALL.
MAYBE SATOU-SAN WILL PRAISE US?
YURA (FLICKER)

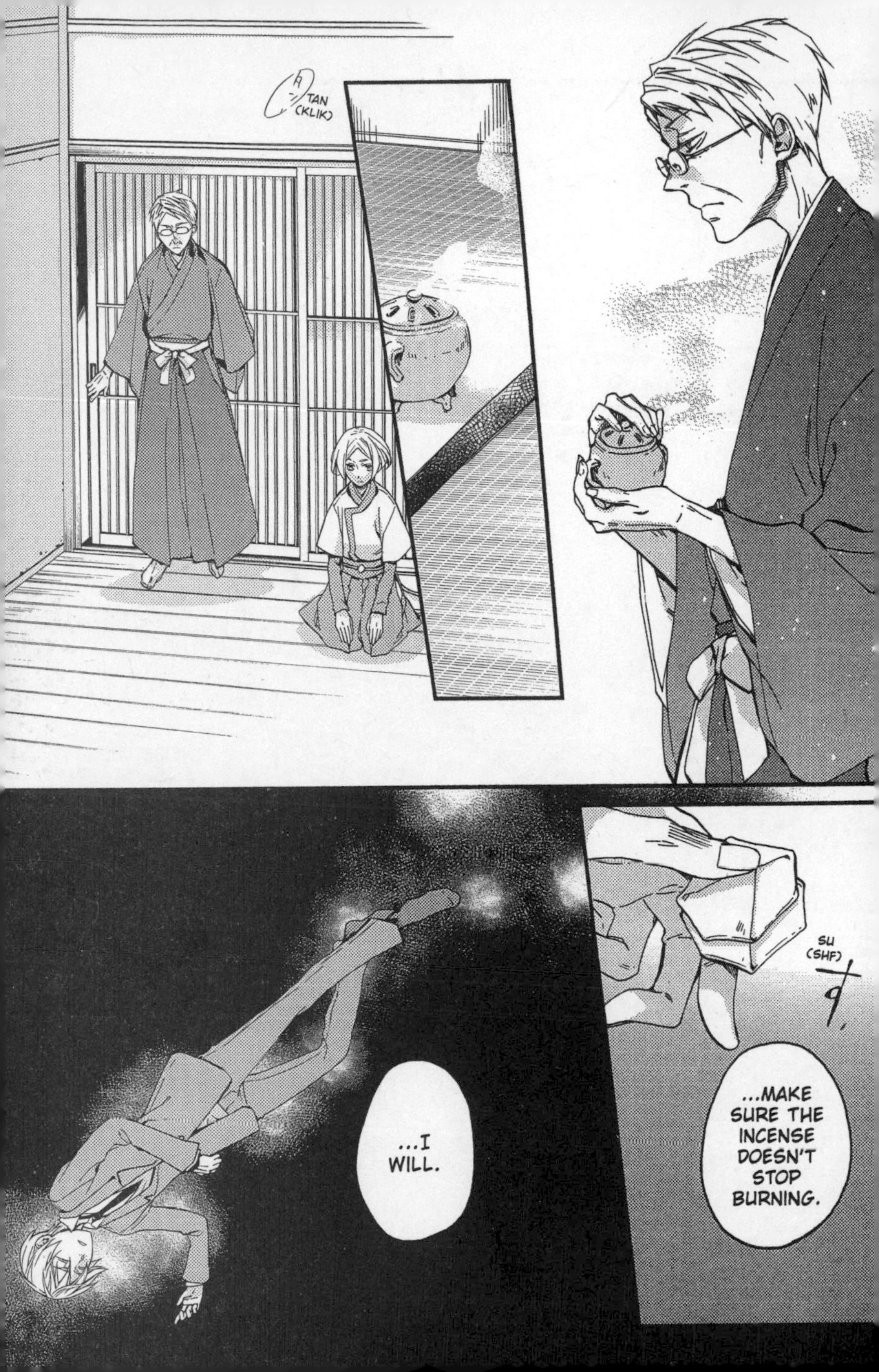
TAN (KLIK)
SU (SHF)
...MAKE SURE THE INCENSE DOESN'T STOP BURNING.
...I WILL.

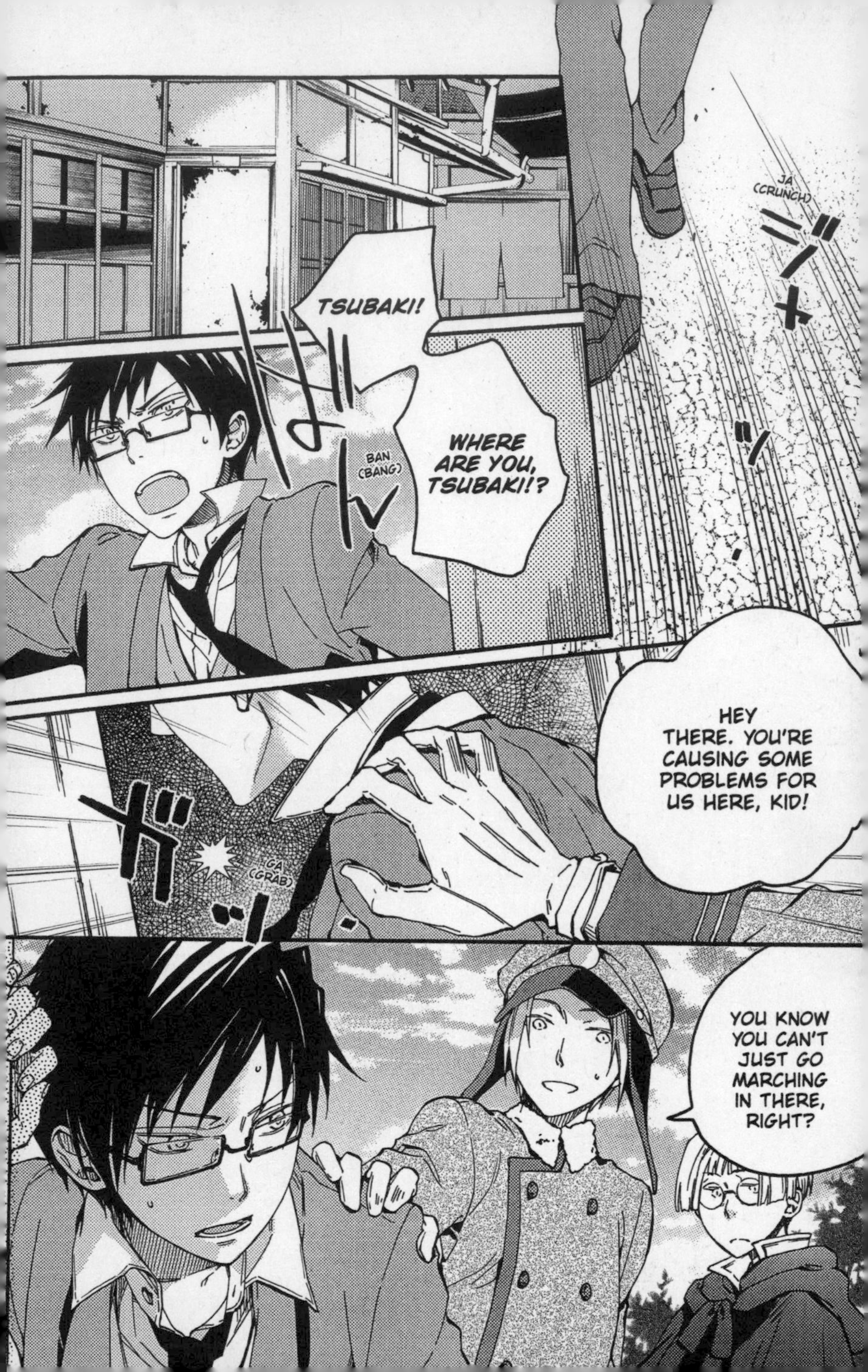
JA (CRUNCH)
TSUBAKI!
WHERE ARE YOU, TSUBAKI!?
BAN (BANG)
HEY THERE. YOU'RE CAUSING SOME PROBLEMS FOR US HERE, KID!
GA (GRAB)
YOU KNOW YOU CAN'T JUST GO MARCHING IN THERE, RIGHT?

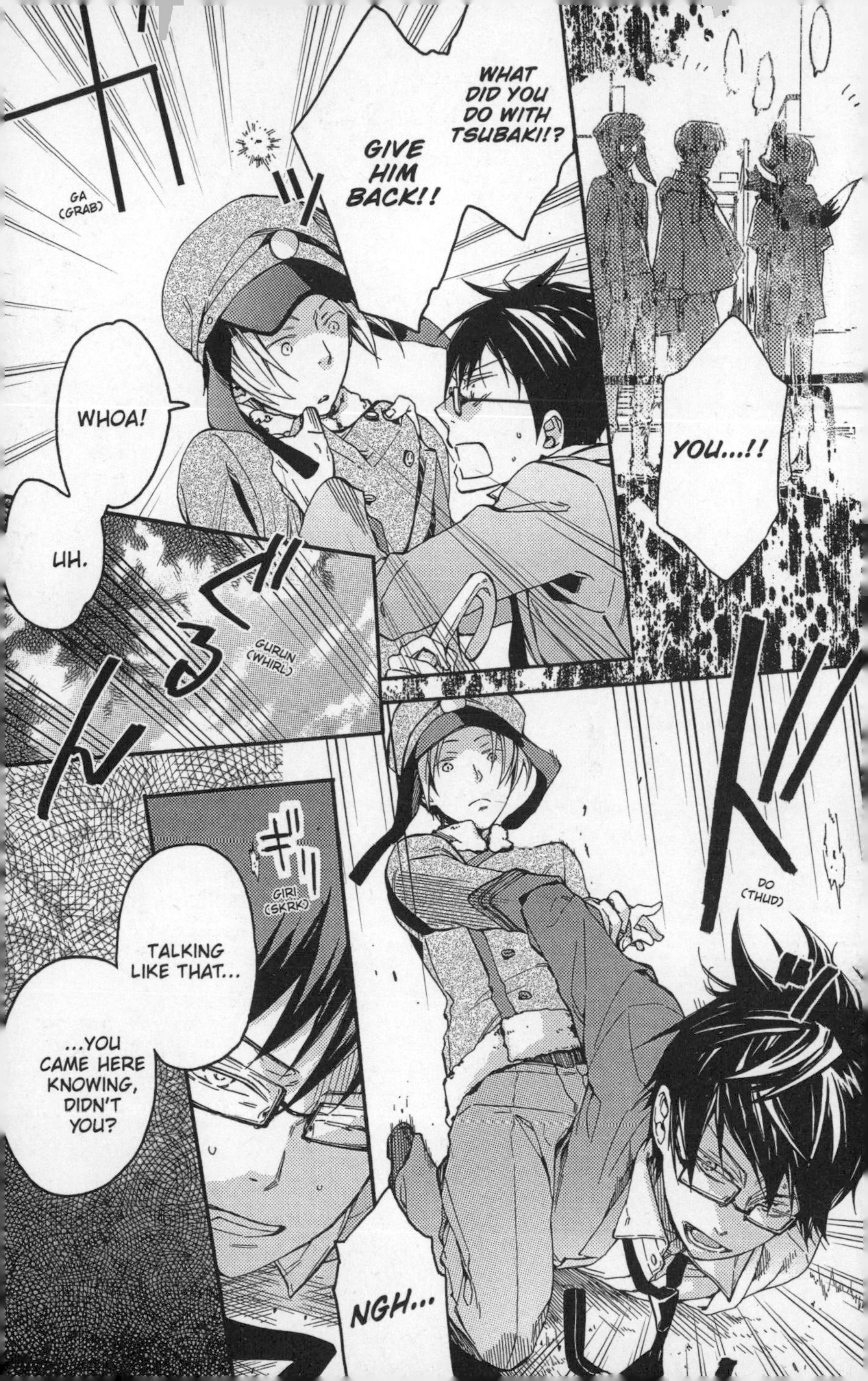
YOU...!!
WHAT DID YOU DO WITH TSUBAKI!!?
GIVE HIM BACK!!
GA (GRAB)
WHOA!
UH.
GURUN (WHIRL)
DO (THUD)
NGH...
GIRI (SKRK)
TALKING LIKE THAT...
...YOU CAME HERE KNOWING, DIDN'T YOU?

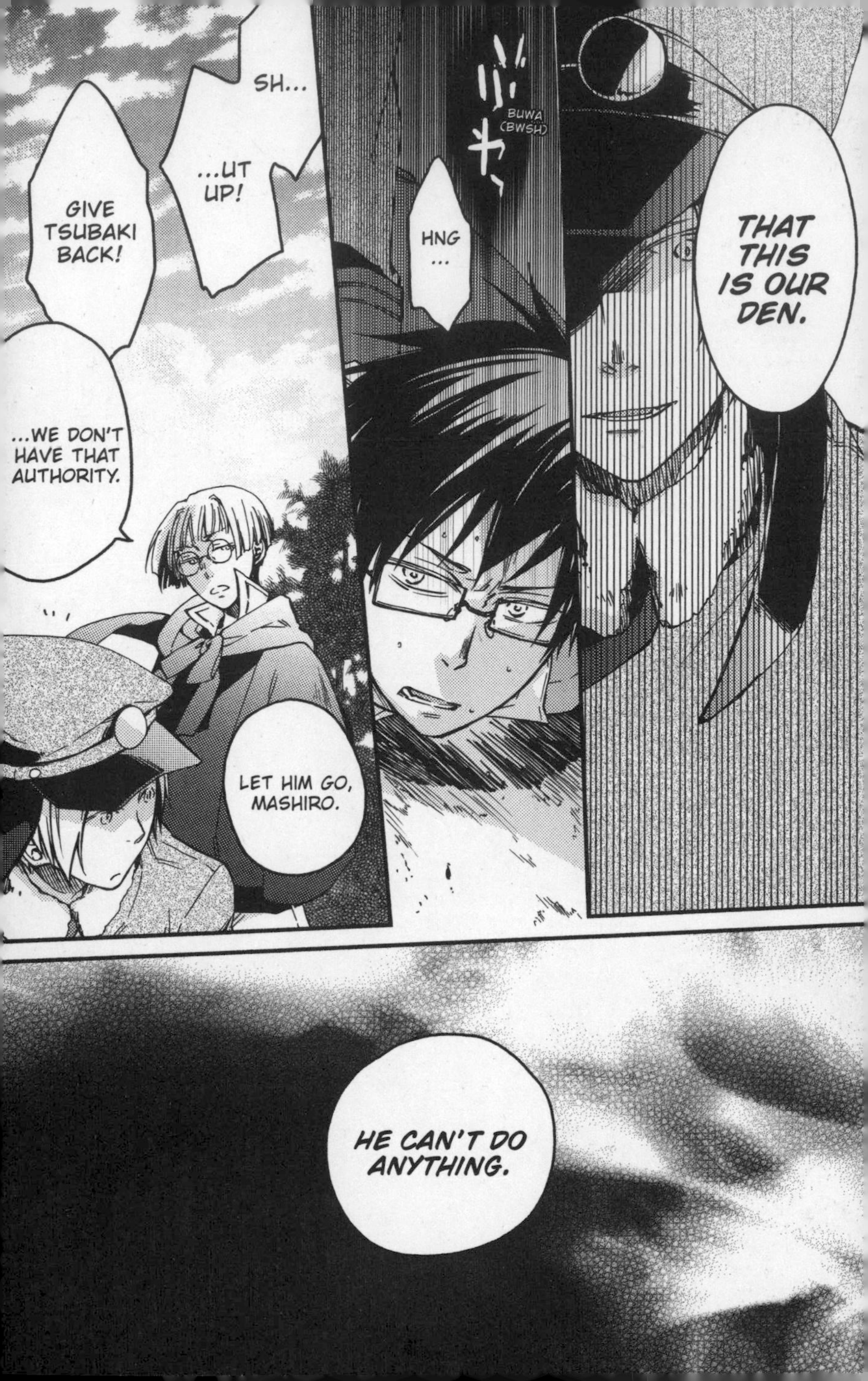
THAT THIS IS OUR DEN.
BUWA (BWSH)
HNG ...
SH...
...UT UP!
GIVE TSUBAKI BACK!
...WE DON'T HAVE THAT AUTHORITY.
LET HIM GO, MASHIRO.
HE CAN'T DO ANYTHING.

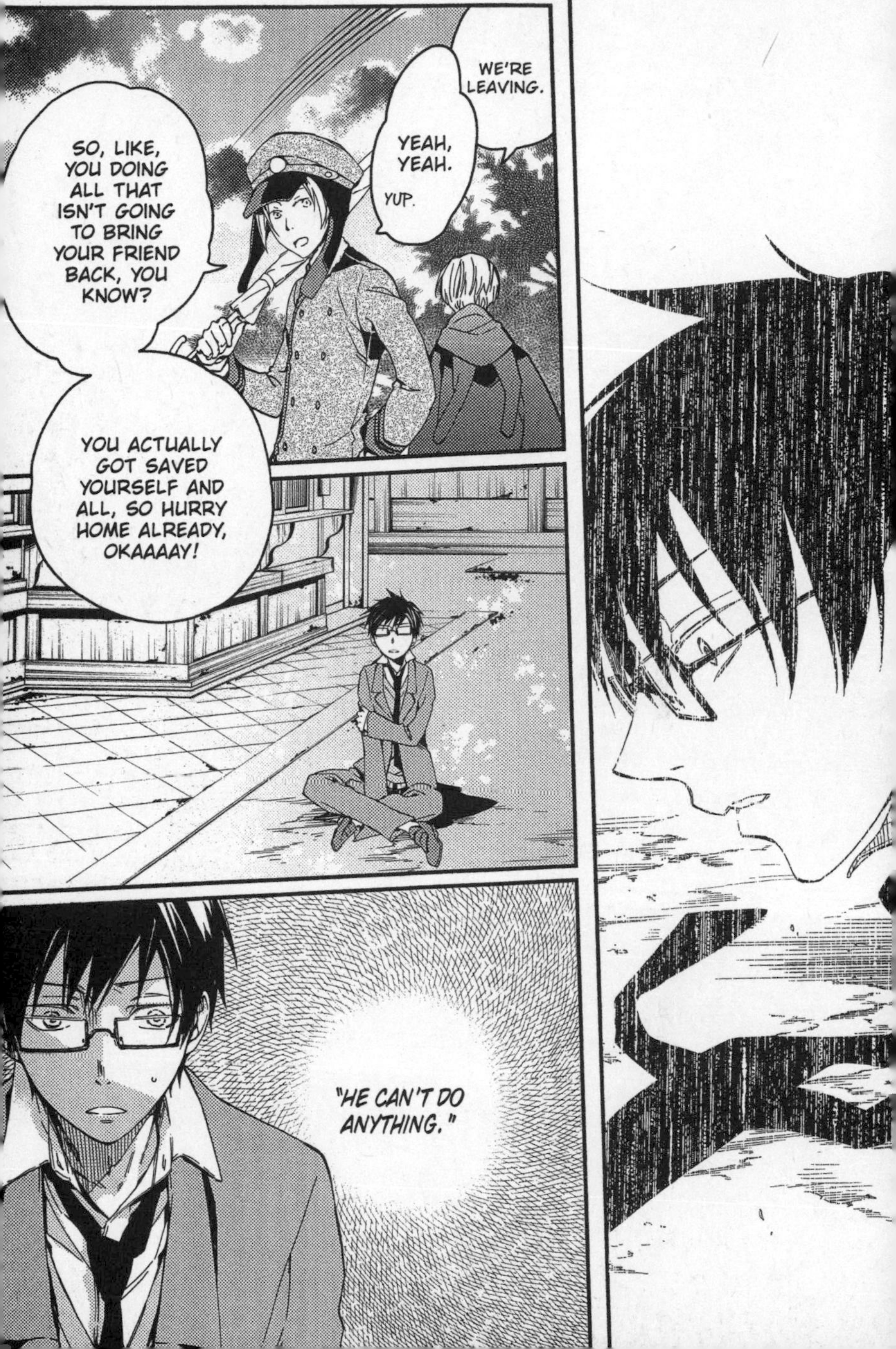
WE'RE LEAVING.
YEAH, YEAH.
YUP.
SO, LIKE, YOU DOING ALL THAT ISN'T GOING TO BRING YOUR FRIEND BACK, YOU KNOW?
YOU ACTUALLY GOT SAVED YOURSELF AND ALL, SO HURRY HOME ALREADY, OKAAAAY!
"HE CAN'T DO ANYTHING."

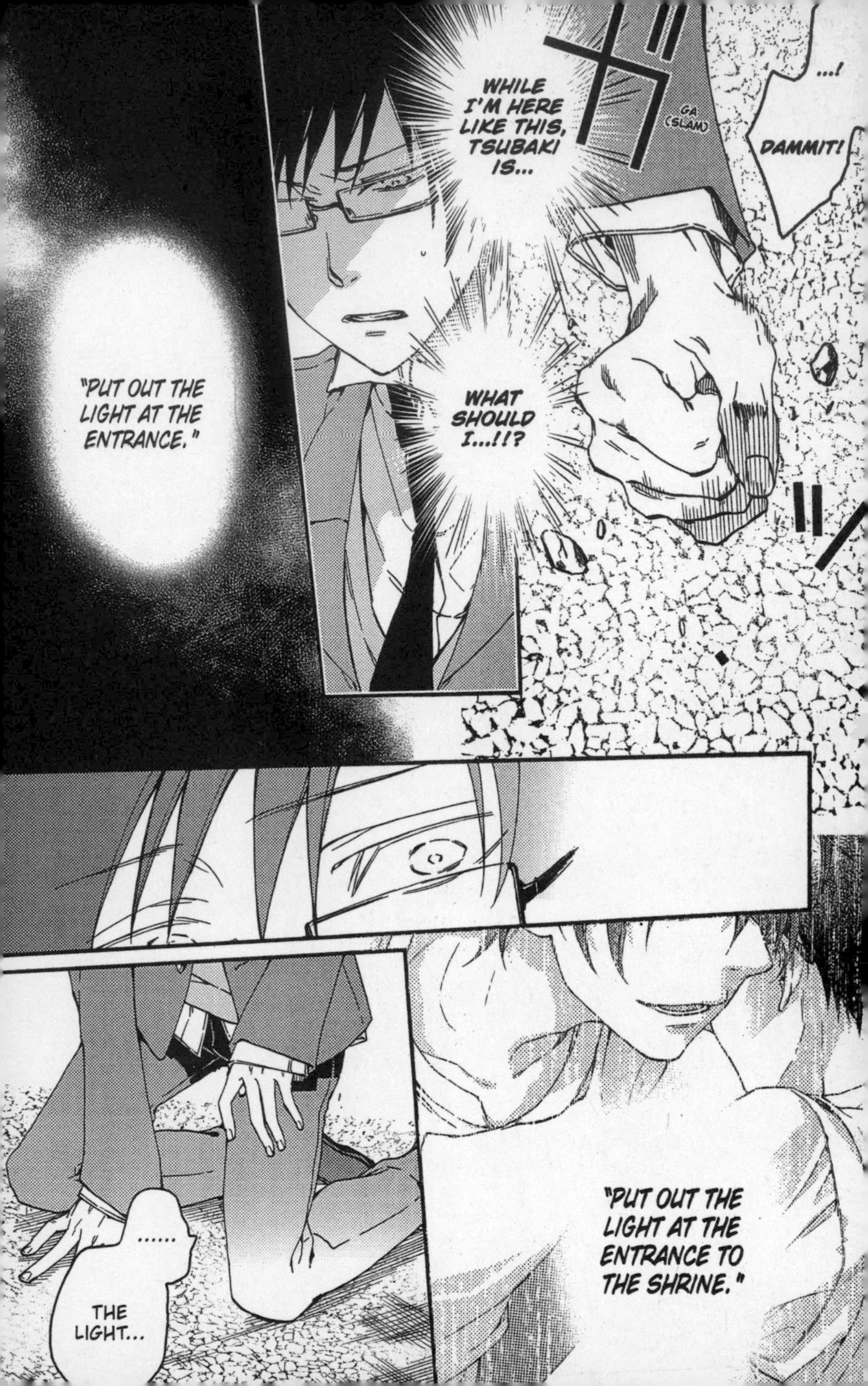

...!
DAMMIT!
GA (SLAM)
WHILE I'M HERE LIKE THIS, TSUBAKI IS...
WHAT SHOULD I...!!?
"PUT OUT THE LIGHT AT THE ENTRANCE."
"PUT OUT THE LIGHT AT THE ENTRANCE TO THE SHRINE."
......
THE LIGHT...

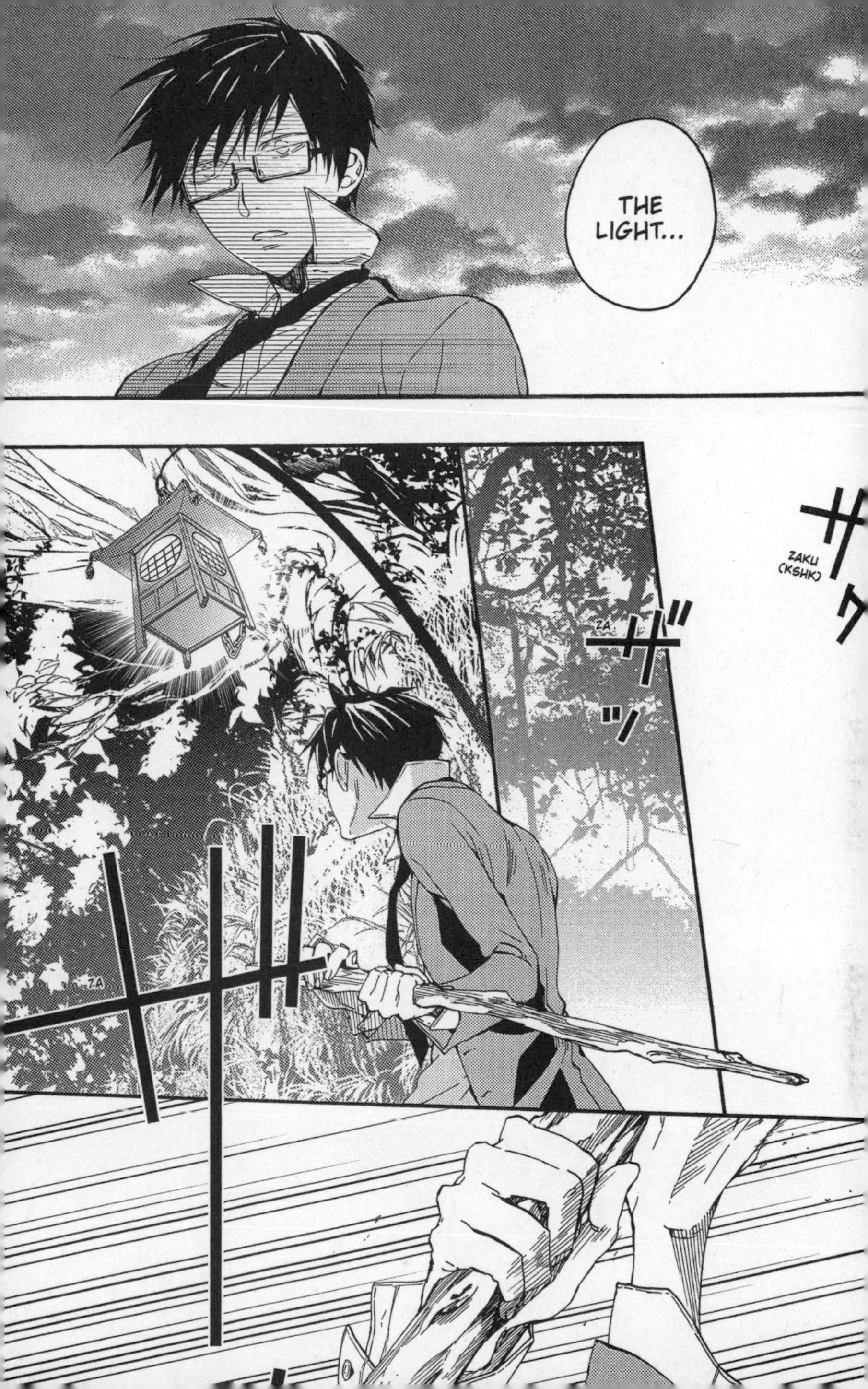
THE LIGHT...
サク
ZAKU (KSHK)
ザッ
ZA
ZA

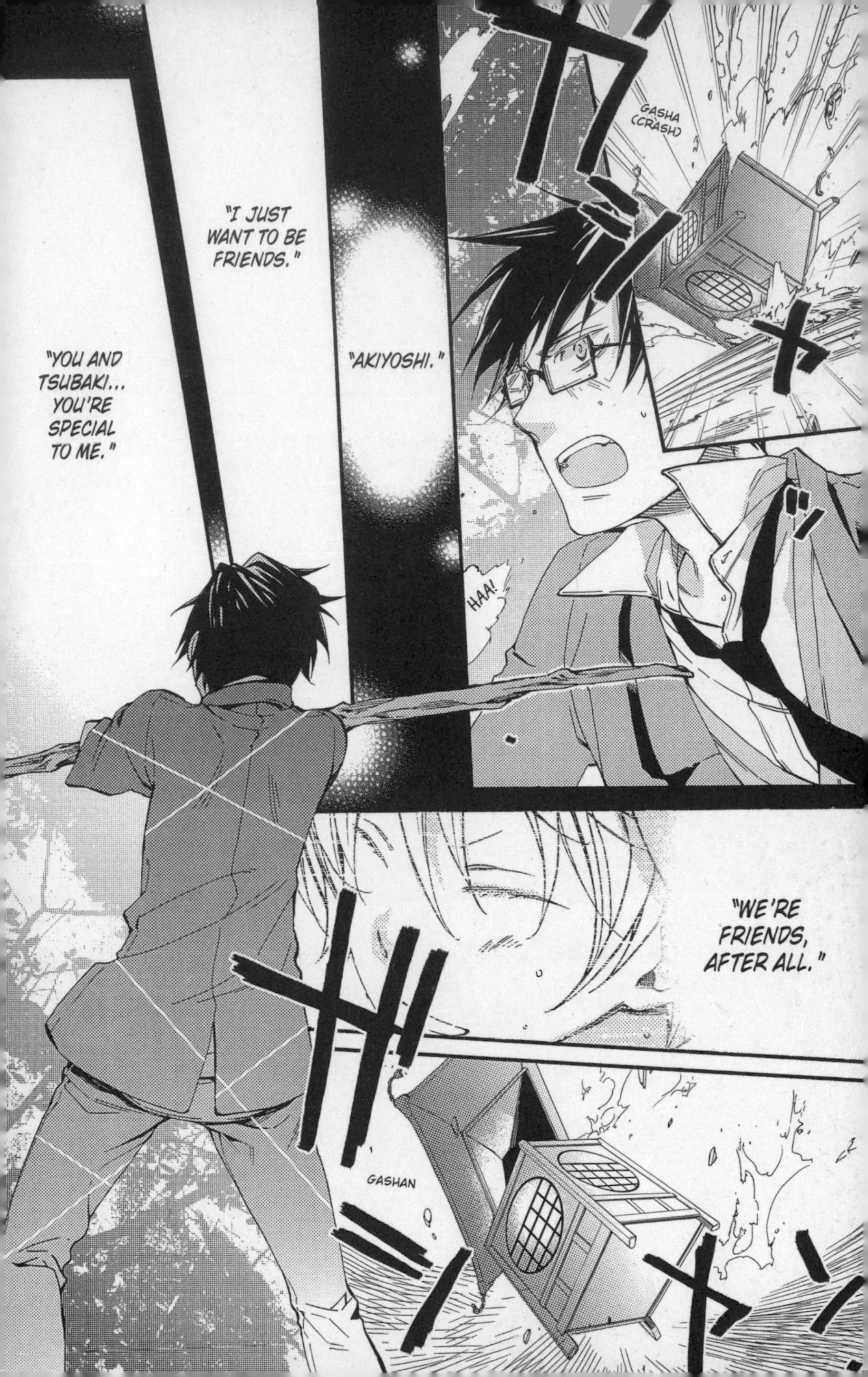
GASHA (CRASH)
HAA!
"AKIYOSHI."
"I JUST WANT TO BE FRIENDS."
"WE'RE FRIENDS, AFTER ALL."
GASHAN
"YOU AND TSUBAKI... YOU'RE SPECIAL TO ME."

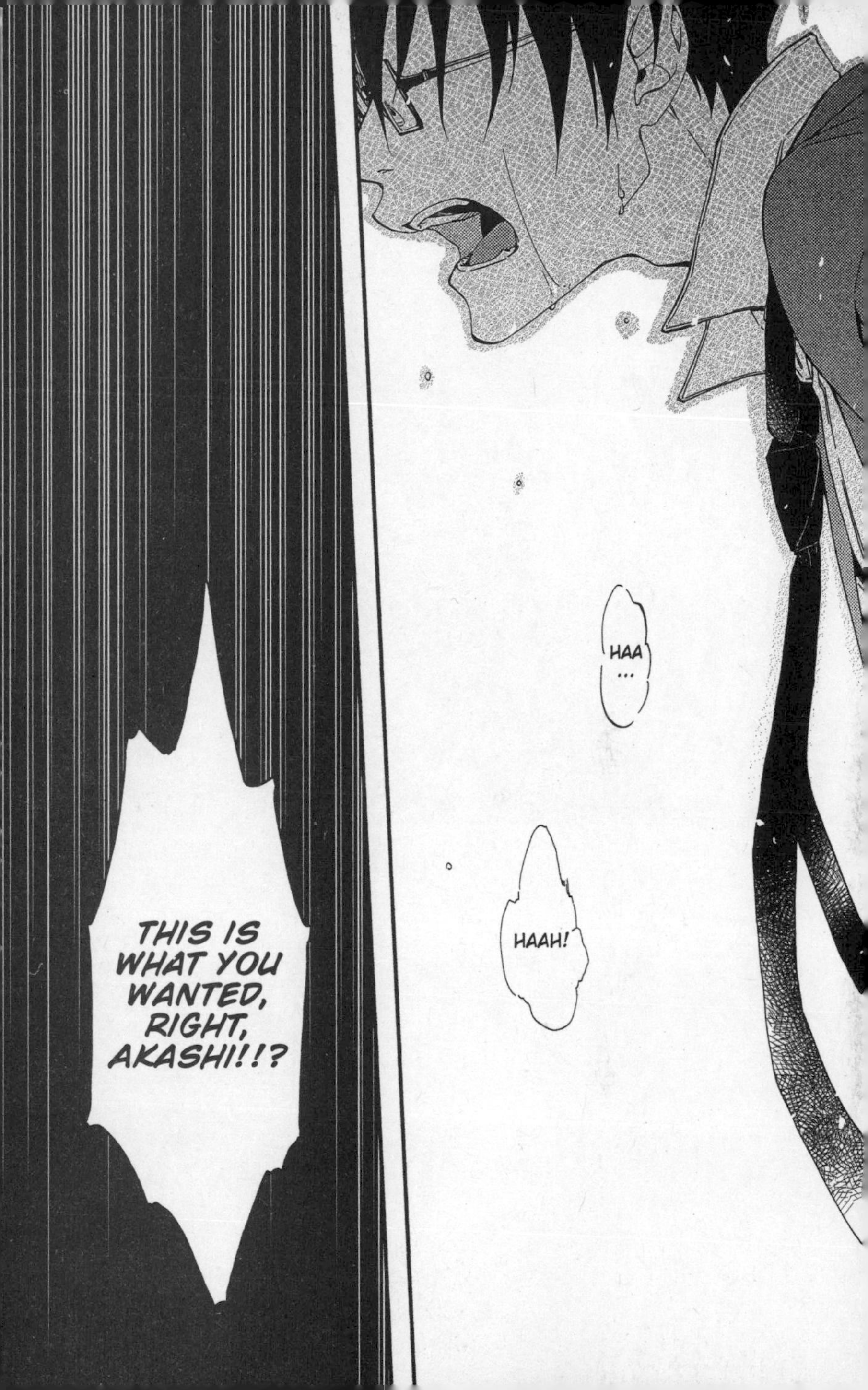
HAA ...
HAAH!
THIS IS WHAT YOU WANTED, RIGHT, AKASHI!!?

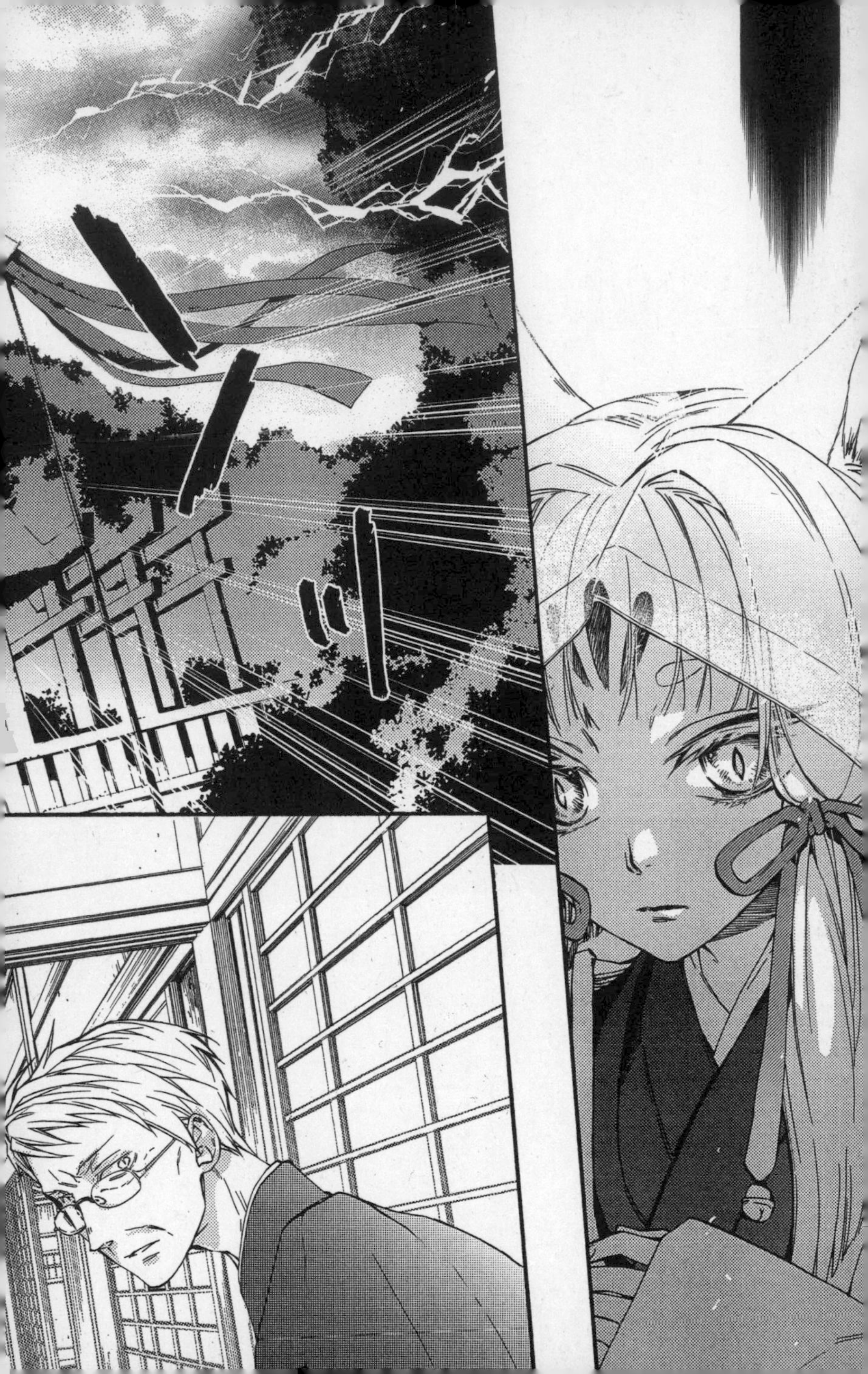

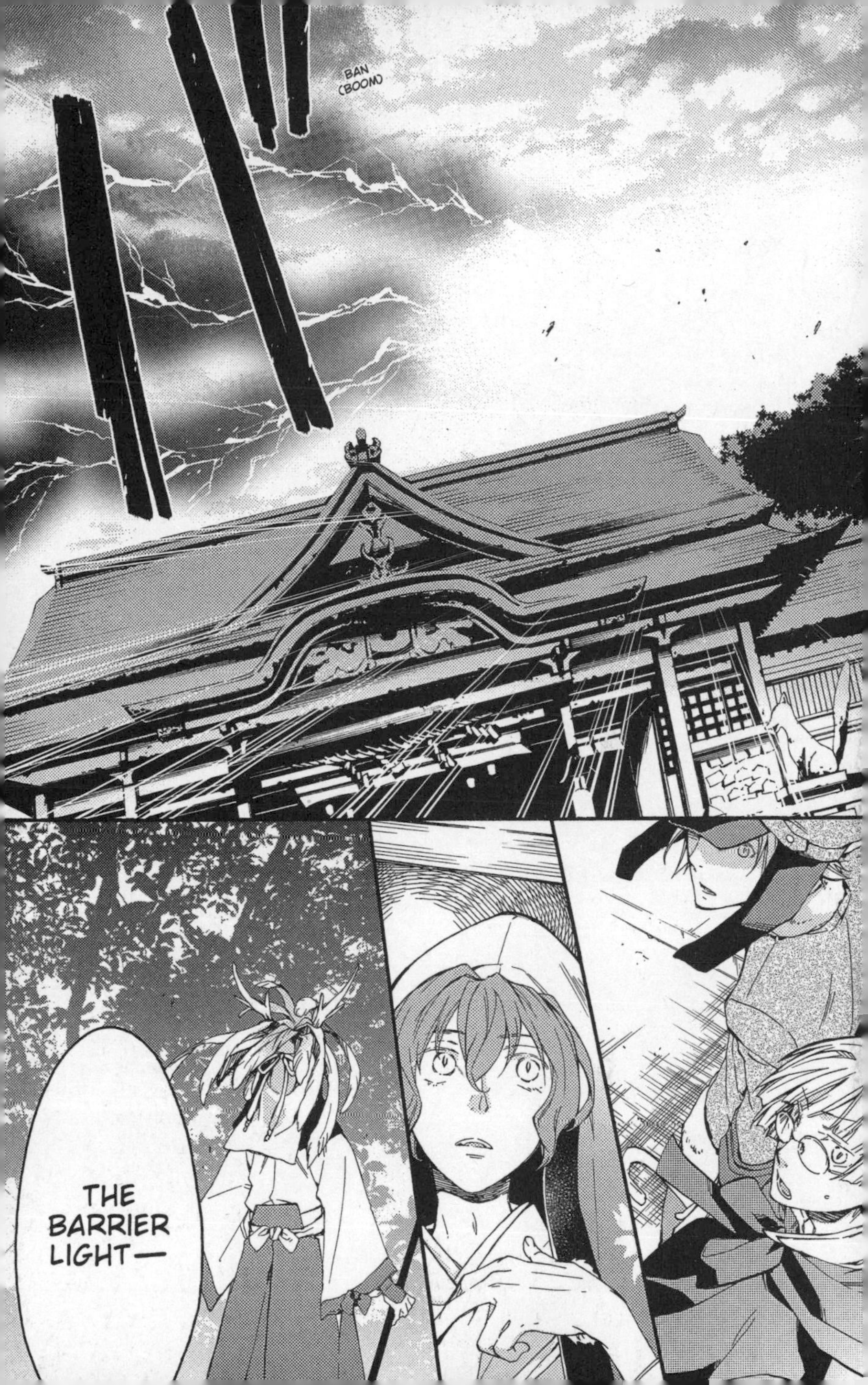
BAN
(BOOM)
THE BARRIER LIGHT—

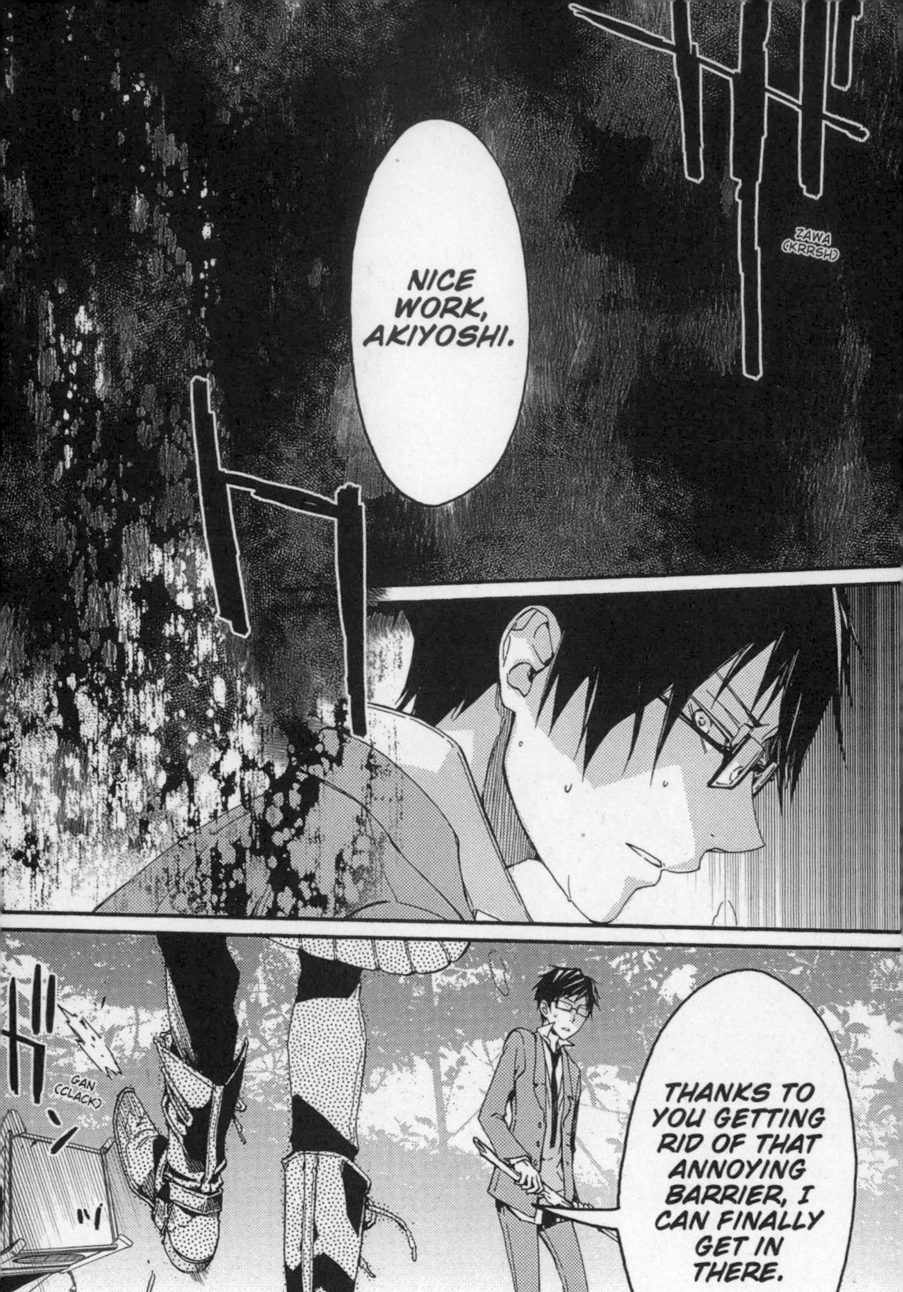
ZAWA (KRRSH)
NICE WORK, AKIYOSHI.
THANKS TO YOU GETTING RID OF THAT ANNOYING BARRIER, I CAN FINALLY GET IN THERE.
GAN (CLACK)

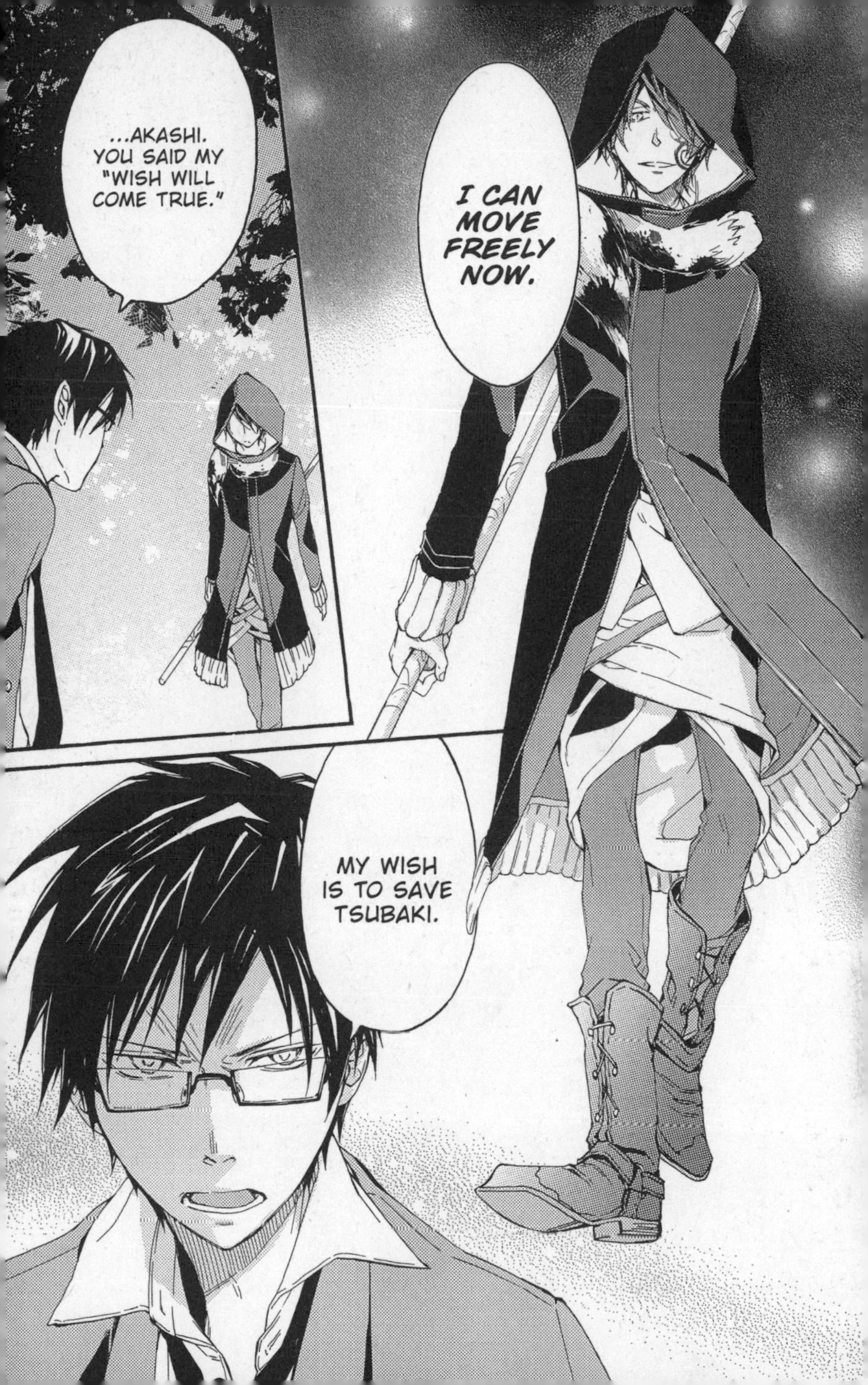
I CAN MOVE FREELY NOW.
...AKASHI. YOU SAID MY "WISH WILL COME TRUE."
MY WISH IS TO SAVE TSUBAKI.

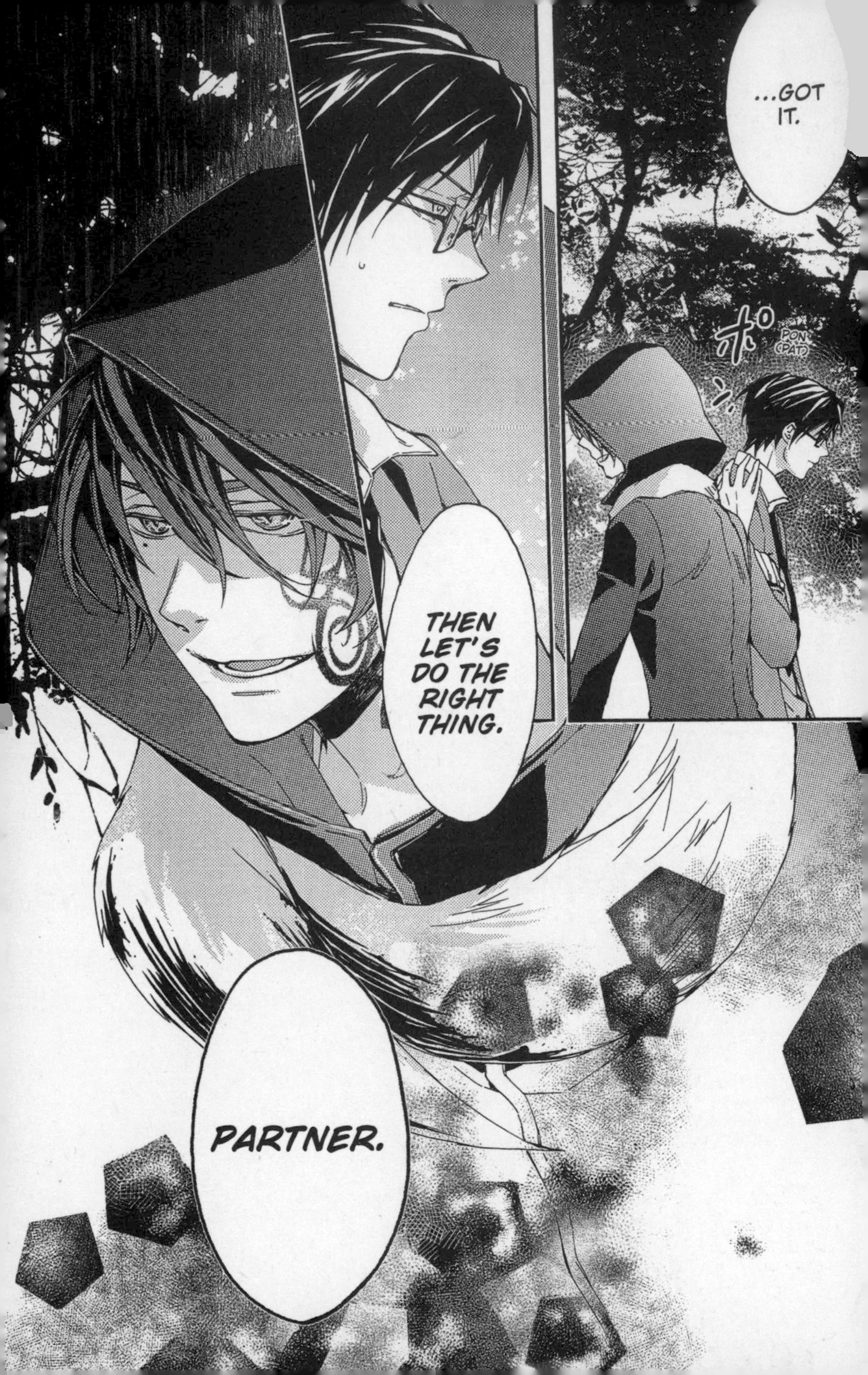
...GOT IT.
PON (PAT)
THEN LET'S DO THE RIGHT THING.
PARTNER.

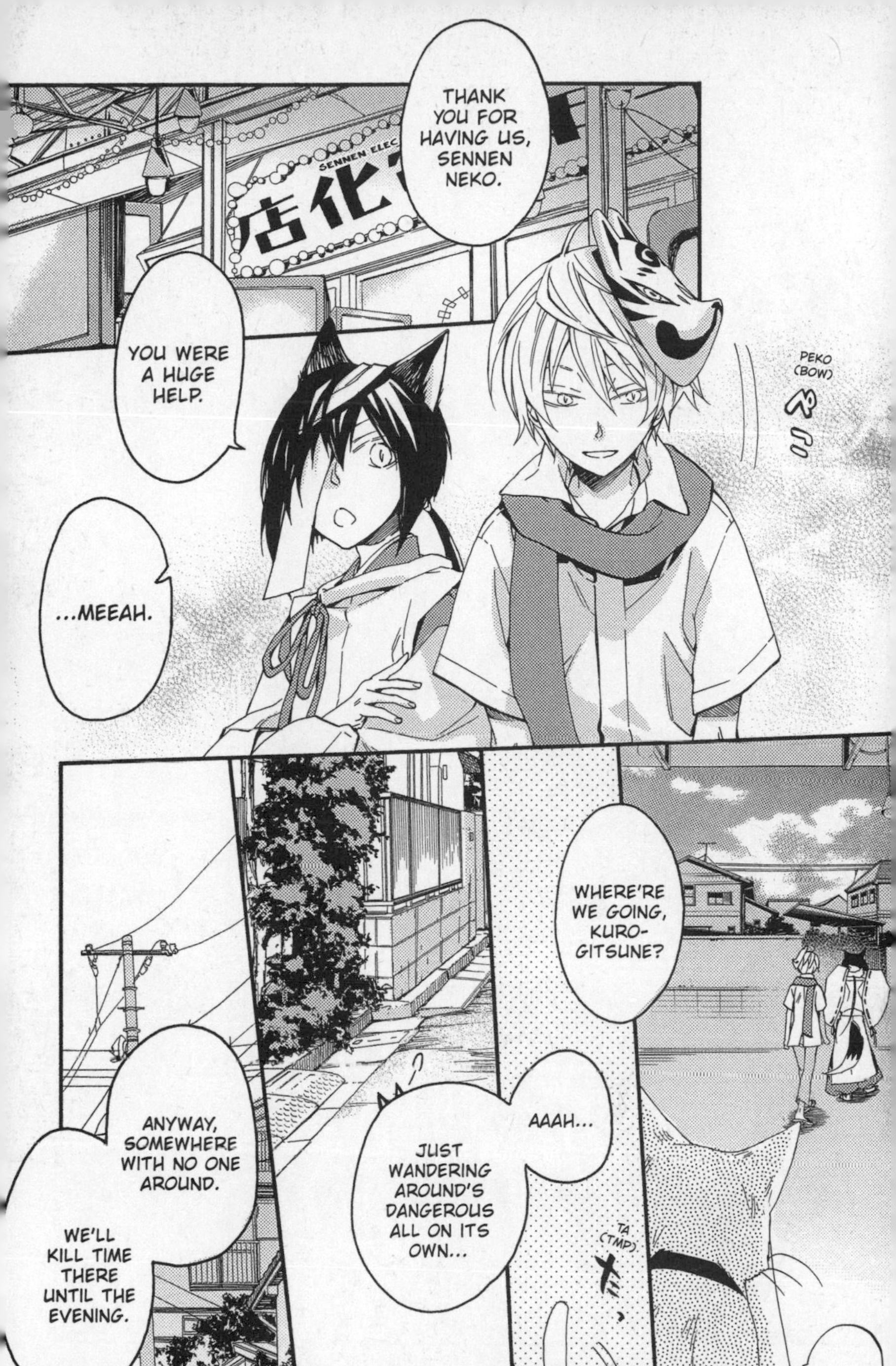

SENNEN ELEC
店化
THANK YOU FOR HAVING US, SENNEN NEKO.
PEKO (BOW)
YOU WERE A HUGE HELP.
...MEEAH.
WHERE'RE WE GOING, KURO-GITSUNE?
AAAH...
JUST WANDERING AROUND'S DANGEROUS ALL ON ITS OWN...
TA (TMP)
......
ANYWAY, SOMEWHERE WITH NO ONE AROUND.
WE'LL KILL TIME THERE UNTIL THE EVENING.

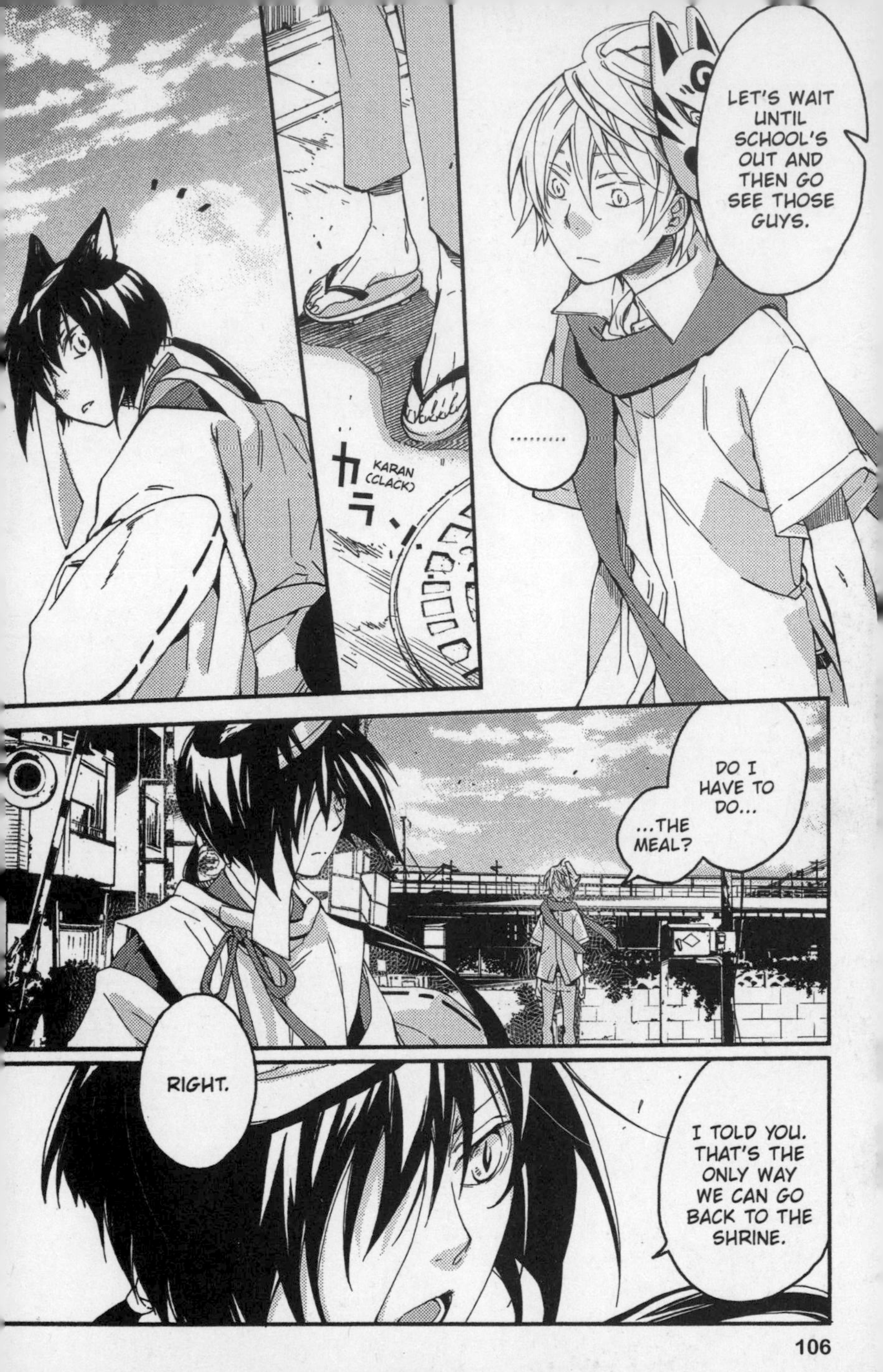

LET'S WAIT UNTIL SCHOOL'S OUT AND THEN GO SEE THOSE GUYS.
....
カラン
KARAN (CLACK)
DO I HAVE TO DO...
...THE MEAL?
I TOLD YOU. THAT'S THE ONLY WAY WE CAN GO BACK TO THE SHRINE.
RIGHT.

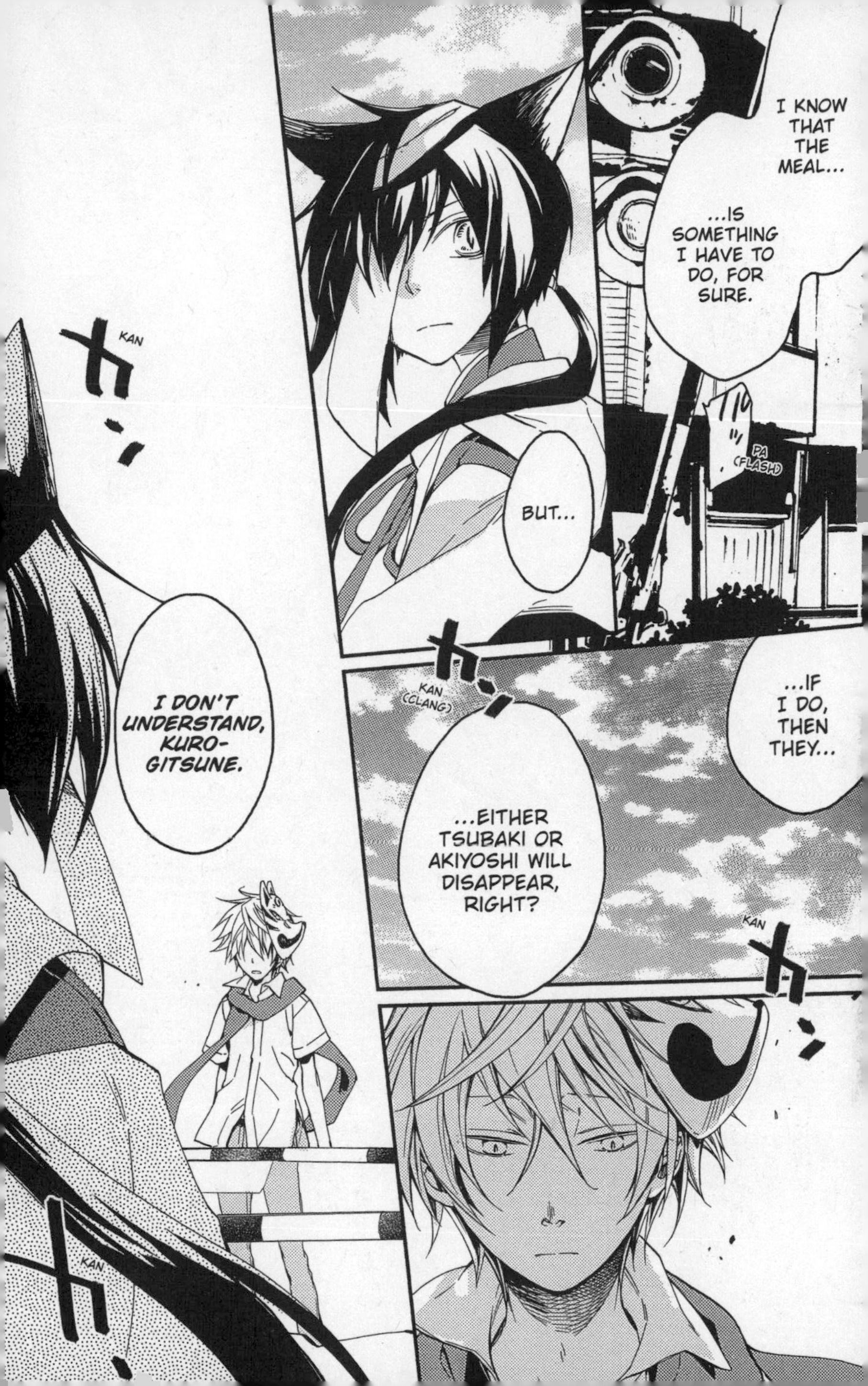
I KNOW THAT THE MEAL...
...IS SOMETHING I HAVE TO DO, FOR SURE.
PA (FLASH)
BUT...
...IF I DO, THEN THEY...
KAN (CLANG)
...EITHER TSUBAKI OR AKIYOSHI WILL DISAPPEAR, RIGHT?
KAN
KAN
I DON'T UNDERSTAND, KURO-GITSUNE.
KAN

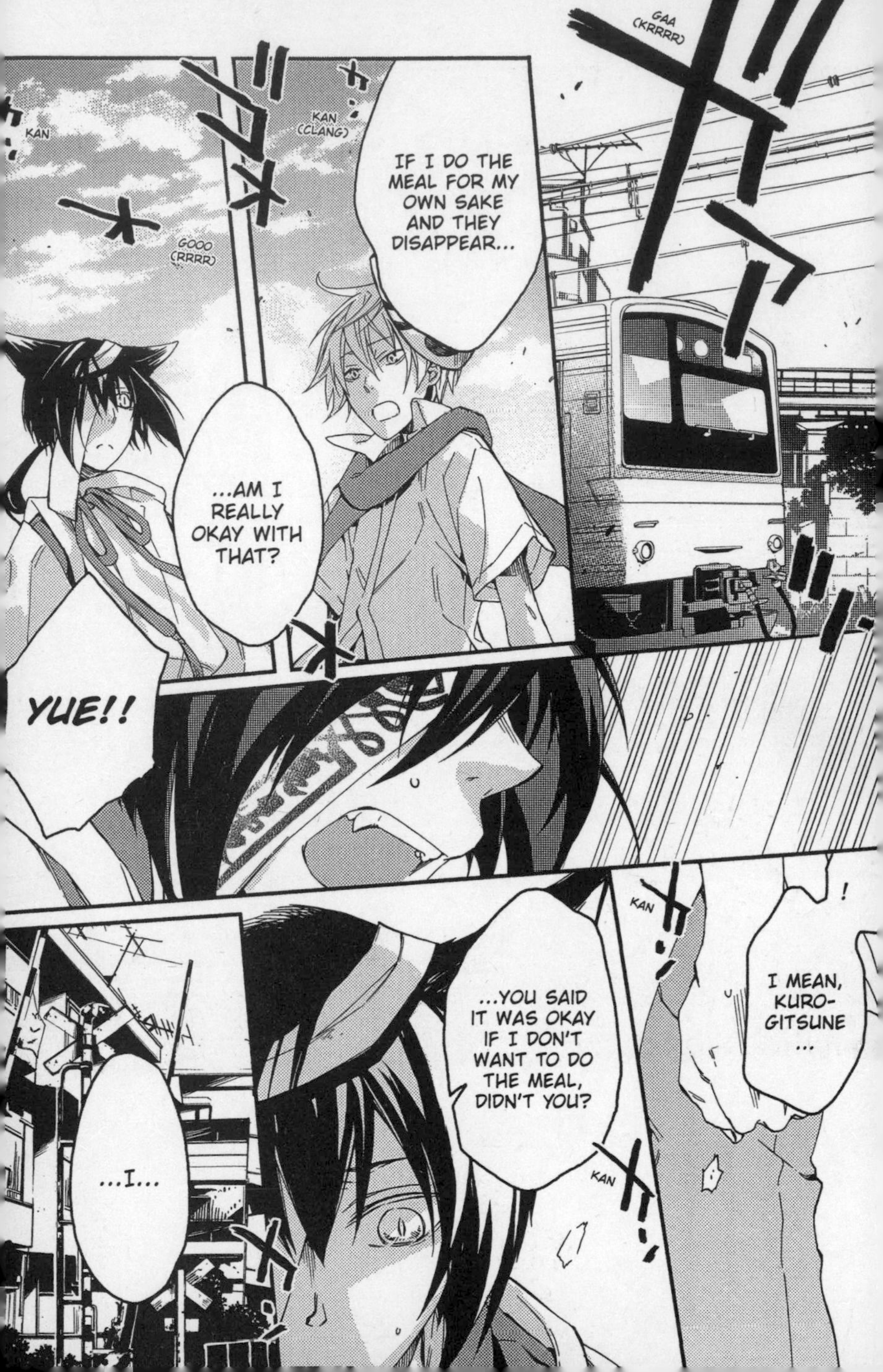
GAA (KRRRR)
KAN (CLANG)
IF I DO THE MEAL FOR MY OWN SAKE AND THEY DISAPPEAR...
KAN
GOOO (RRRR)
...AM I REALLY OKAY WITH THAT?
YUE!!
KAN
I MEAN, KURO-GITSUNE ...
!
...YOU SAID IT WAS OKAY IF I DON'T WANT TO DO THE MEAL, DIDN'T YOU?
KAN
...I...

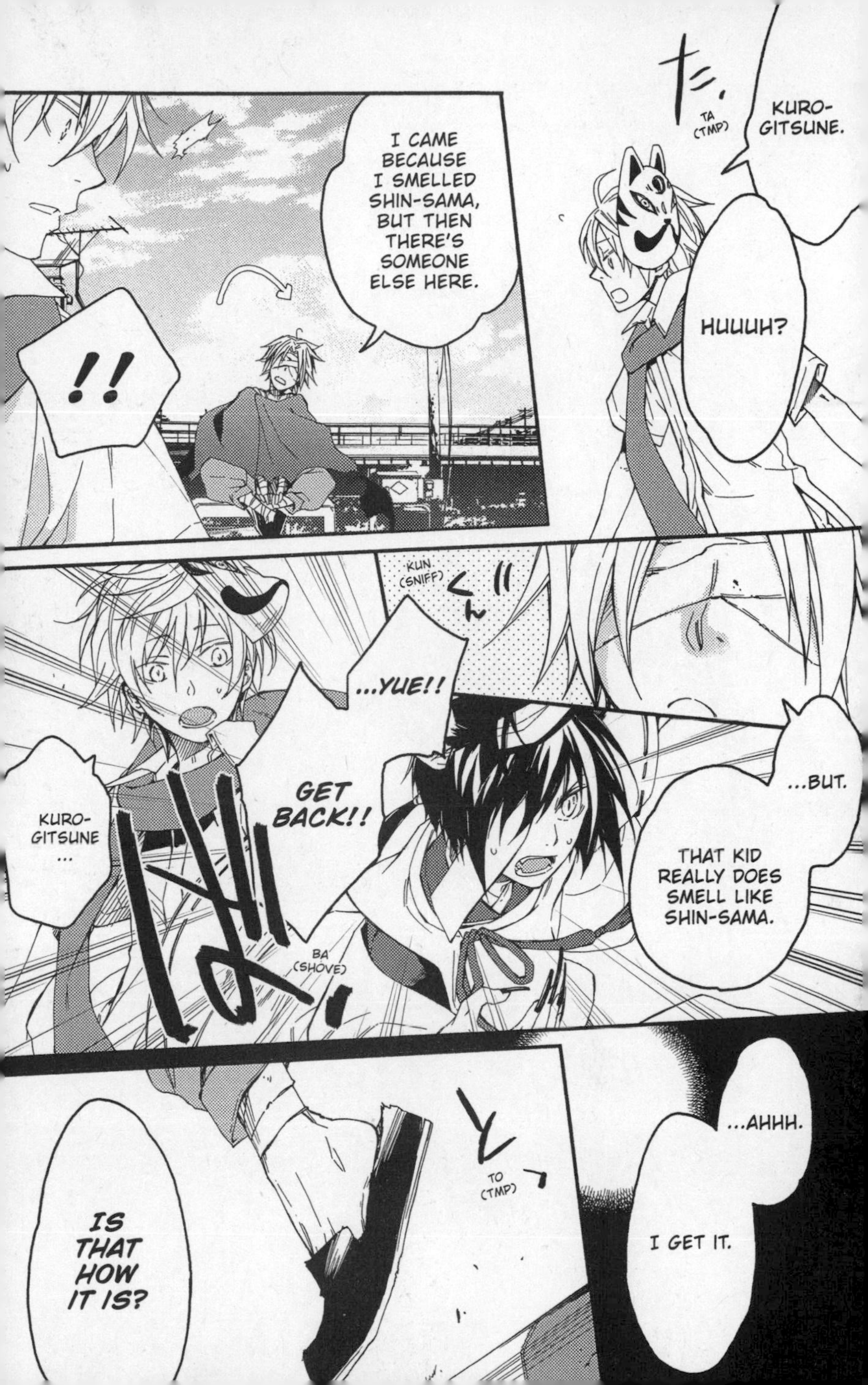

TA (TMP)
KURO-GITSUNE.
HUUUH?
I CAME BECAUSE I SMELLED SHIN-SAMA, BUT THEN THERE'S SOMEONE ELSE HERE.
!!
KUN (SNIFF)
...BUT.
THAT KID REALLY DOES SMELL LIKE SHIN-SAMA.
...YUE!!
GET BACK!!
BA (SHOVE)
KURO-GITSUNE ...
...AHHH.
I GET IT.
TO (TMP)
IS THAT HOW IT IS?

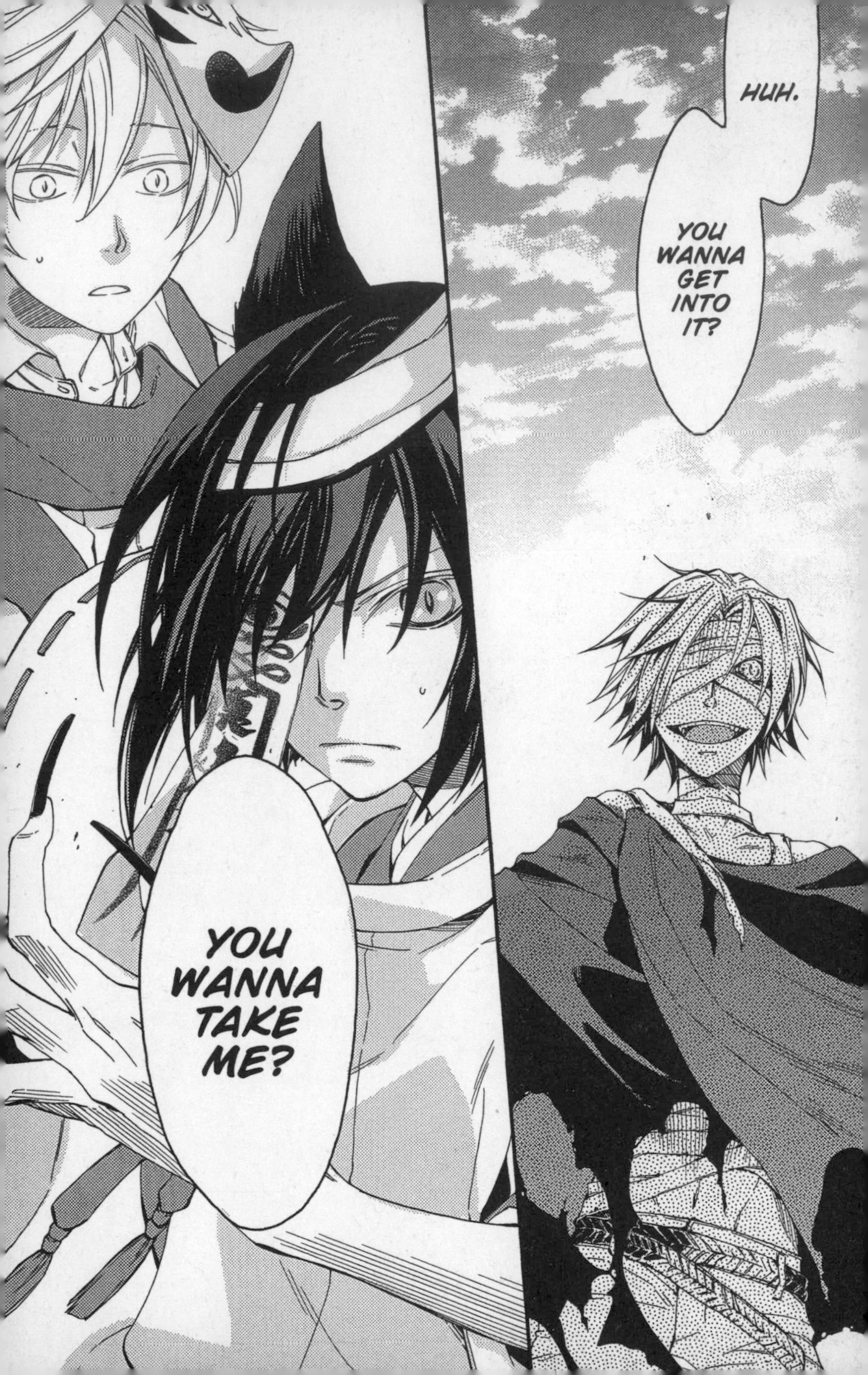
HUH.
YOU WANNA GET INTO IT?
YOU WANNA TAKE ME?

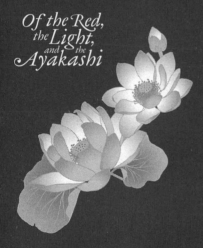

Of the Red,
the Light,
and the
Ayakashi

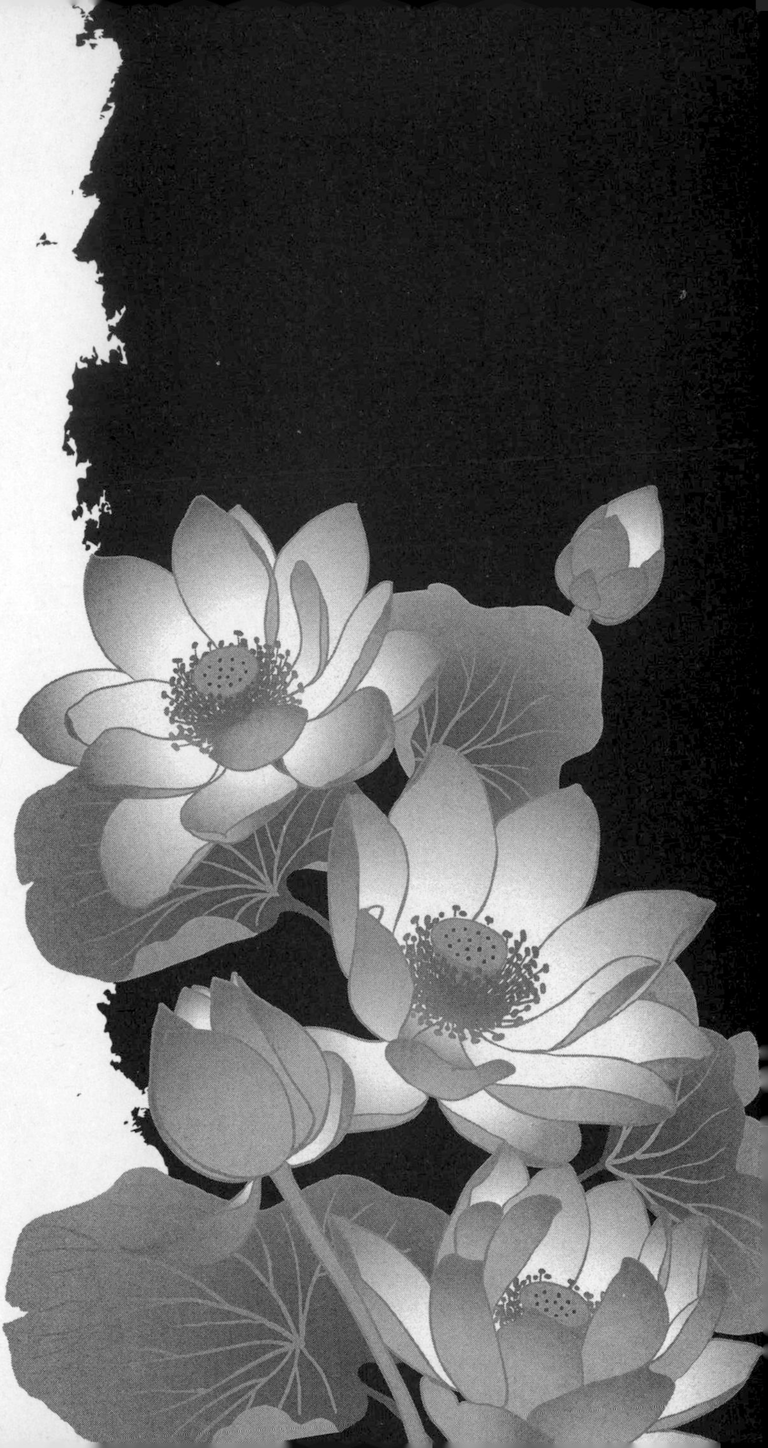

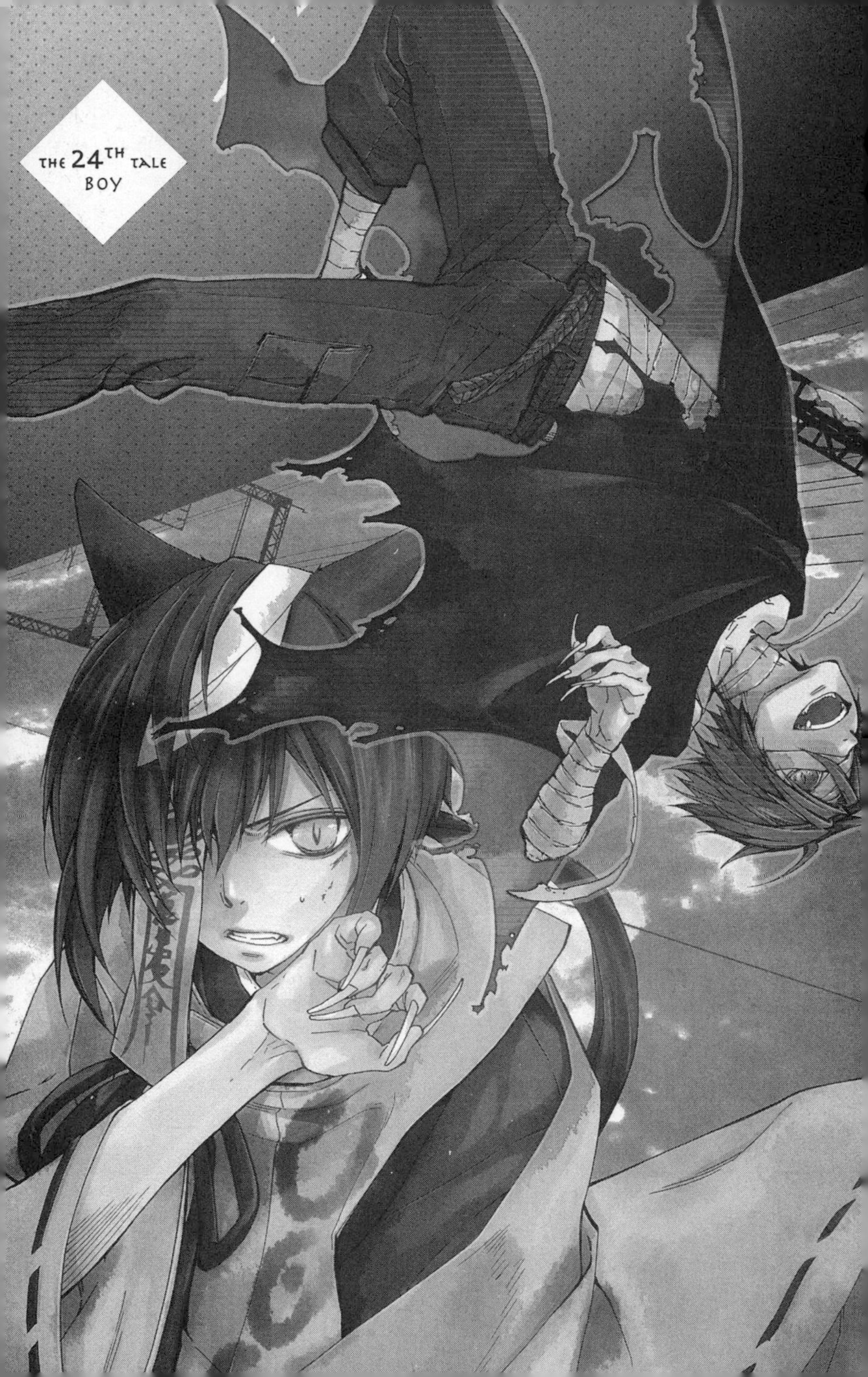
THE 24TH TALE
BOY

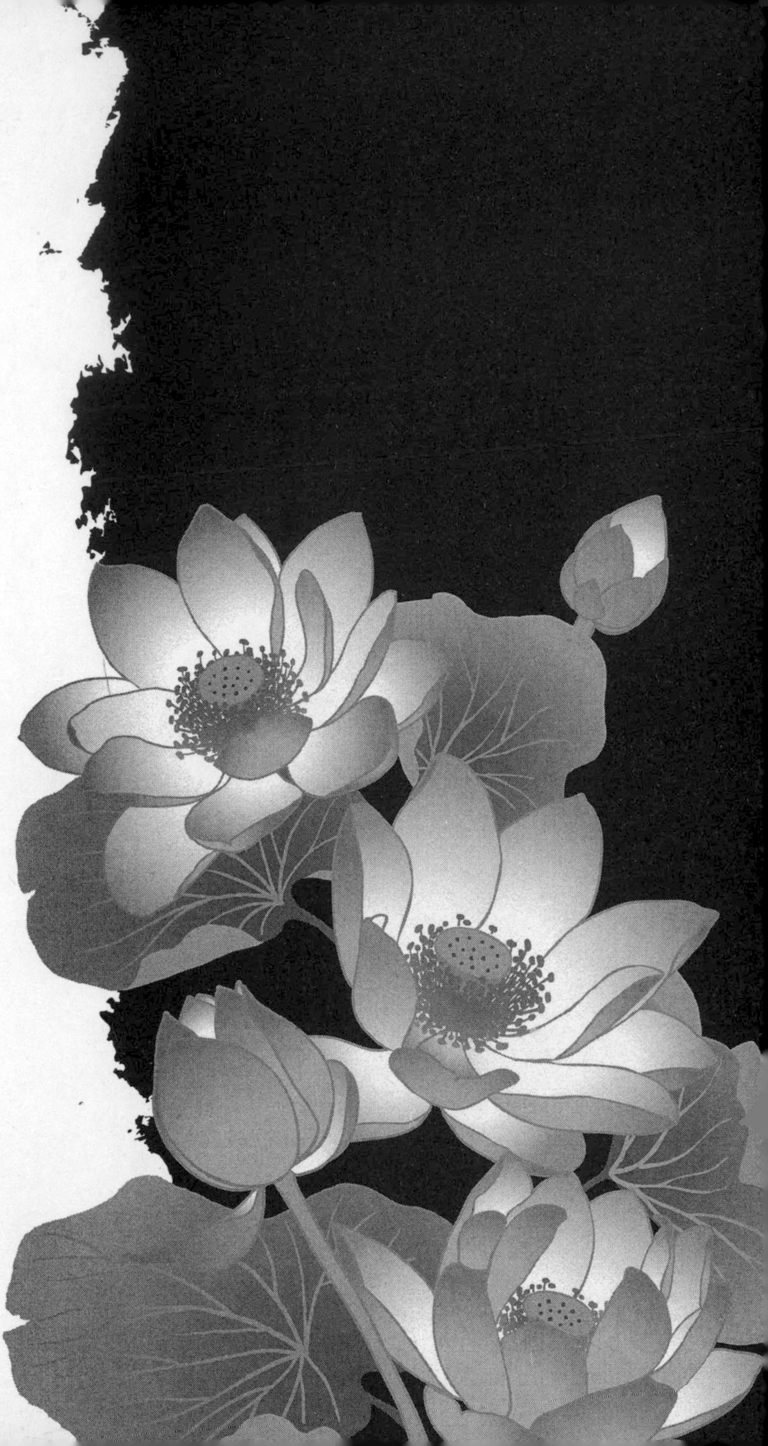

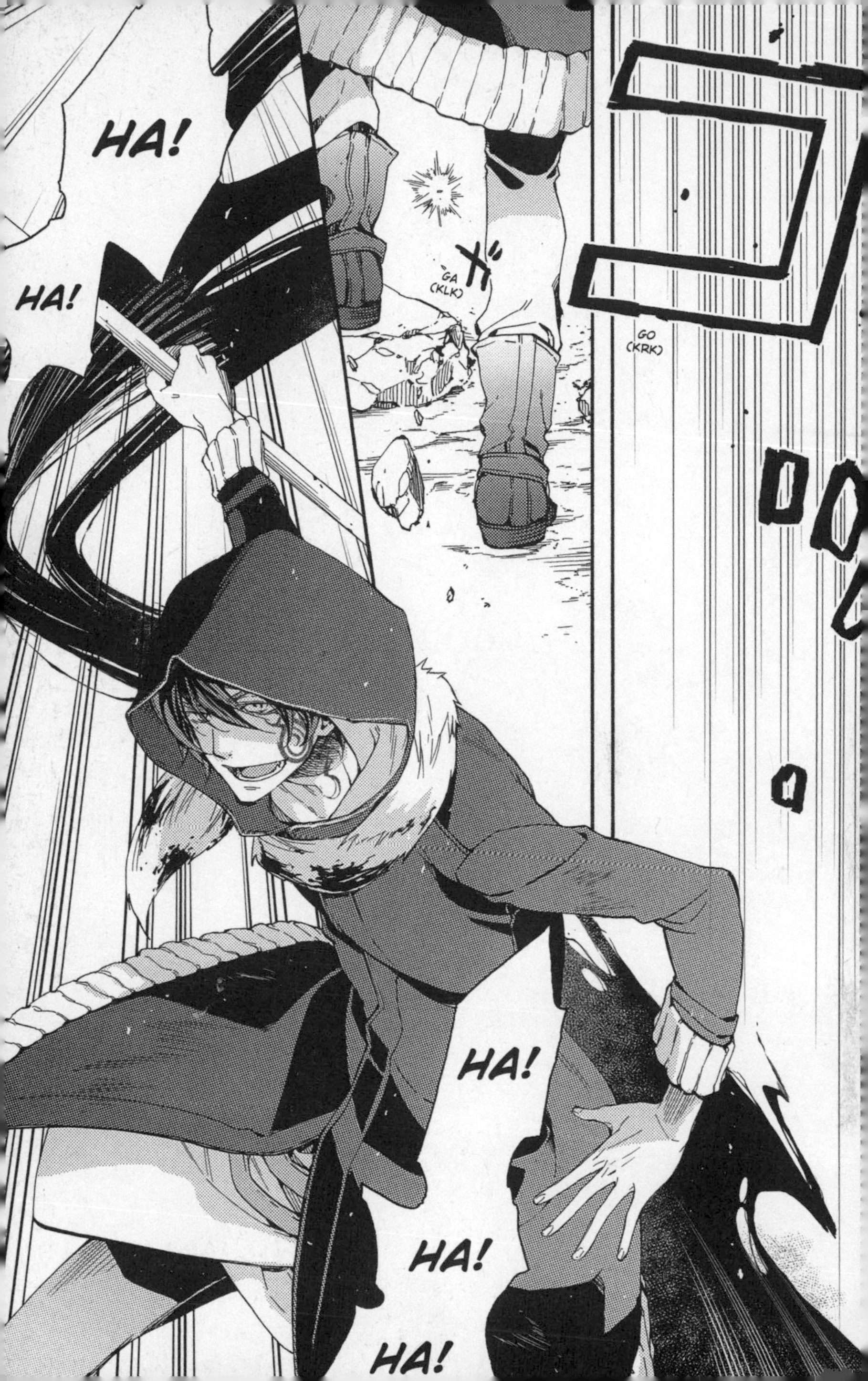
GO
(KRK)
GA
(KLK)
HA!
HA!
HA!
HA!
HA!

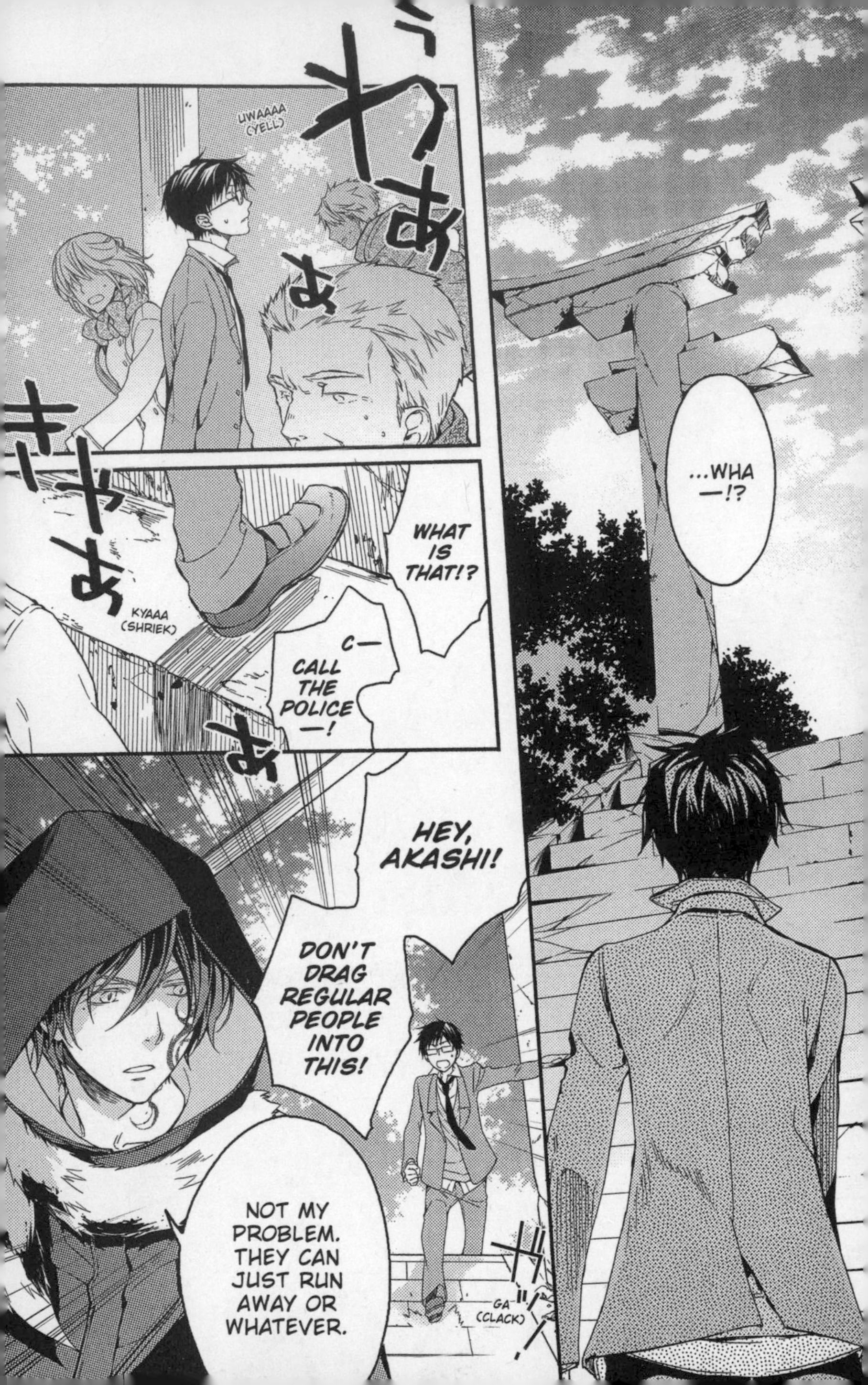
...WHA—!?
うわあぁ
UWAAAA (YELL)
きゃあぁ
KYAAA (SHRIEK)
WHAT IS THAT!?
C— CALL THE POLICE—!
HEY, AKASHI!
DON'T DRAG REGULAR PEOPLE INTO THIS!
NOT MY PROBLEM. THEY CAN JUST RUN AWAY OR WHATEVER.
GA (CLACK)

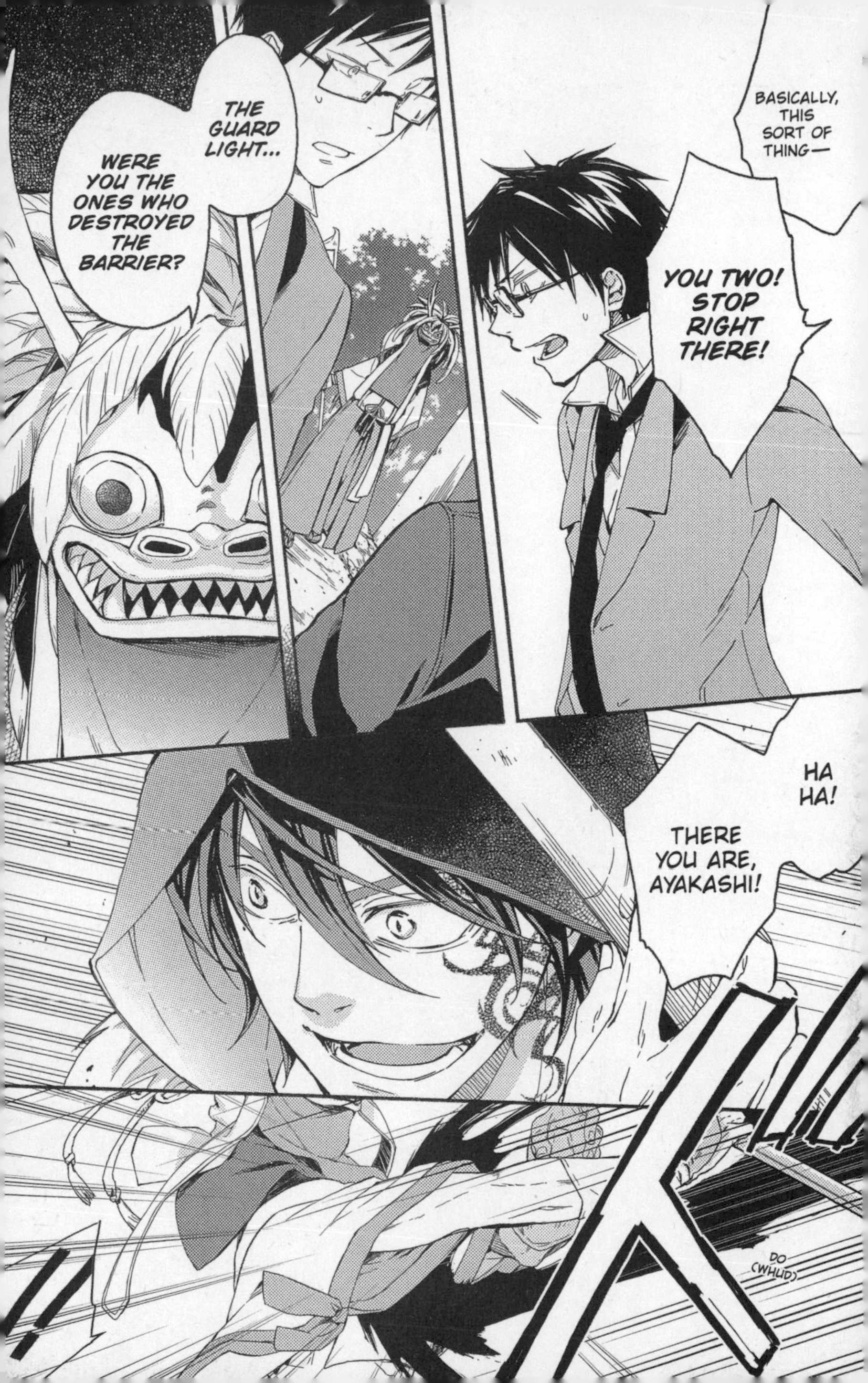
BASICALLY, THIS SORT OF THING—
YOU TWO! STOP RIGHT THERE!
THE GUARD LIGHT...
WERE YOU THE ONES WHO DESTROYED THE BARRIER?
HA HA!
THERE YOU ARE, AYAKASHI!
DO (WHUD)

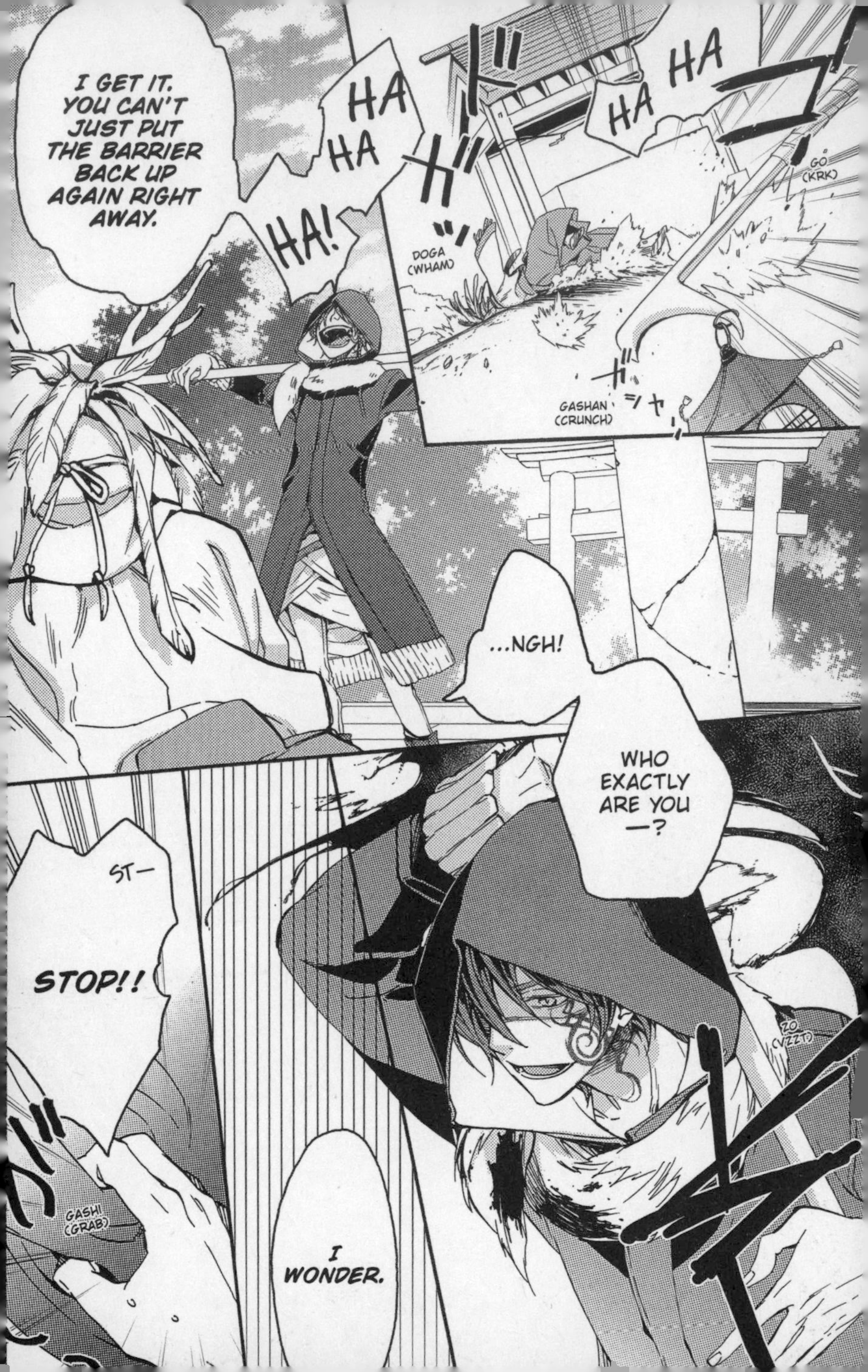
HA HA
GO (KRK)
DOGA (WHAM)
GASHAN (CRUNCH)
HA HA HA!
I GET IT. YOU CAN'T JUST PUT THE BARRIER BACK UP AGAIN RIGHT AWAY.
...NGH!
WHO EXACTLY ARE YOU —?
ZO (VZZT)
I WONDER.
ST—
STOP!!
GASHI (GRAB)

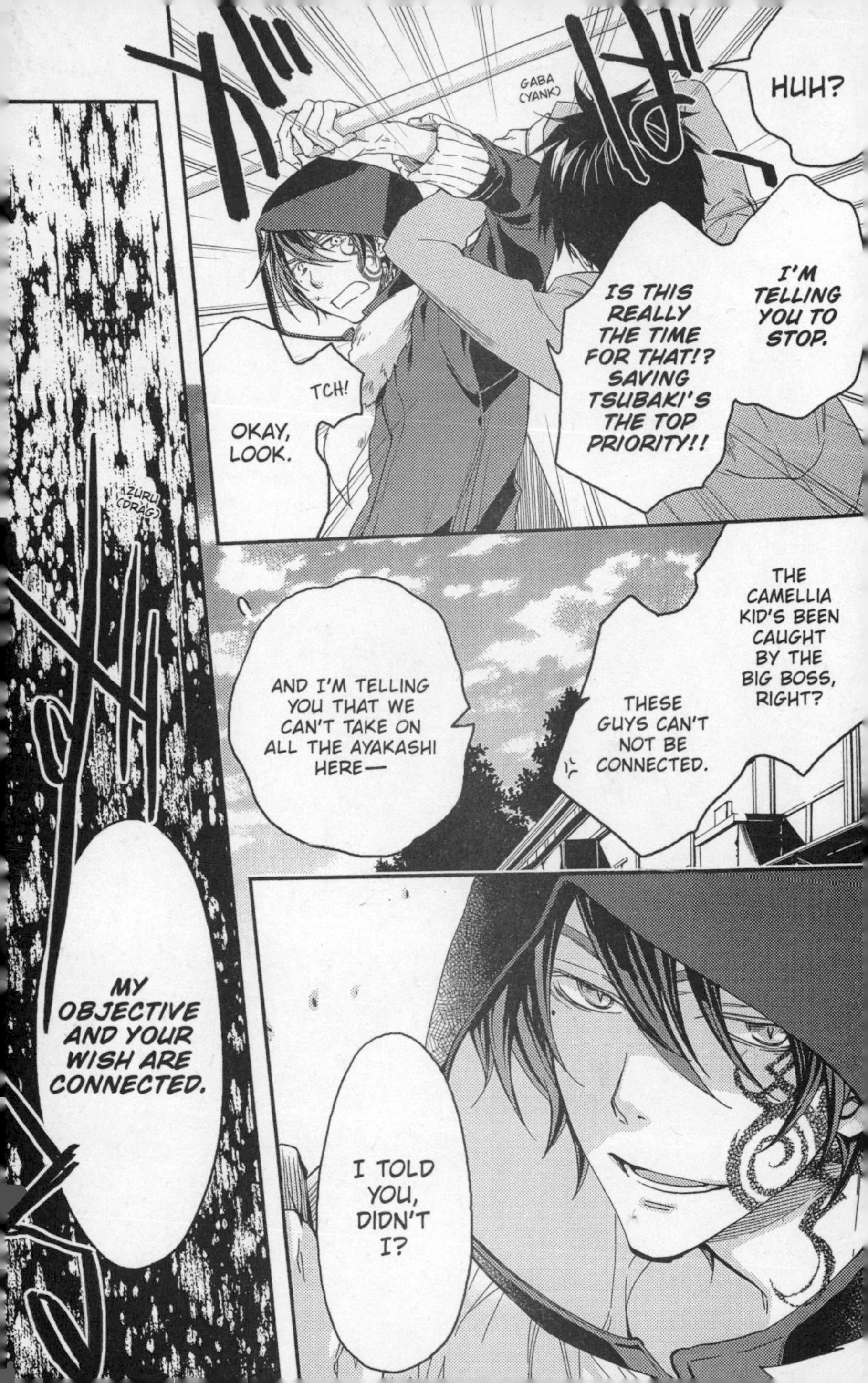
HUH?
GABA (YANK)
I'M TELLING YOU TO STOP.
IS THIS REALLY THE TIME FOR THAT!? SAVING TSUBAKI'S THE TOP PRIORITY!!
TCH!
OKAY, LOOK.
THE CAMELLIA KID'S BEEN CAUGHT BY THE BIG BOSS, RIGHT?
THESE GUYS CAN'T NOT BE CONNECTED.
AND I'M TELLING YOU THAT WE CAN'T TAKE ON ALL THE AYAKASHI HERE—
I TOLD YOU, DIDN'T I?
ZURU (DRAG)
MY OBJECTIVE AND YOUR WISH ARE CONNECTED.

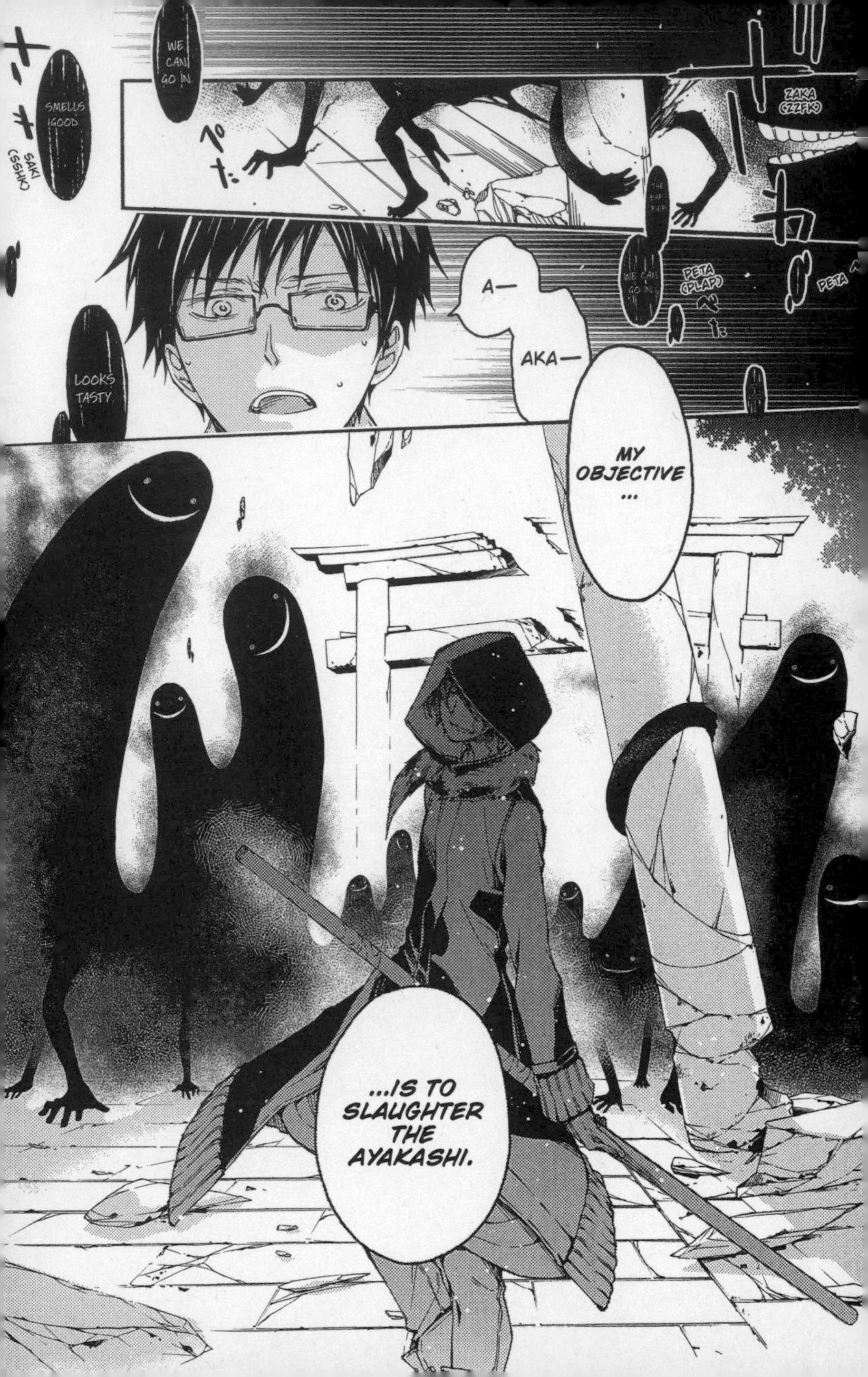

ZAKA (ZZFK)
WE CAN GO IN.
SMELLS GOOD.
SAKI (SSHK)
PETA
PETA (PLAP)
WE CAN GO IN.
A—
AKA—
LOOKS TASTY.
MY OBJECTIVE ...
...IS TO SLAUGHTER THE AYAKASHI.

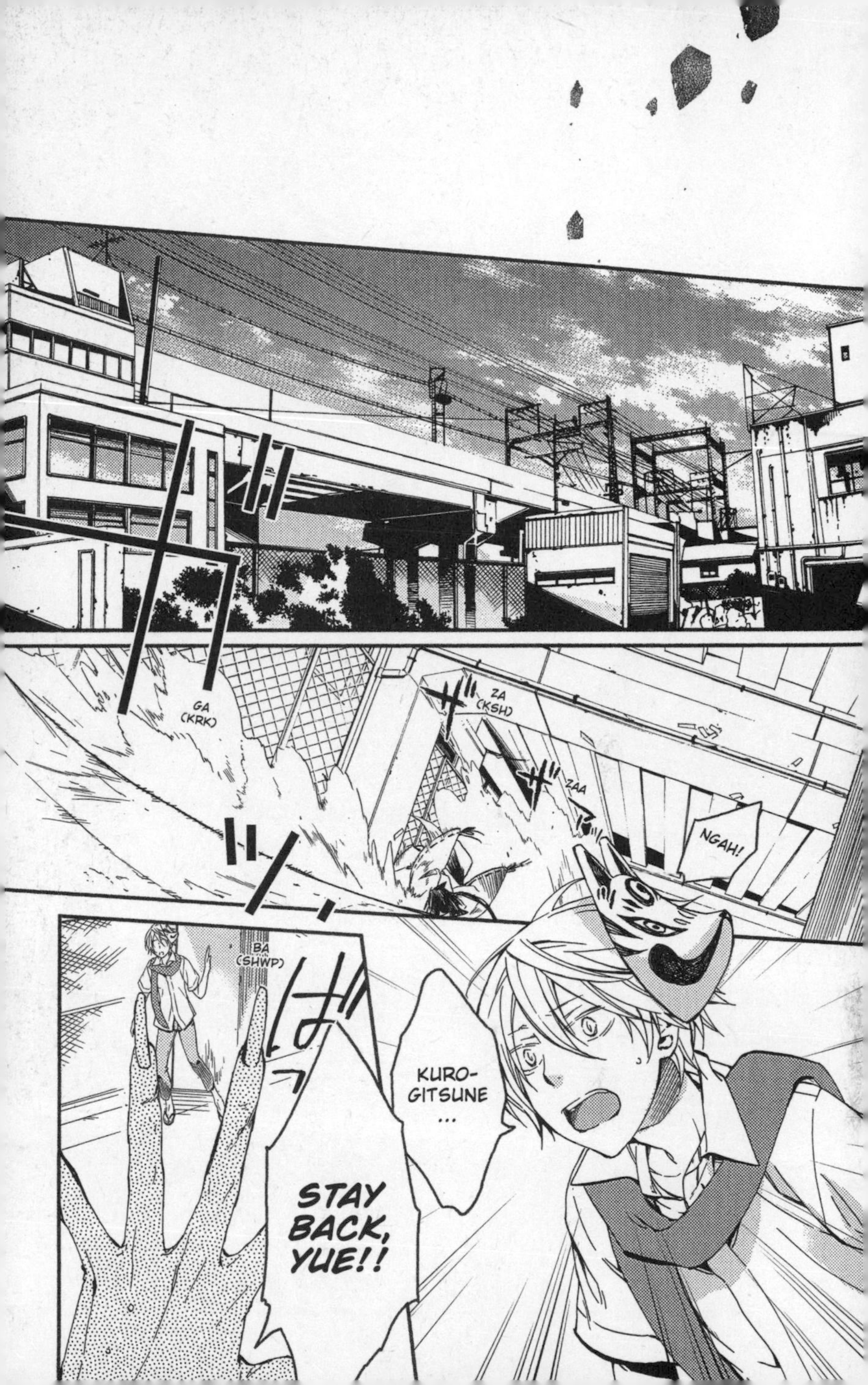

ZA
(KSH)
ZAA
NGAH!
GA
(KRK)
KURO-
GITSUNE
...
STAY
BACK,
YUE!!
BA
(SHWP)

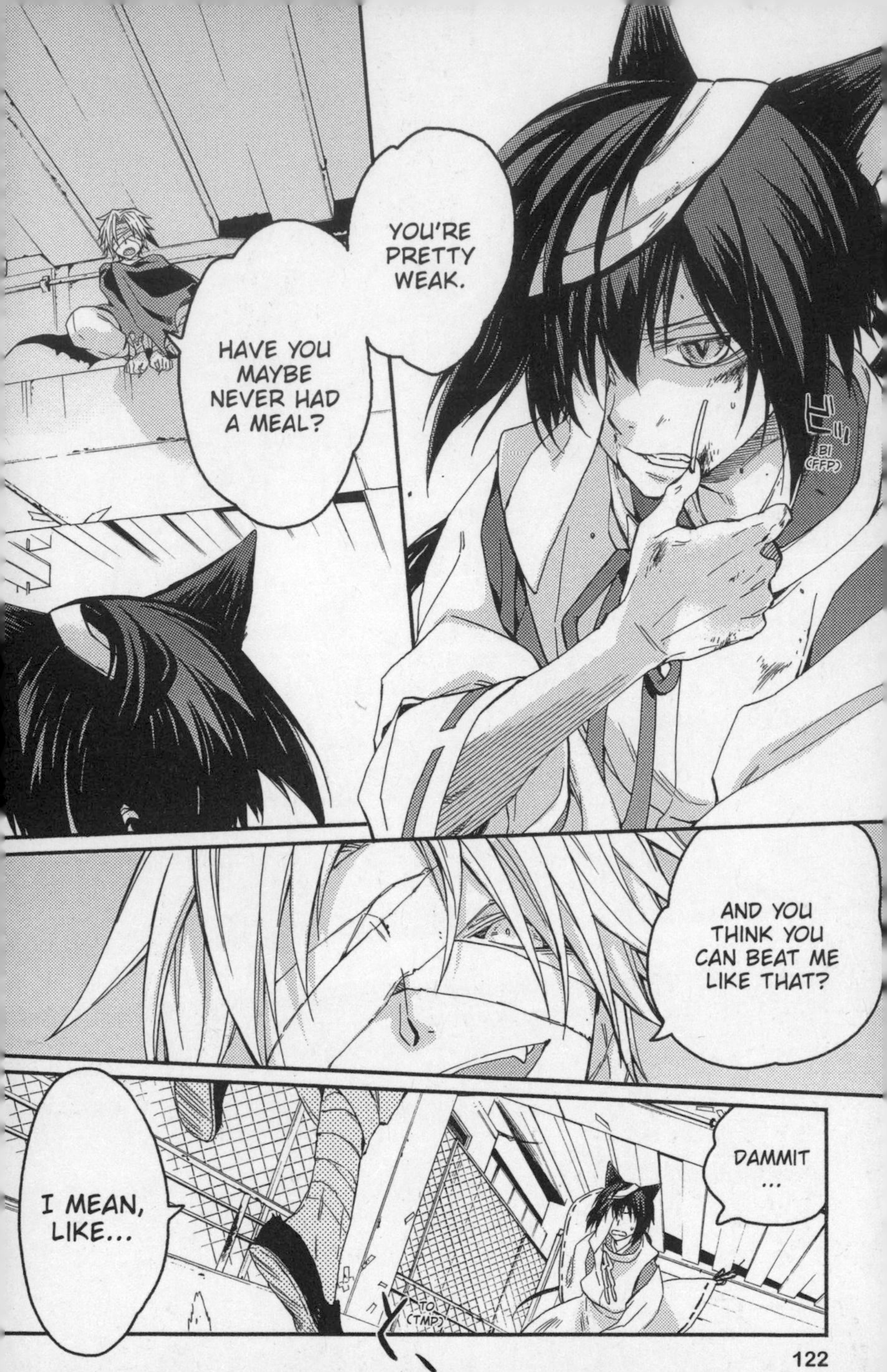

YOU'RE PRETTY WEAK.
HAVE YOU MAYBE NEVER HAD A MEAL?
BI (FFP)
AND YOU THINK YOU CAN BEAT ME LIKE THAT?
DAMMIT ...
TO (TMP)
I MEAN, LIKE...

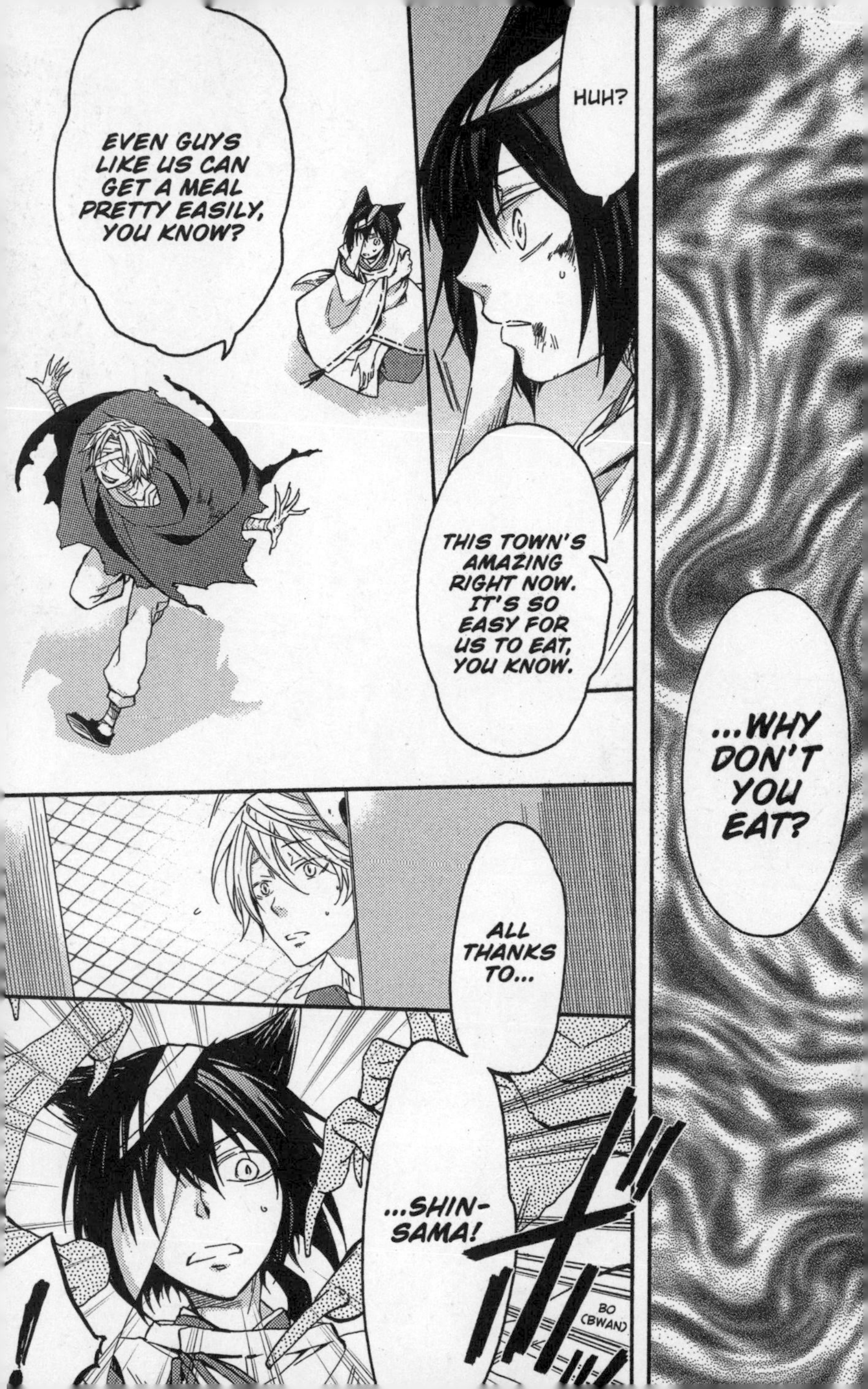
...WHY DON'T YOU EAT?
HUH?
THIS TOWN'S AMAZING RIGHT NOW. IT'S SO EASY FOR US TO EAT, YOU KNOW.
EVEN GUYS LIKE US CAN GET A MEAL PRETTY EASILY, YOU KNOW?
ALL THANKS TO...
...SHIN-SAMA!
BO (BWAN)

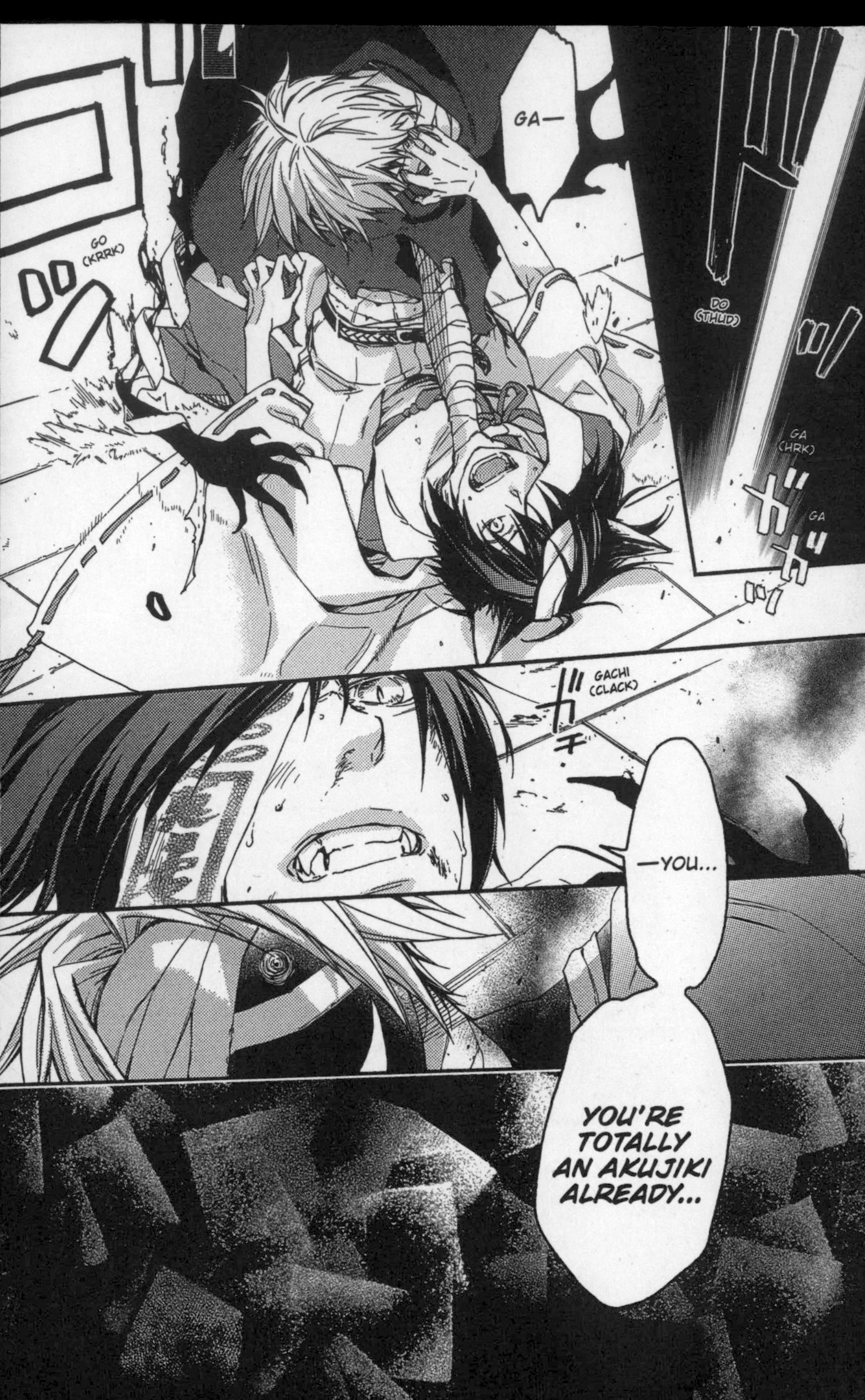
GA—
DO (THUD)
GA (HRK)
GA
GO (KRRK)
GACHI (CLACK)
—YOU...
YOU'RE TOTALLY AN AKUJIKI ALREADY...

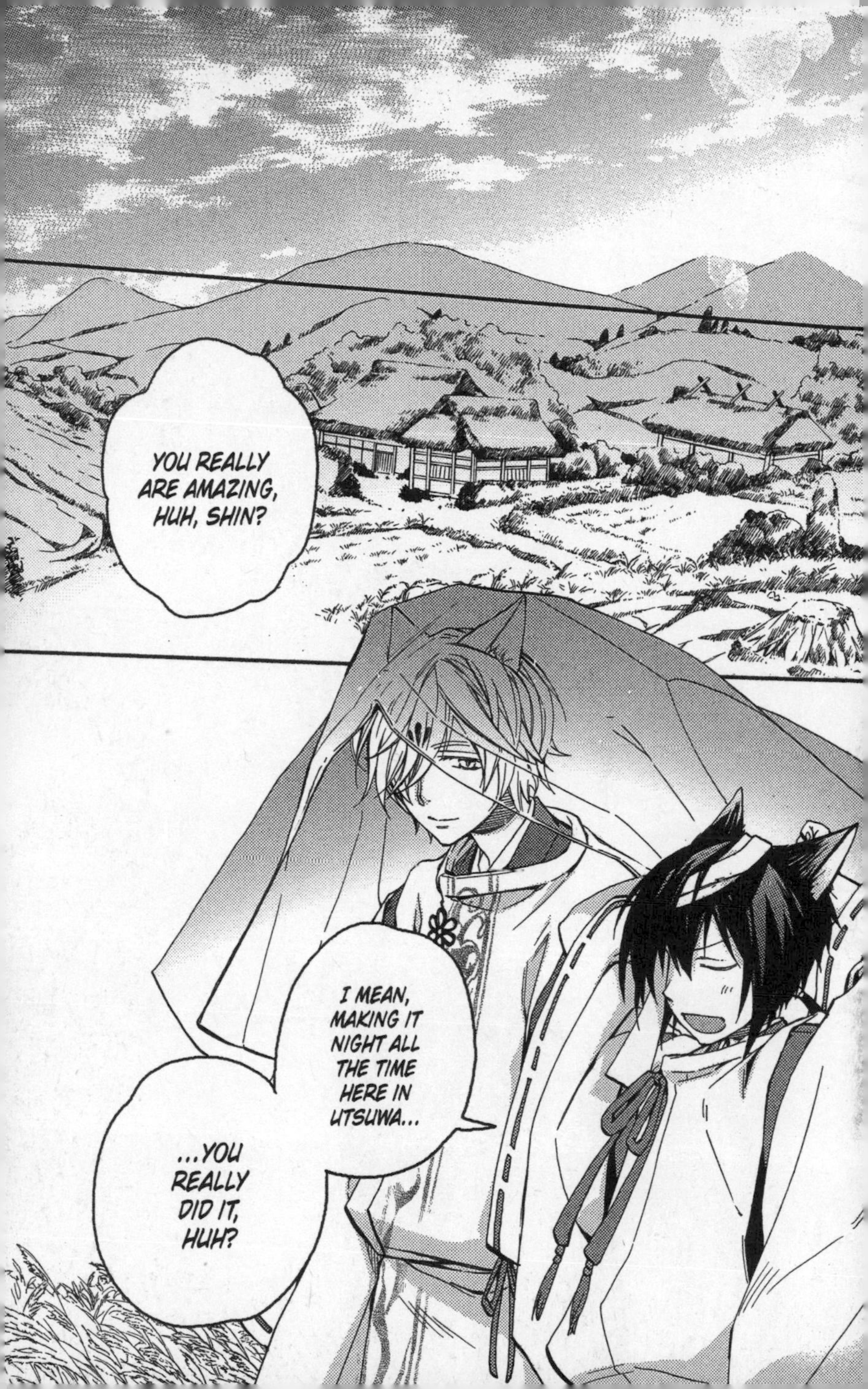
YOU REALLY ARE AMAZING, HUH, SHIN?
I MEAN, MAKING IT NIGHT ALL THE TIME HERE IN UTSUWA...
...YOU REALLY DID IT, HUH?

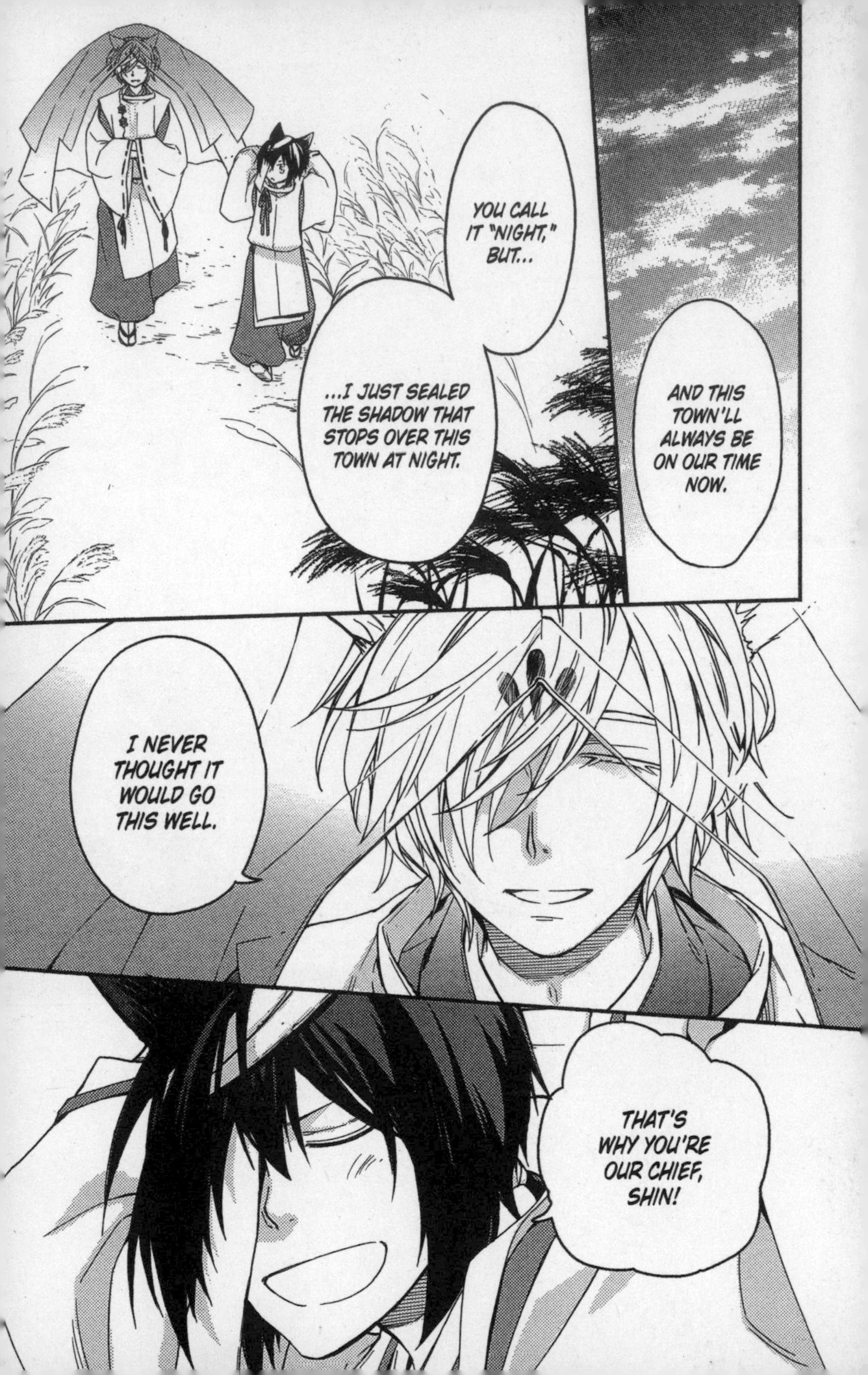
AND THIS TOWN'LL ALWAYS BE ON OUR TIME NOW.
YOU CALL IT "NIGHT," BUT...
...I JUST SEALED THE SHADOW THAT STOPS OVER THIS TOWN AT NIGHT.
I NEVER THOUGHT IT WOULD GO THIS WELL.
THAT'S WHY YOU'RE OUR CHIEF, SHIN!

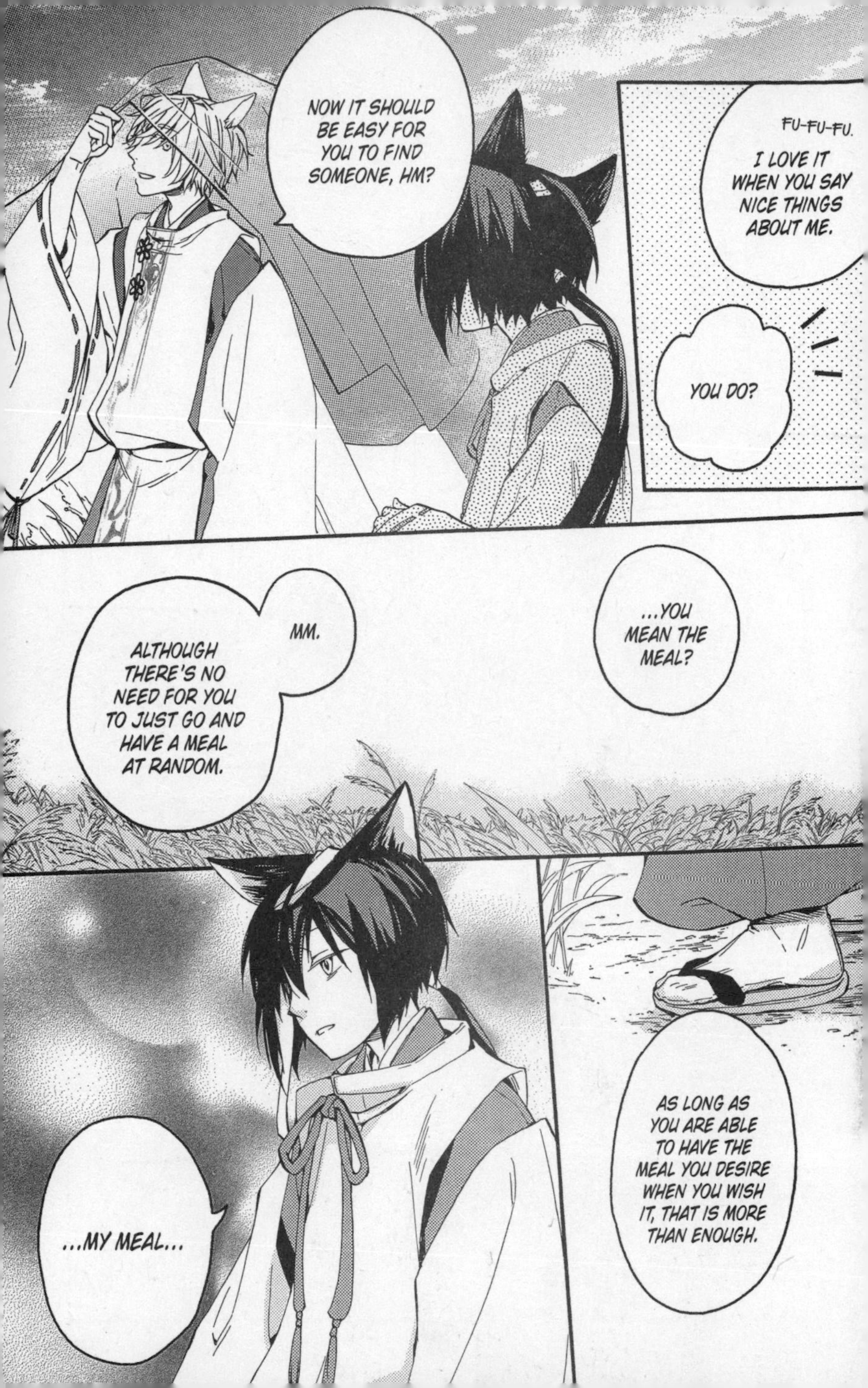
FU-FU-FU.
I LOVE IT WHEN YOU SAY NICE THINGS ABOUT ME.
YOU DO?
NOW IT SHOULD BE EASY FOR YOU TO FIND SOMEONE, HM?
...YOU MEAN THE MEAL?
MM.
ALTHOUGH THERE'S NO NEED FOR YOU TO JUST GO AND HAVE A MEAL AT RANDOM.
AS LONG AS YOU ARE ABLE TO HAVE THE MEAL YOU DESIRE WHEN YOU WISH IT, THAT IS MORE THAN ENOUGH.
...MY MEAL...

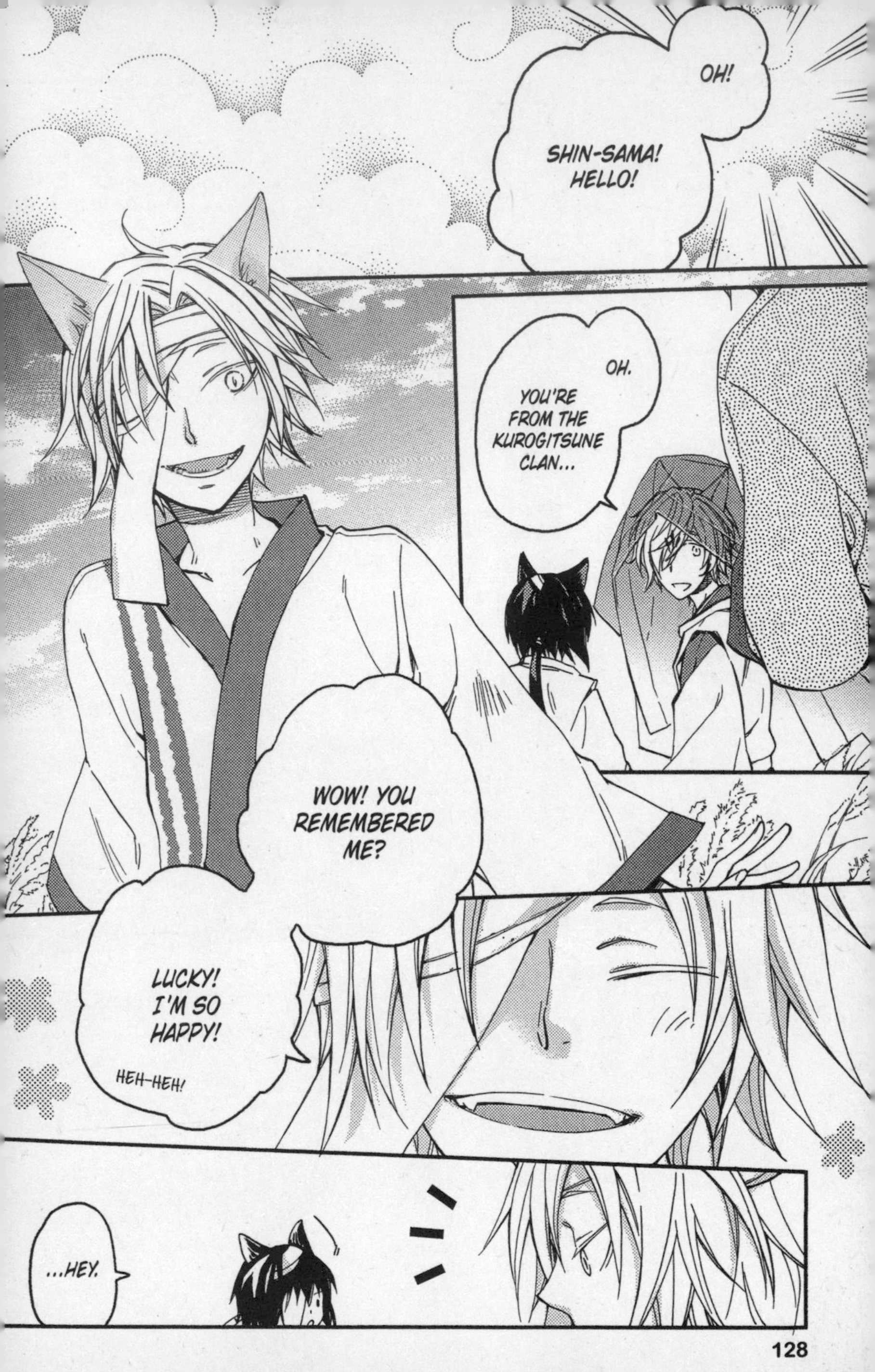
OH!
SHIN-SAMA! HELLO!
OH.
YOU'RE FROM THE KUROGITSUNE CLAN...
WOW! YOU REMEMBERED ME?
LUCKY! I'M SO HAPPY!
HEH-HEH!
...HEY.

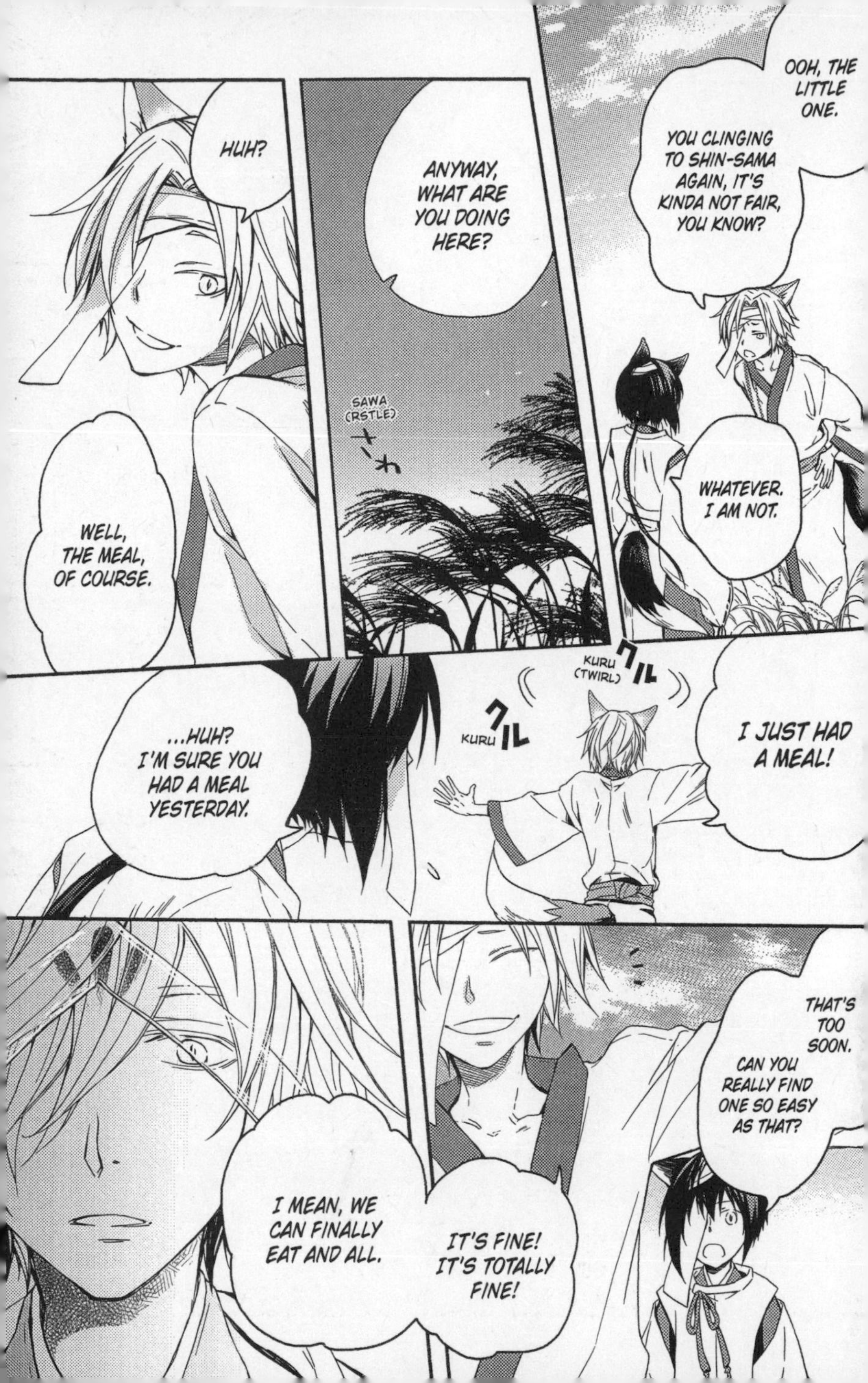
OOH, THE LITTLE ONE.
YOU CLINGING TO SHIN-SAMA AGAIN, IT'S KINDA NOT FAIR, YOU KNOW?
WHATEVER. I AM NOT.
ANYWAY, WHAT ARE YOU DOING HERE?
SAWA (RSTLE)
HUH?
WELL, THE MEAL, OF COURSE.
KURU (TWIRL)
KURU
I JUST HAD A MEAL!
...HUH? I'M SURE YOU HAD A MEAL YESTERDAY.
THAT'S TOO SOON.
CAN YOU REALLY FIND ONE SO EASY AS THAT?
IT'S FINE! IT'S TOTALLY FINE!
I MEAN, WE CAN FINALLY EAT AND ALL.

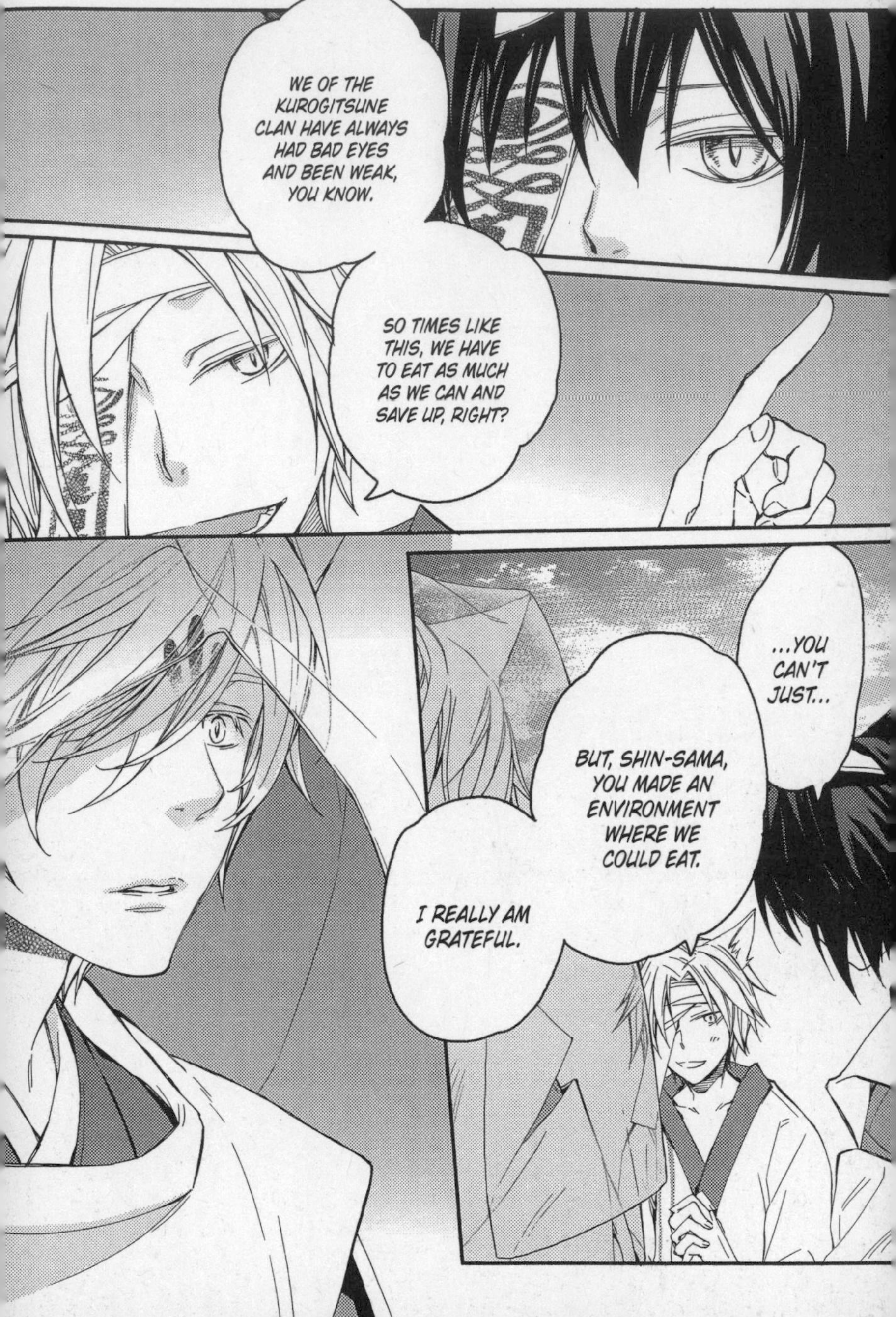
WE OF THE KUROGITSUNE CLAN HAVE ALWAYS HAD BAD EYES AND BEEN WEAK, YOU KNOW.
SO TIMES LIKE THIS, WE HAVE TO EAT AS MUCH AS WE CAN AND SAVE UP, RIGHT?
...YOU CAN'T JUST...
BUT, SHIN-SAMA, YOU MADE AN ENVIRONMENT WHERE WE COULD EAT.
I REALLY AM GRATEFUL.

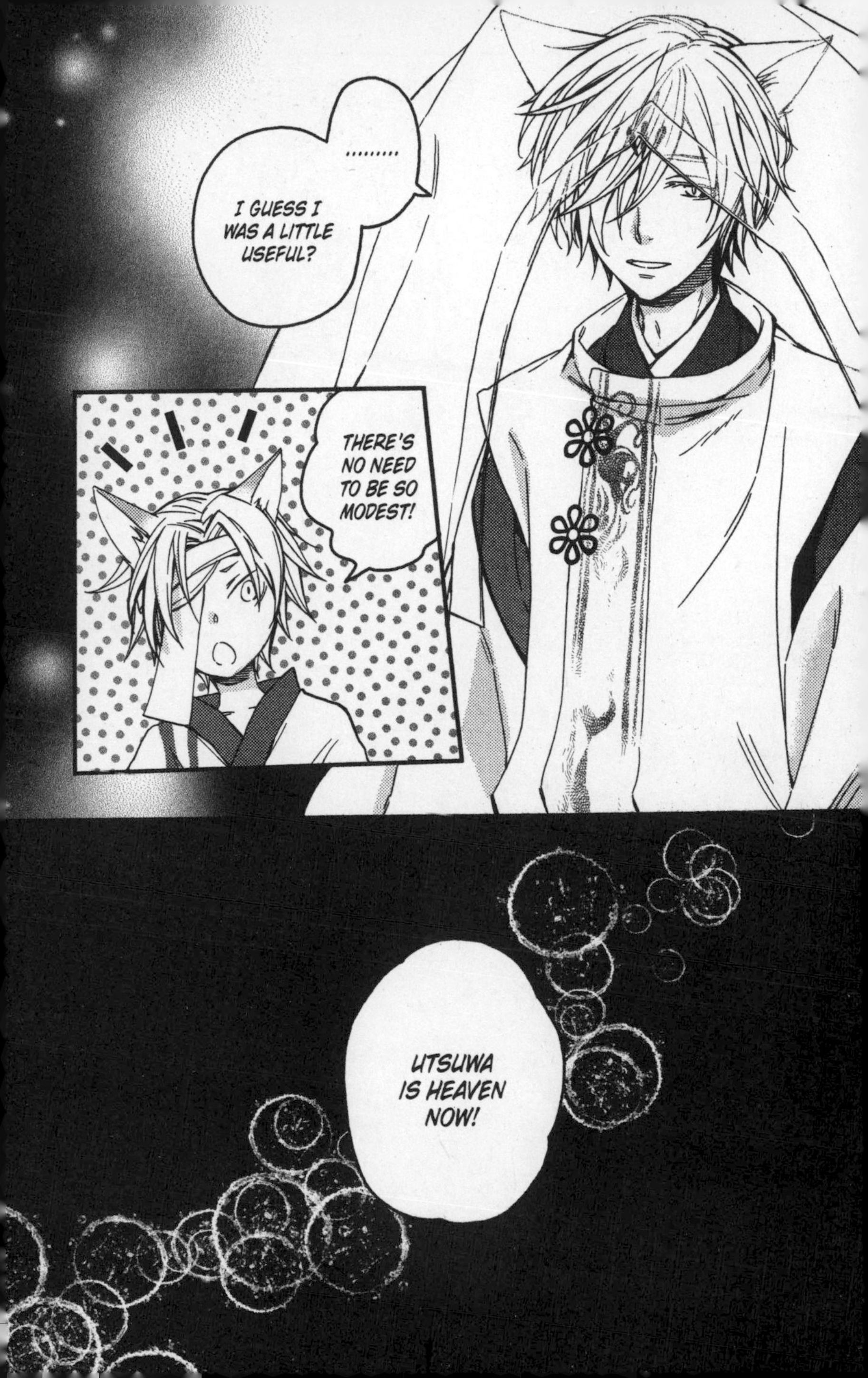
....
I GUESS I WAS A LITTLE USEFUL?
THERE'S NO NEED TO BE SO MODEST!
UTSUWA IS HEAVEN NOW!

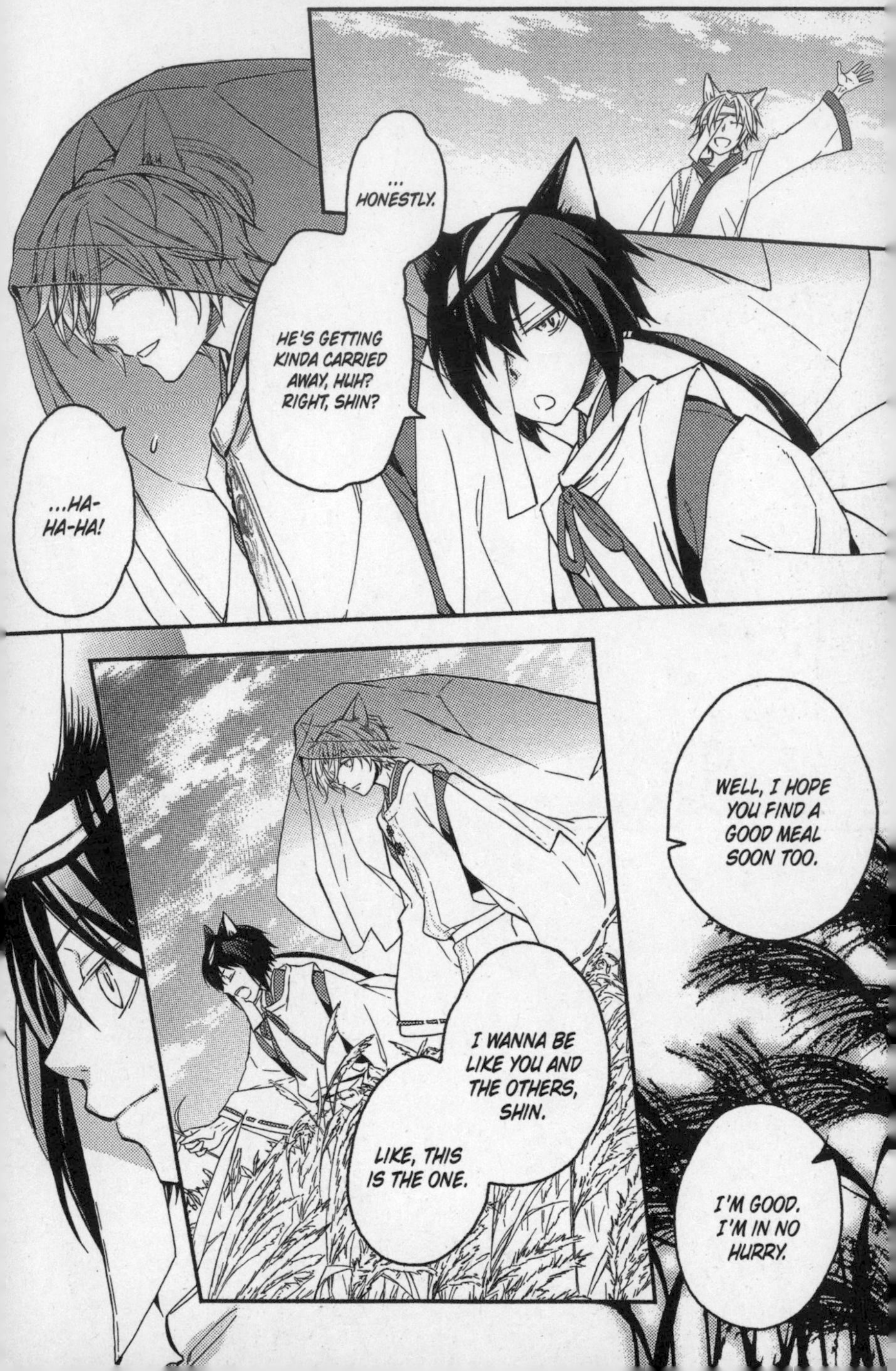
...HONESTLY.
HE'S GETTING KINDA CARRIED AWAY, HUH? RIGHT, SHIN?
...HA-HA-HA!
WELL, I HOPE YOU FIND A GOOD MEAL SOON TOO.
I'M GOOD. I'M IN NO HURRY.
I WANNA BE LIKE YOU AND THE OTHERS, SHIN.
LIKE, THIS IS THE ONE.

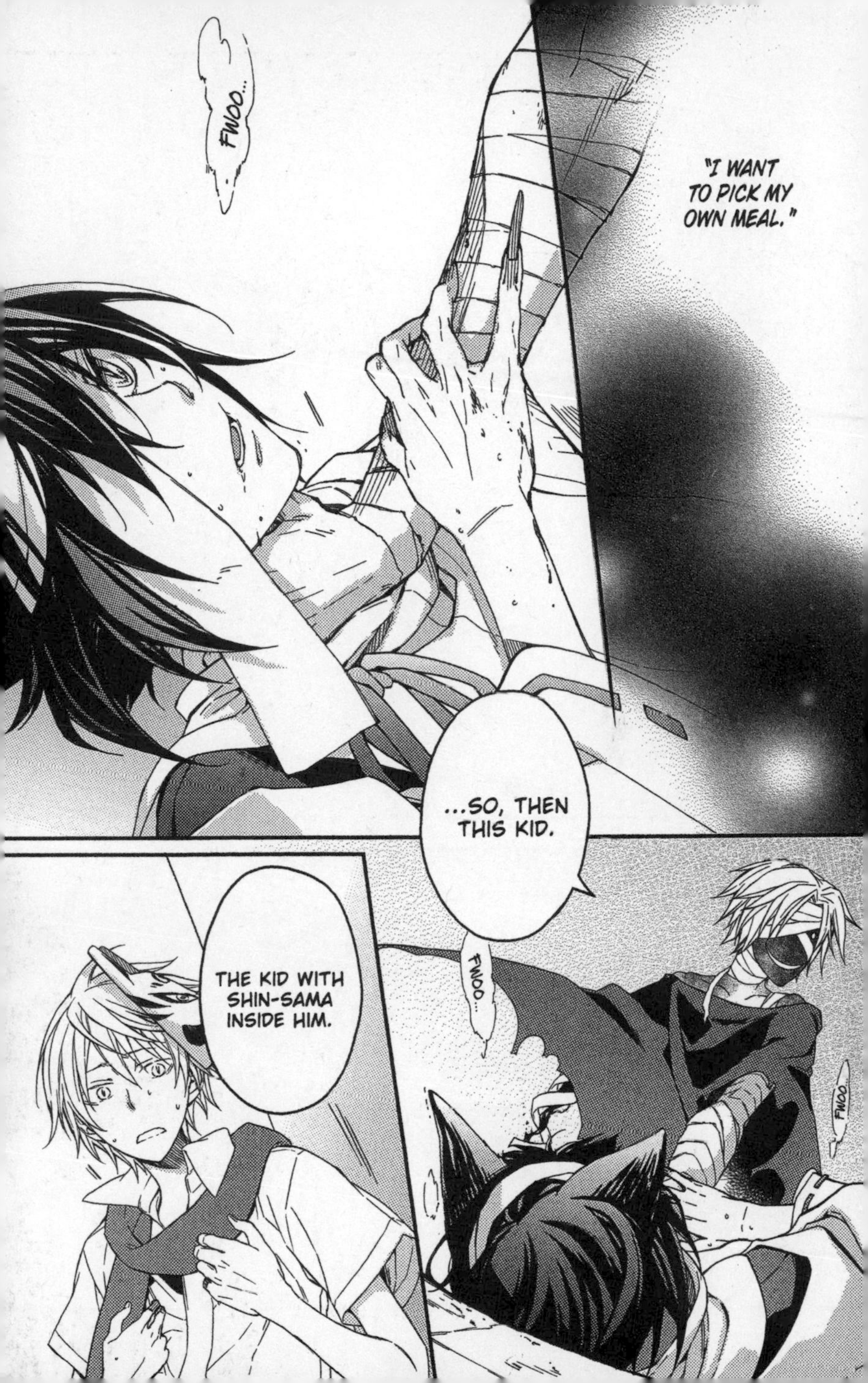
"I WANT TO PICK MY OWN MEAL."
FWOO...
...SO, THEN THIS KID.
FWOO
FWOO...
THE KID WITH SHIN-SAMA INSIDE HIM.

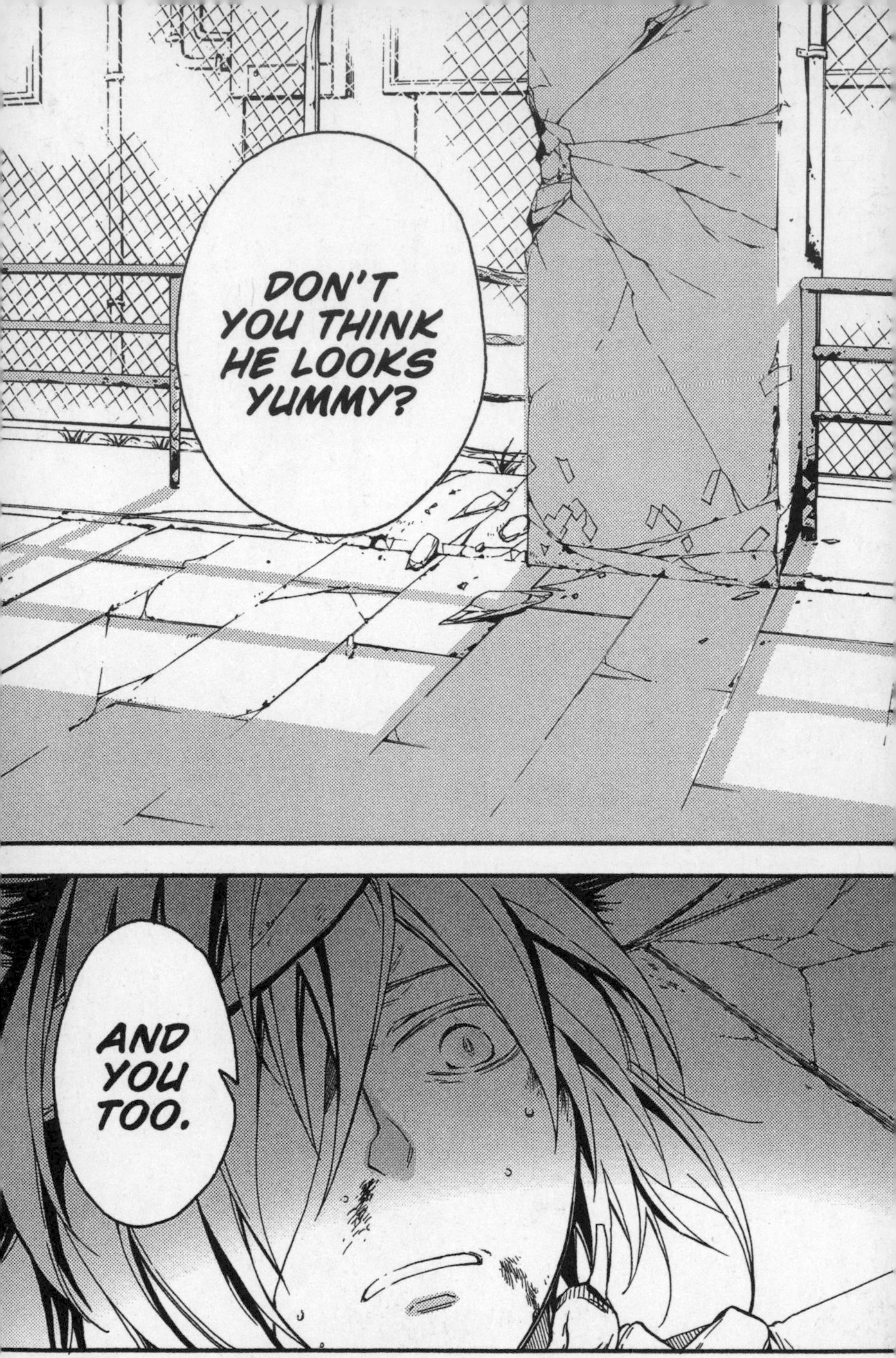
DON'T YOU THINK HE LOOKS YUMMY?
AND YOU TOO.

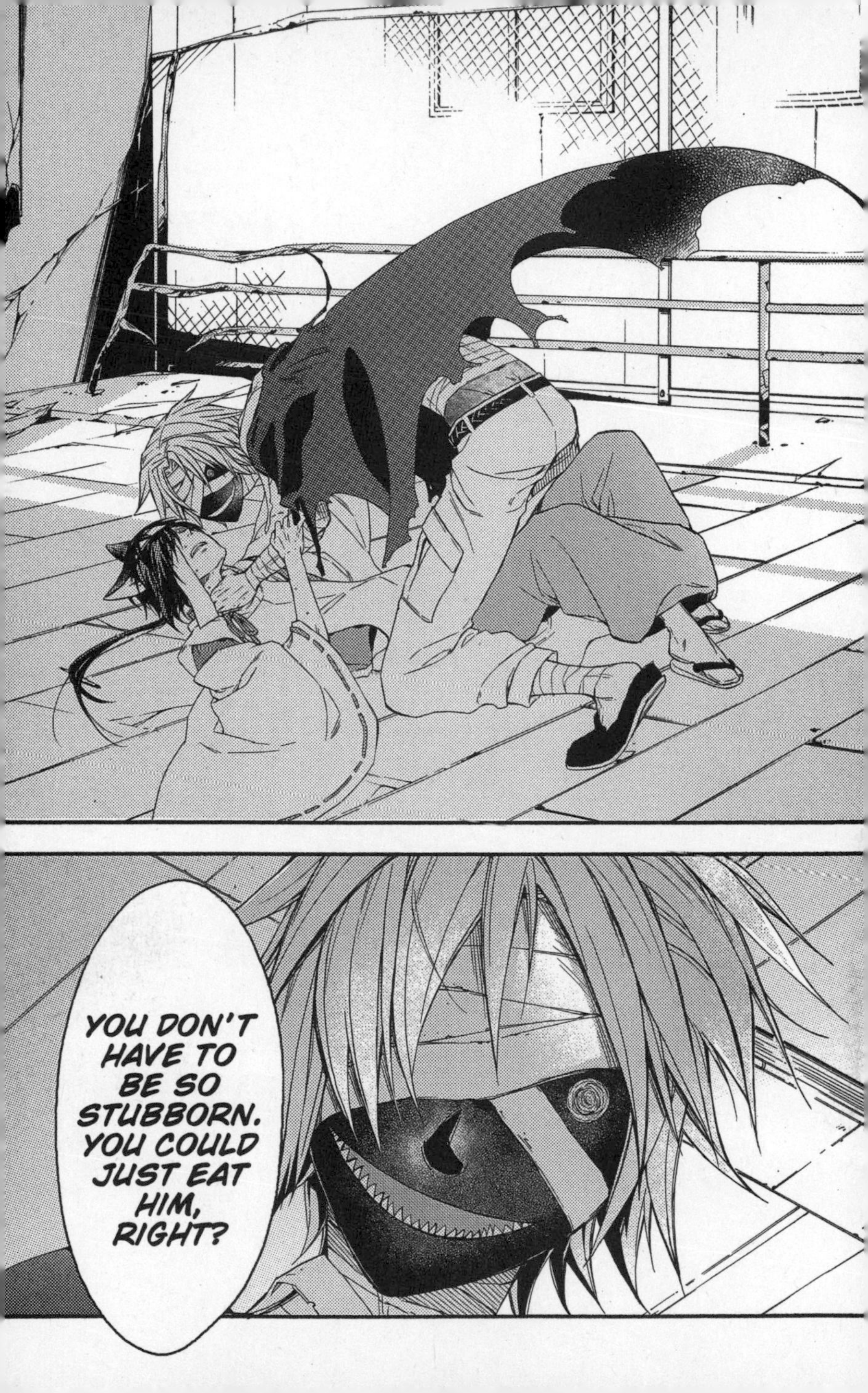
YOU DON'T HAVE TO BE SO STUBBORN. YOU COULD JUST EAT HIM, RIGHT?

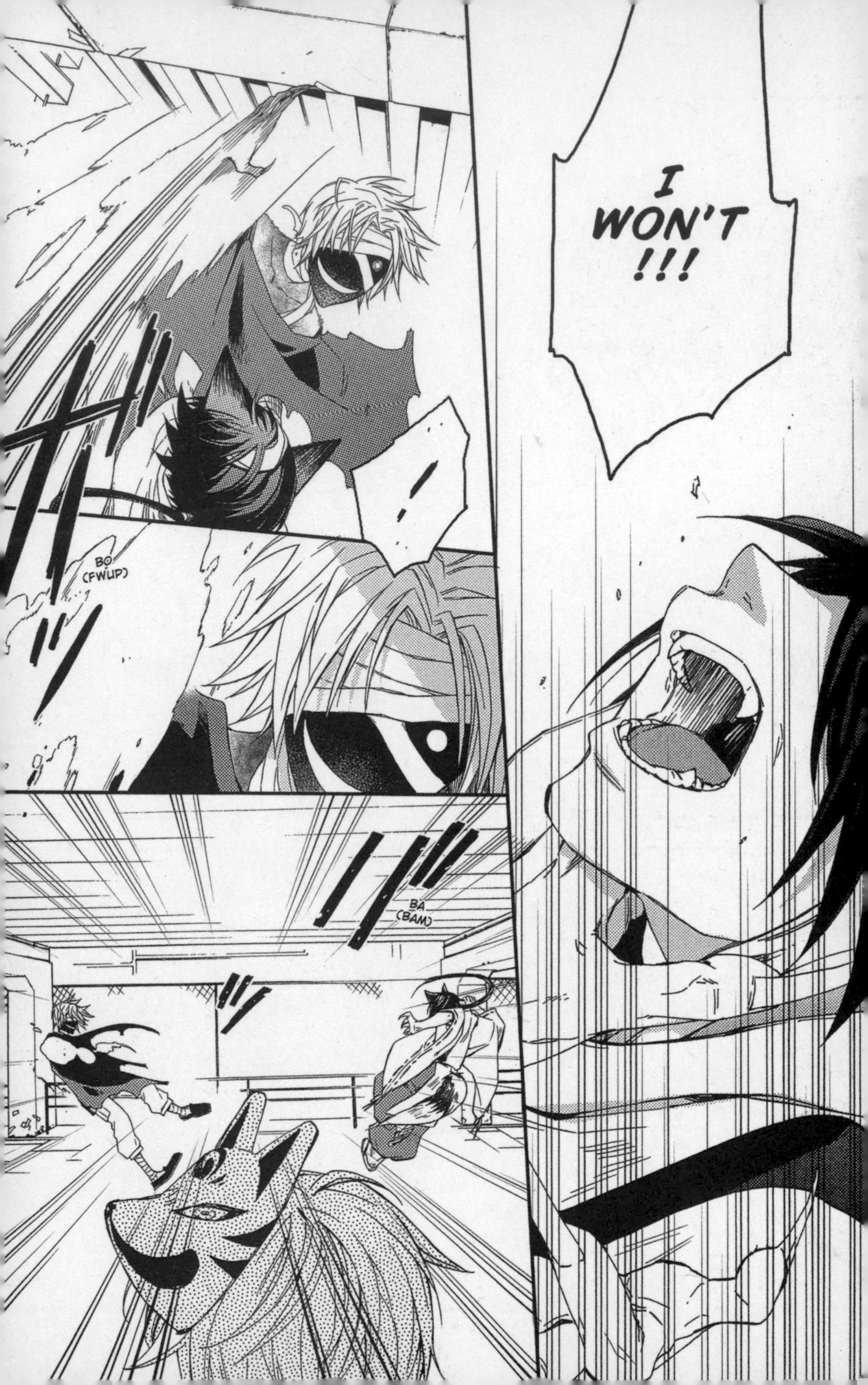
I WON'T !!!
BO (FWUP)
BA (BAM)

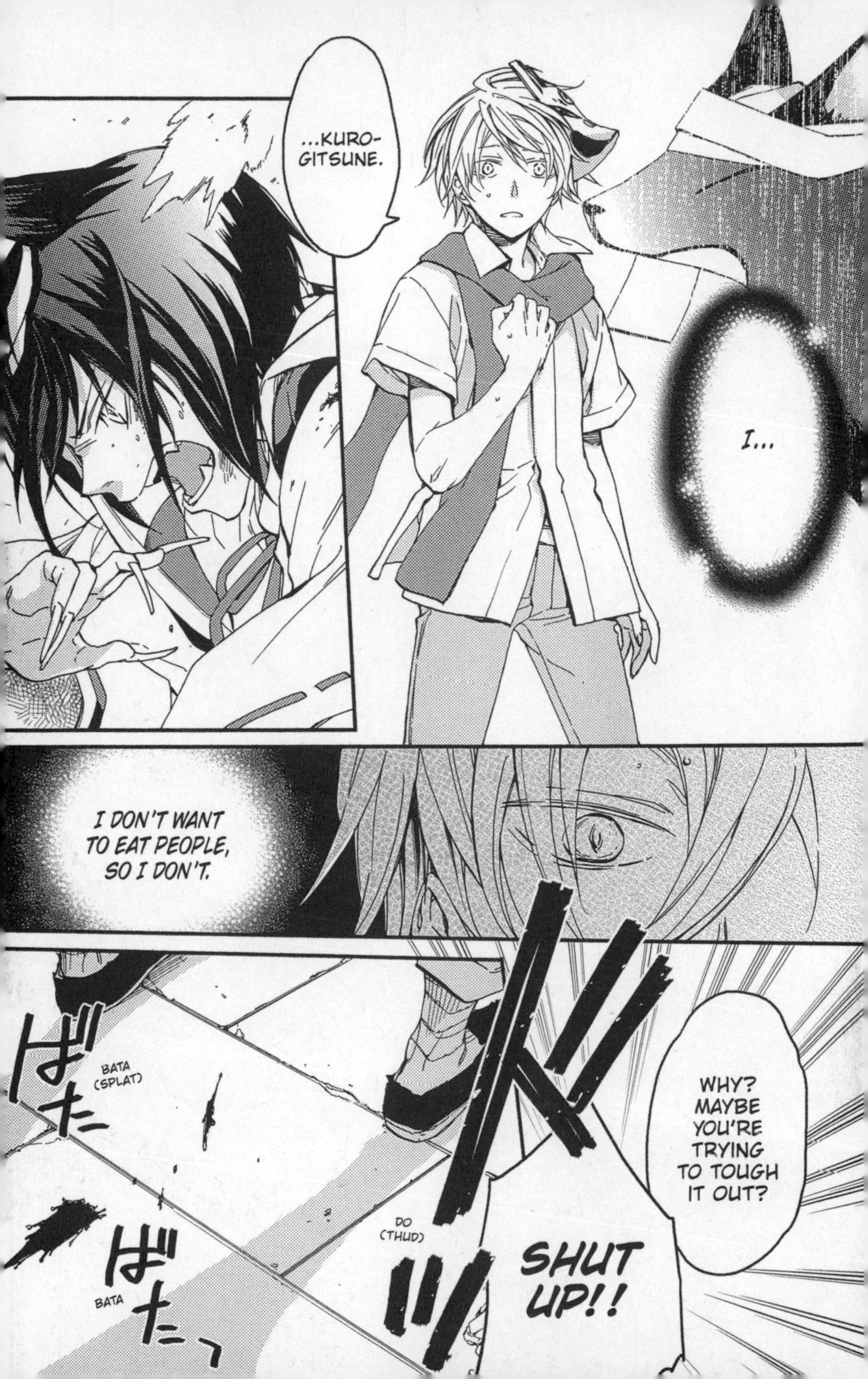
...KURO-GITSUNE.
I...
I DON'T WANT TO EAT PEOPLE, SO I DON'T.
WHY? MAYBE YOU'RE TRYING TO TOUGH IT OUT?
SHUT UP!!
DO (THUD)
ばた
BATA (SPLAT)
ばたっ
BATA

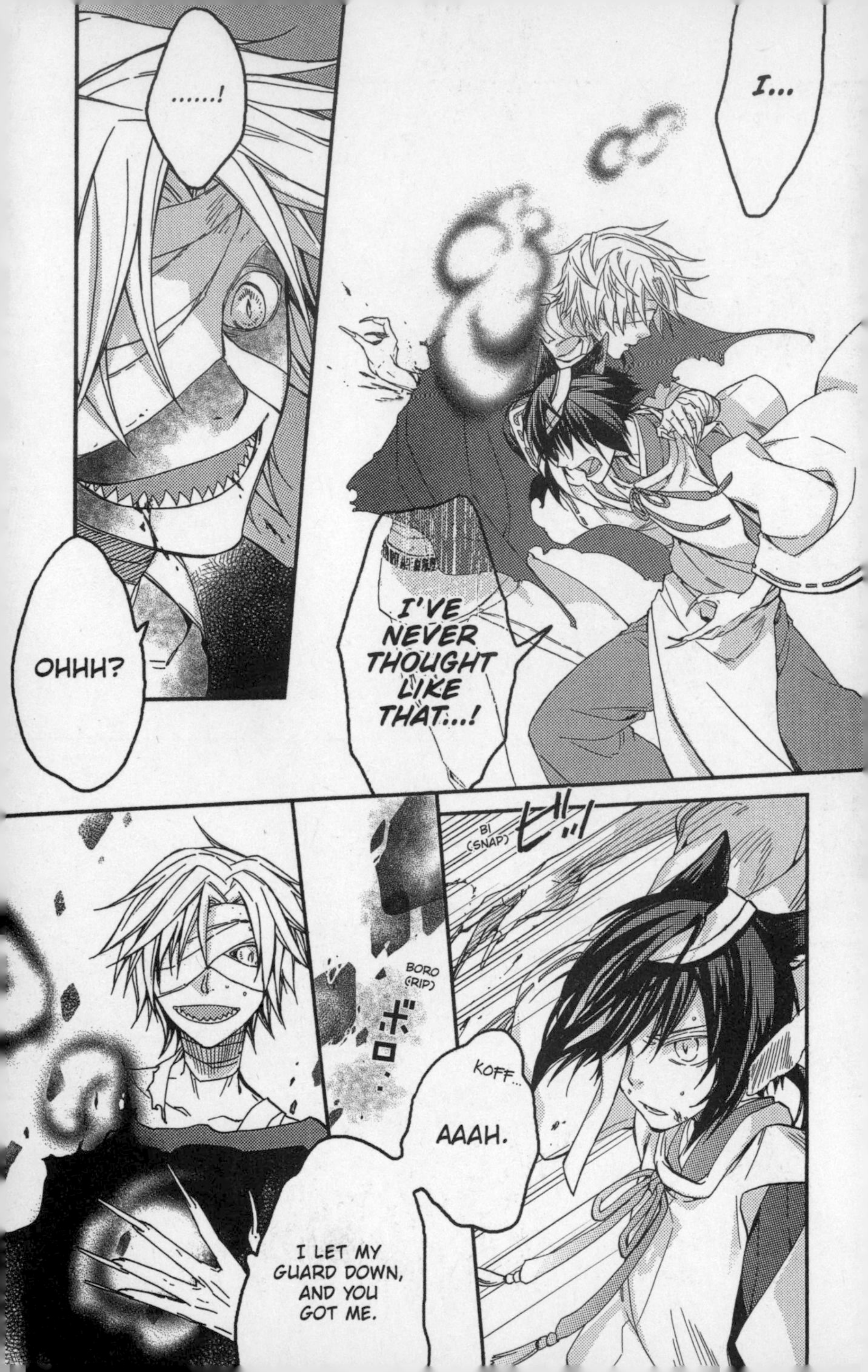
I...
I'VE NEVER THOUGHT LIKE THAT...!
......!
OHHH?
BI (SNAP) ビッ
KOFF...
BORO (RIP) ボロ...
AAAH.
I LET MY GUARD DOWN, AND YOU GOT ME.

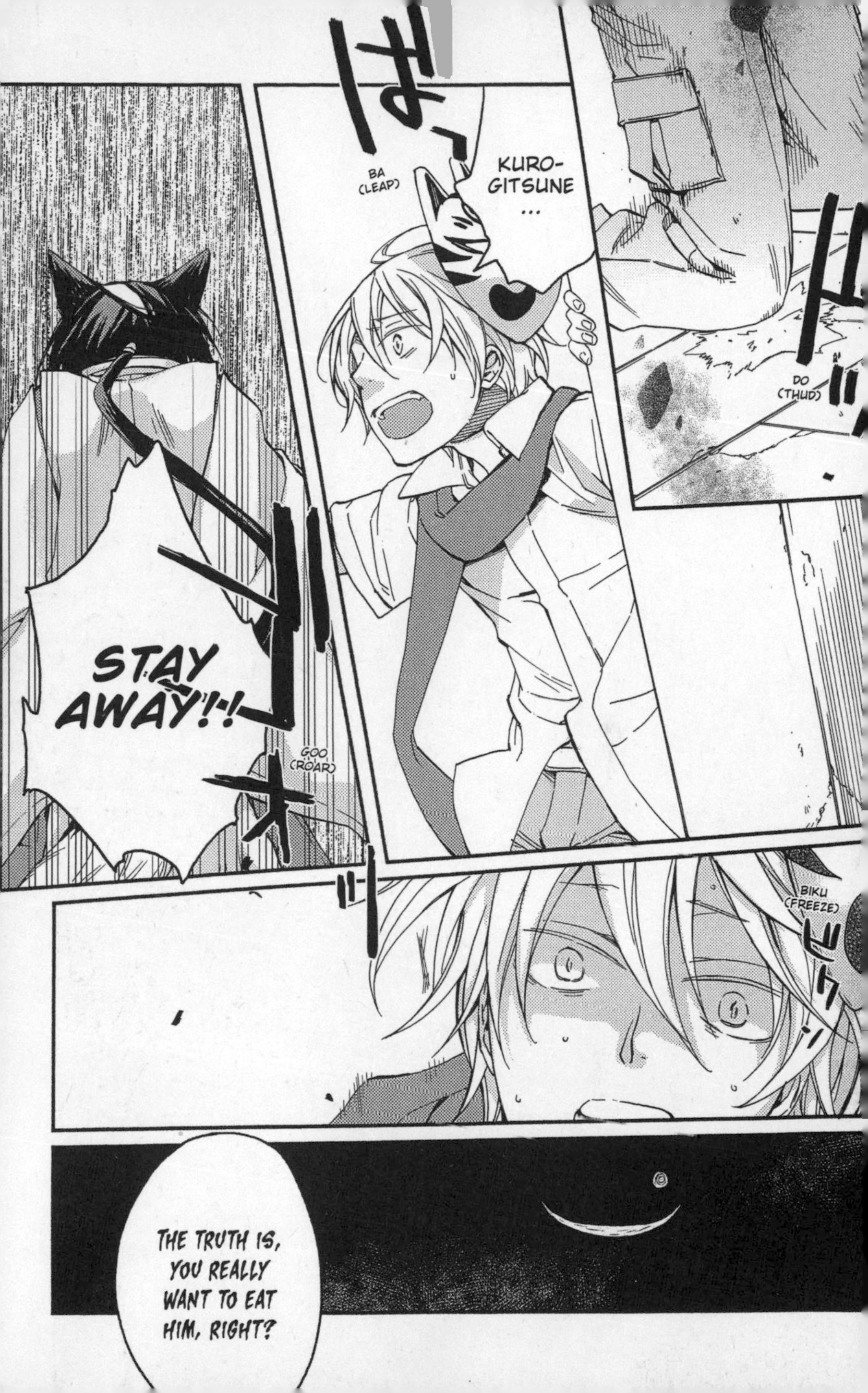
DO (THUD)
KURO-GITSUNE ...
BA (LEAP)
STAY AWAY!!
GOO (ROAR)
BIKU (FREEZE)
THE TRUTH IS, YOU REALLY WANT TO EAT HIM, RIGHT?

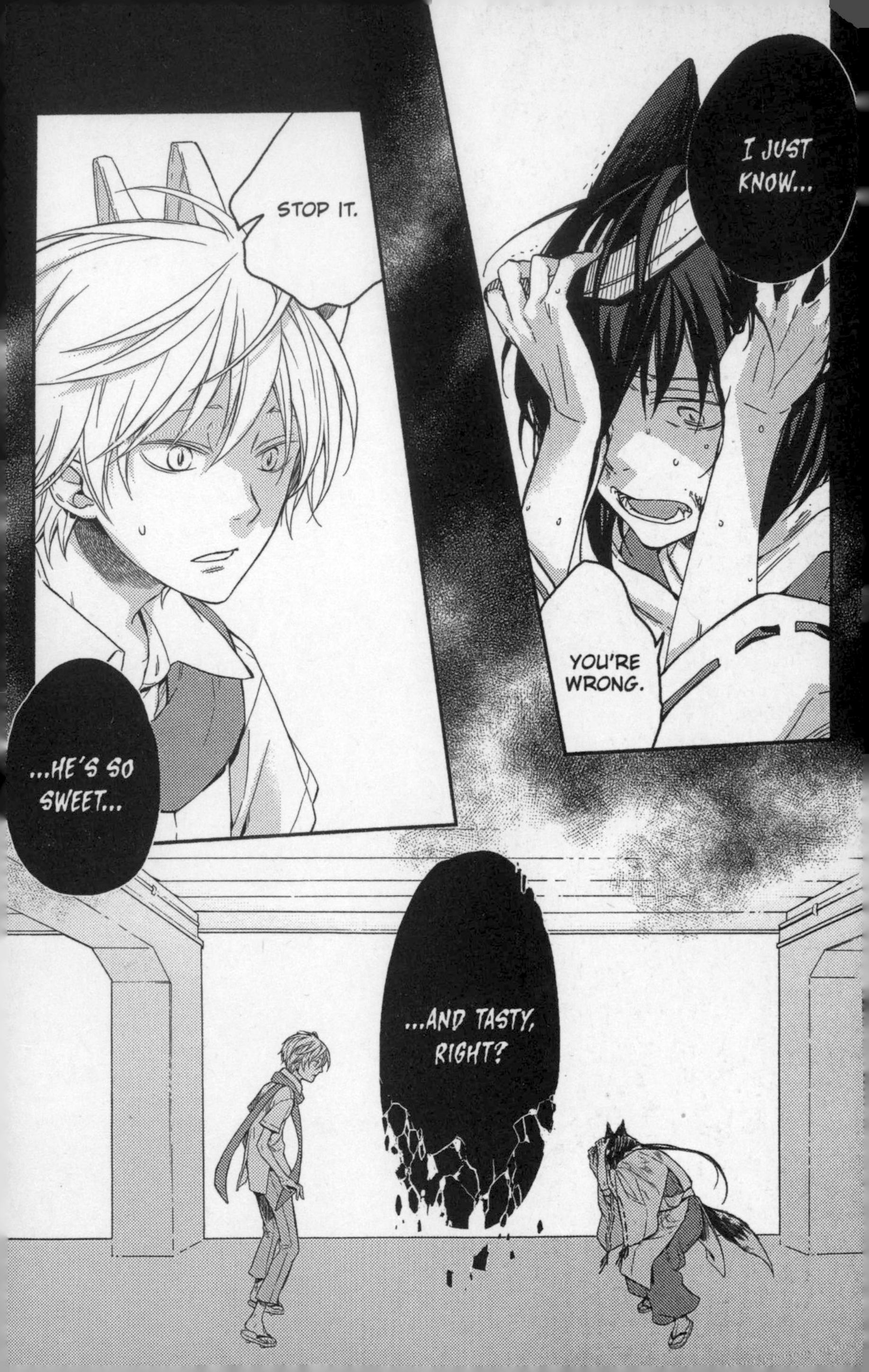
I JUST KNOW...
YOU'RE WRONG.
STOP IT.
...HE'S SO SWEET...
...AND TASTY, RIGHT?

TO BE CONTINUED
IN VOLUME 6

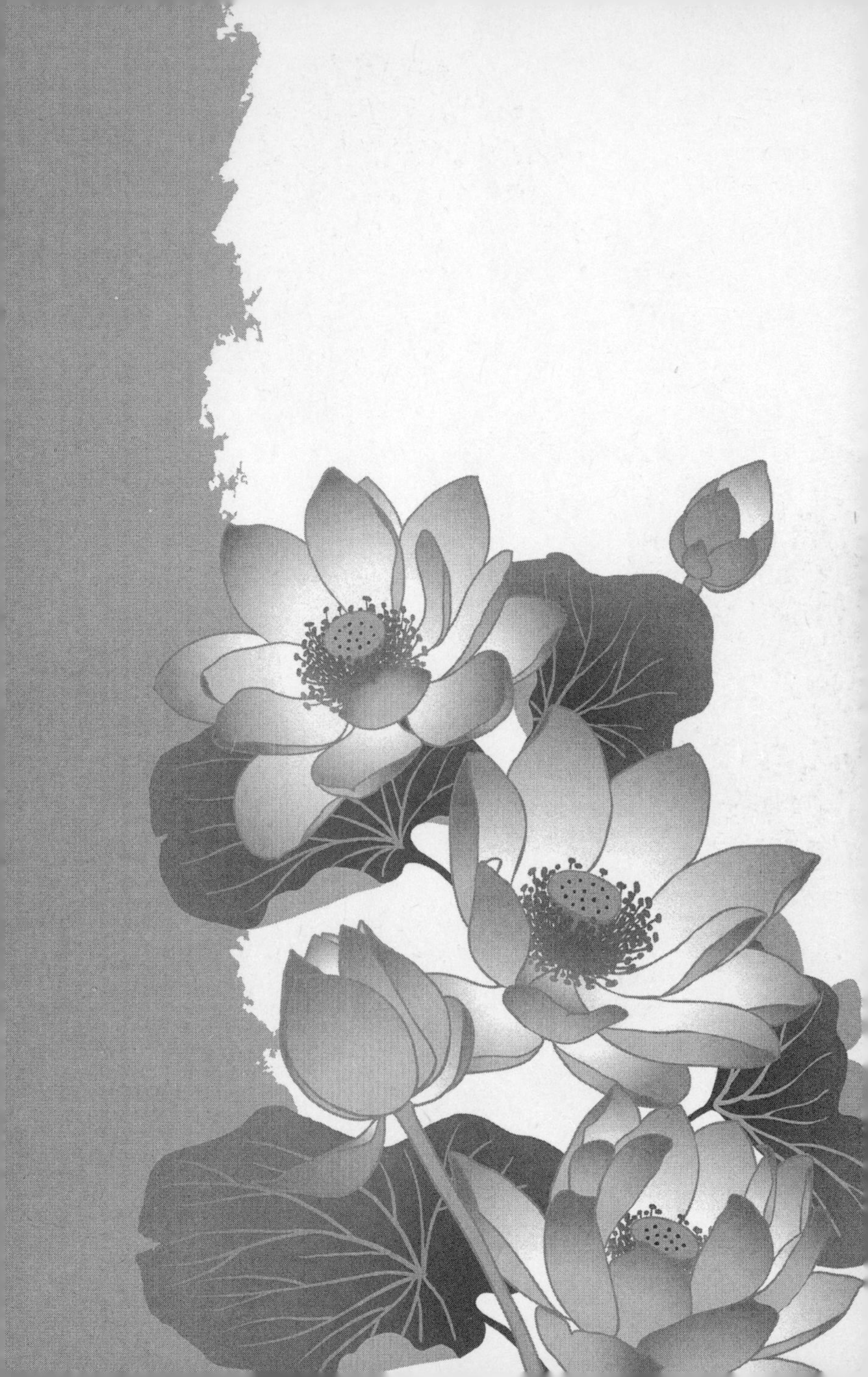

Special Extra

After School with Suzuki-kun

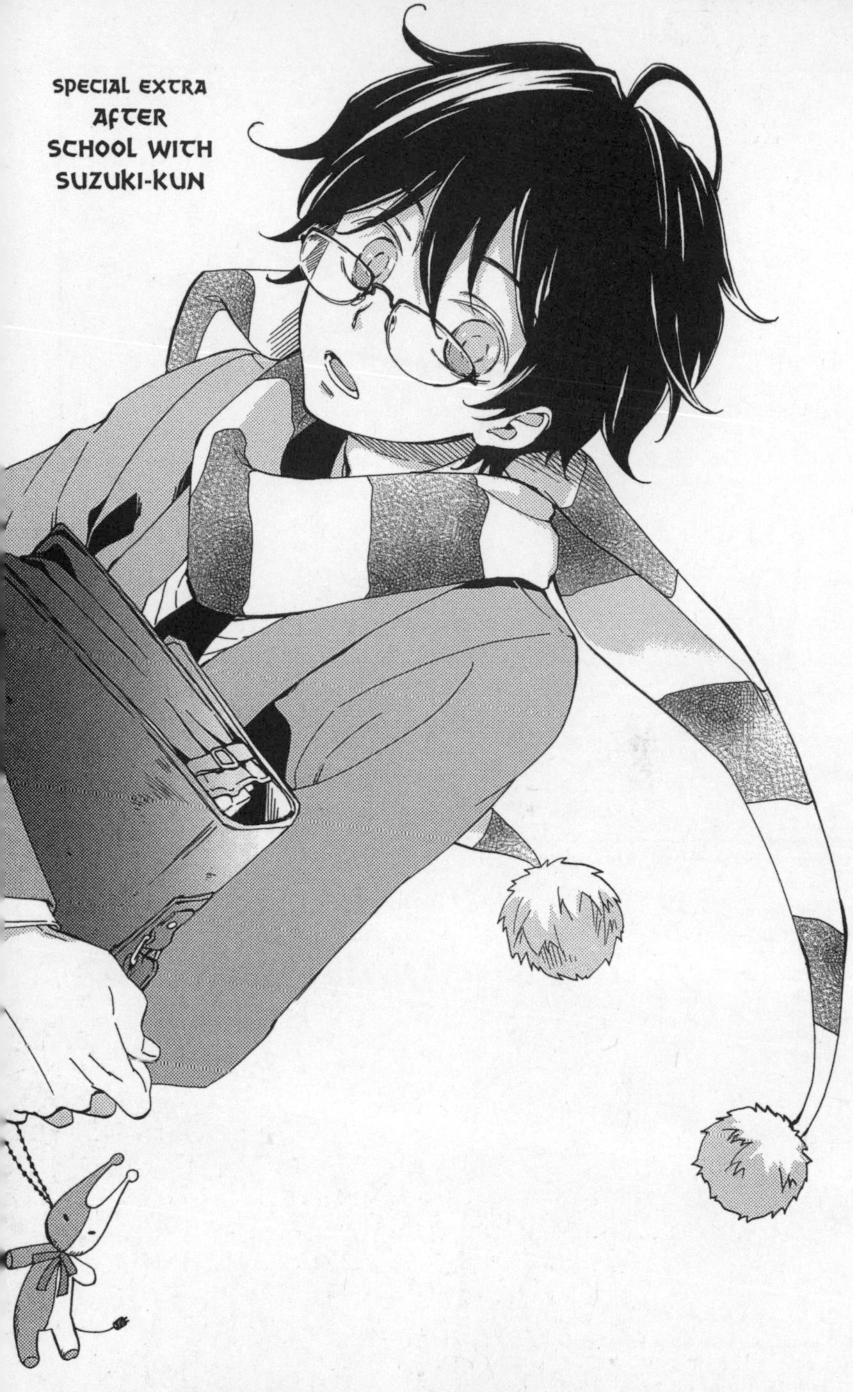

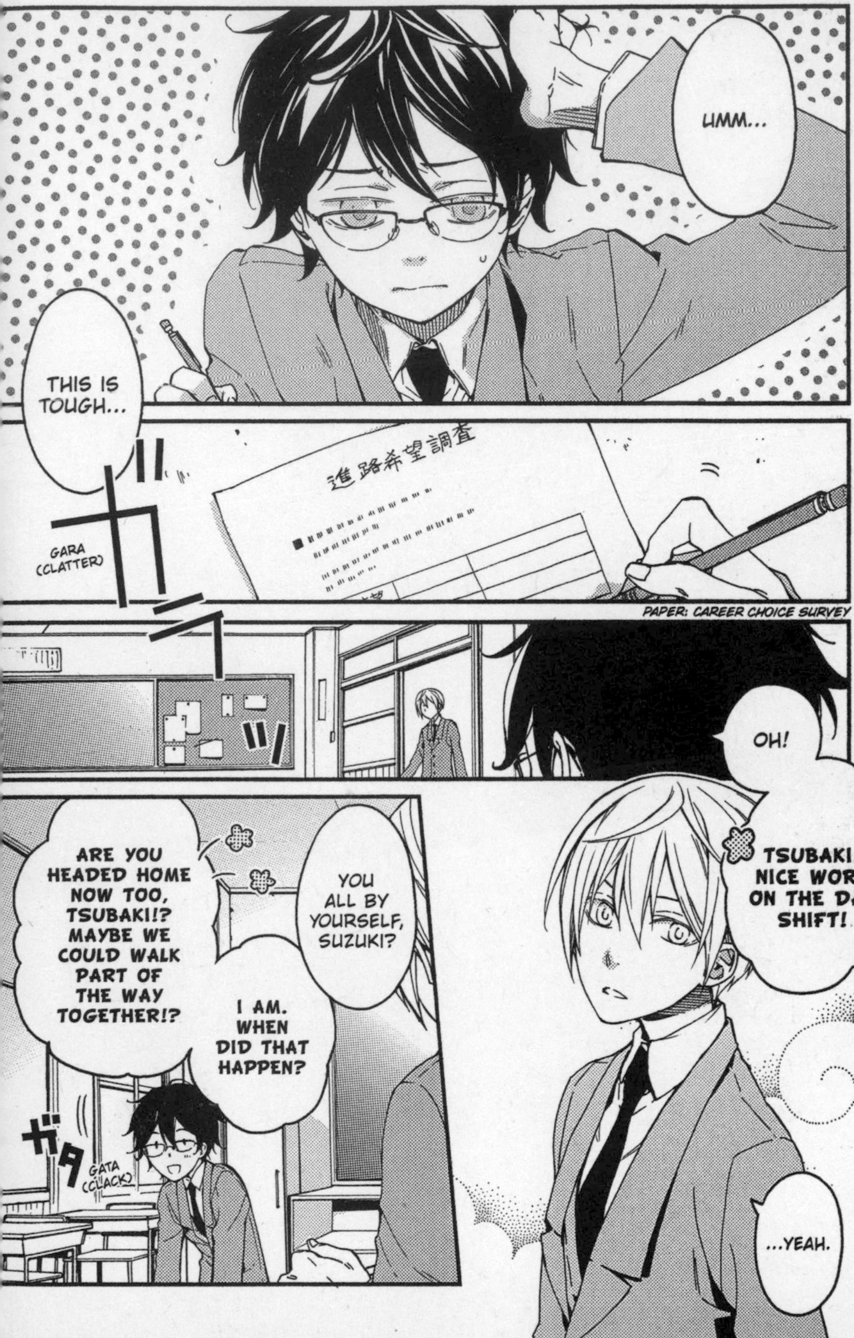
UMM...
THIS IS TOUGH...
進路希望調査
ガラッ
GARA (CLATTER)
PAPER: CAREER CHOICE SURVEY
OH!
TSUBAKI! NICE WORK ON THE DAY SHIFT!
...YEAH.
YOU ALL BY YOURSELF, SUZUKI?
I AM. WHEN DID THAT HAPPEN?
ARE YOU HEADED HOME NOW TOO, TSUBAKI!? MAYBE WE COULD WALK PART OF THE WAY TOGETHER!?
ガタ
GATA (CLACK)

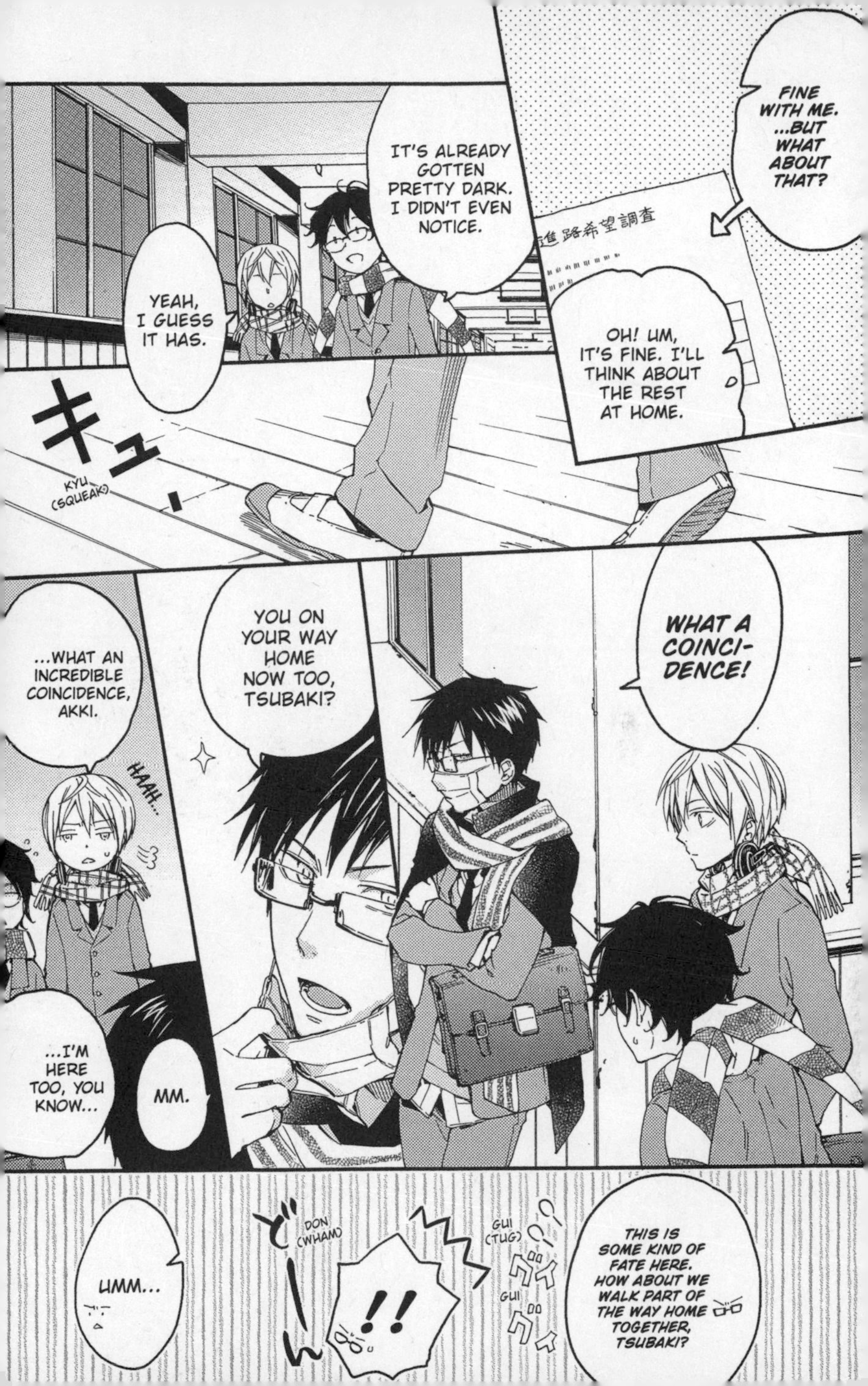
FINE WITH ME. ...BUT WHAT ABOUT THAT?
進路希望調査
OH! UM, IT'S FINE. I'LL THINK ABOUT THE REST AT HOME.
IT'S ALREADY GOTTEN PRETTY DARK. I DIDN'T EVEN NOTICE.
YEAH, I GUESS IT HAS.
キュ
KYU (SQUEAK)
WHAT A COINCI-DENCE!
YOU ON YOUR WAY HOME NOW TOO, TSUBAKI?
...WHAT AN INCREDIBLE COINCIDENCE, AKKI.
HAAH...
MM.
...I'M HERE TOO, YOU KNOW...
THIS IS SOME KIND OF FATE HERE. HOW ABOUT WE WALK PART OF THE WAY HOME TOGETHER, TSUBAKI?
グイ
GUI (TUG)
グイ
GUI
!!
どーん
DON (WHAM)
UMM...

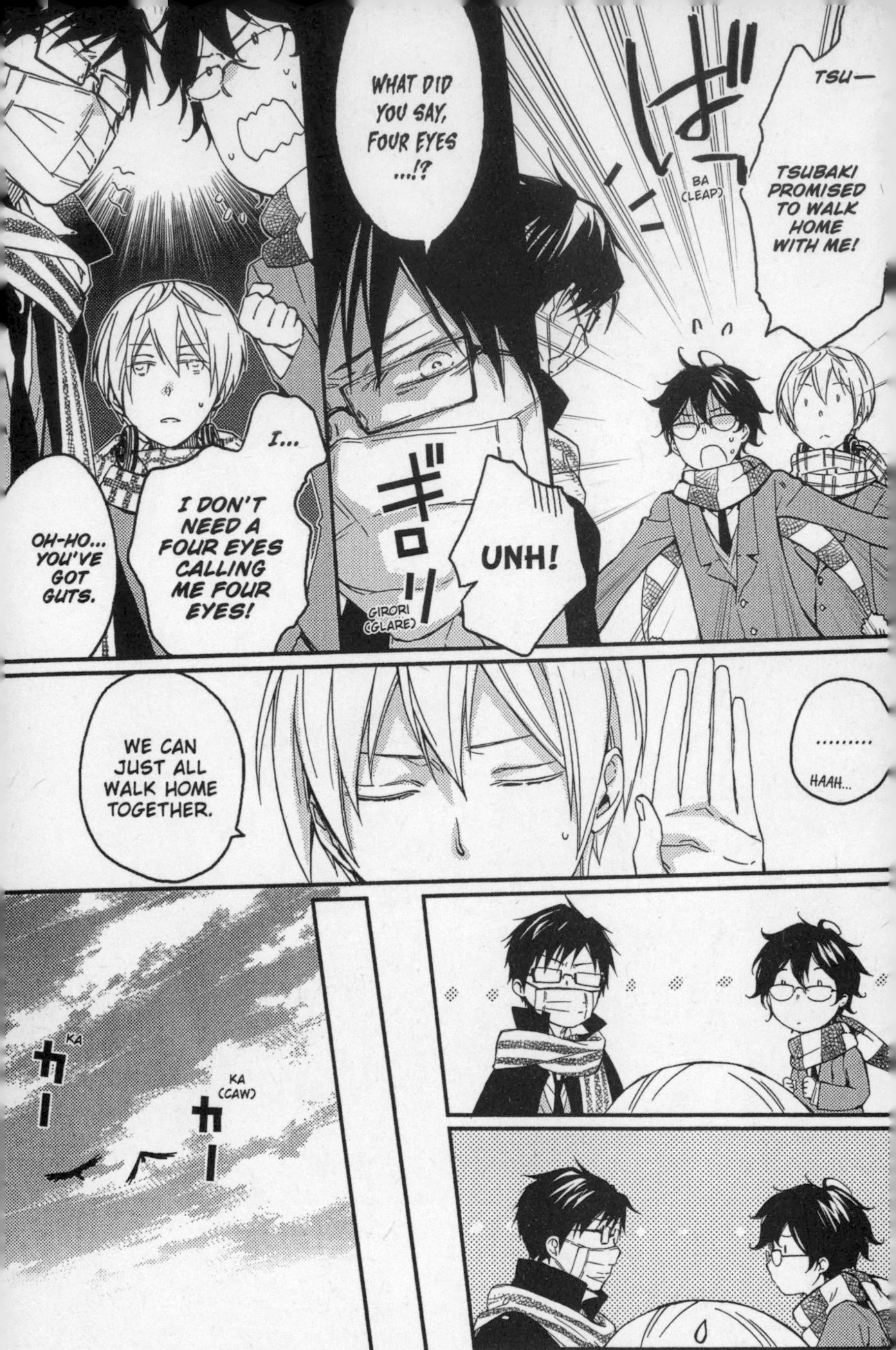
TSU—
TSUBAKI PROMISED TO WALK HOME WITH ME!
BA (LEAP)
WHAT DID YOU SAY, FOUR EYES ...!?
UNH!
GIRORI (GLARE)
I...
I DON'T NEED A FOUR EYES CALLING ME FOUR EYES!
OH-HO... YOU'VE GOT GUTS.
....
HAAH...
WE CAN JUST ALL WALK HOME TOGETHER.
KA (CAW)
KA

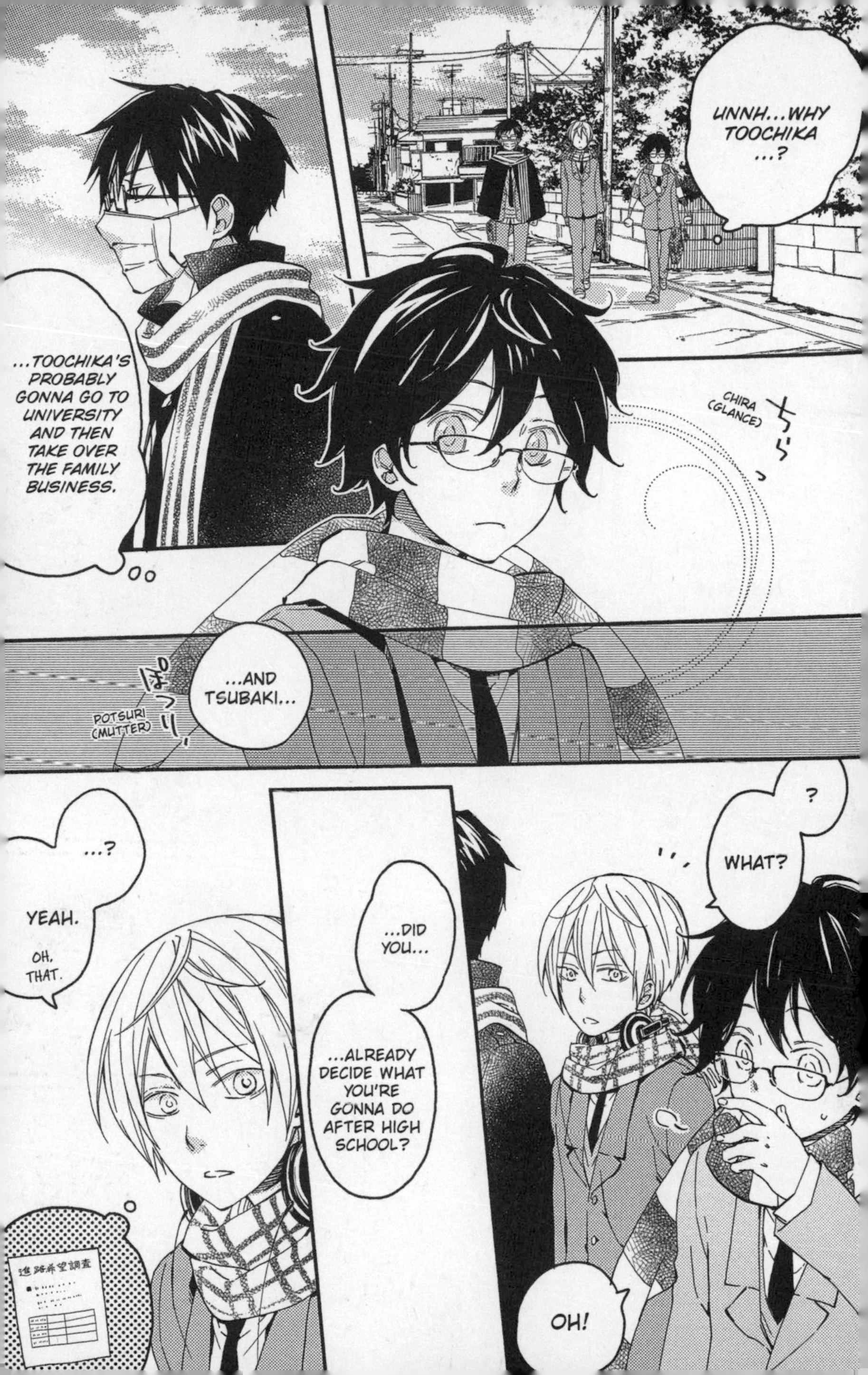
UNNH...WHY TOOCHIKA ...?
...TOOCHIKA'S PROBABLY GONNA GO TO UNIVERSITY AND THEN TAKE OVER THE FAMILY BUSINESS.
CHIRA (GLANCE)
ちら
...AND TSUBAKI...
ぽつり
POTSURI (MUTTER)
?
WHAT?
OH!
...DID YOU...
...ALREADY DECIDE WHAT YOU'RE GONNA DO AFTER HIGH SCHOOL?
...?
YEAH.
OH, THAT.
進路希望調査

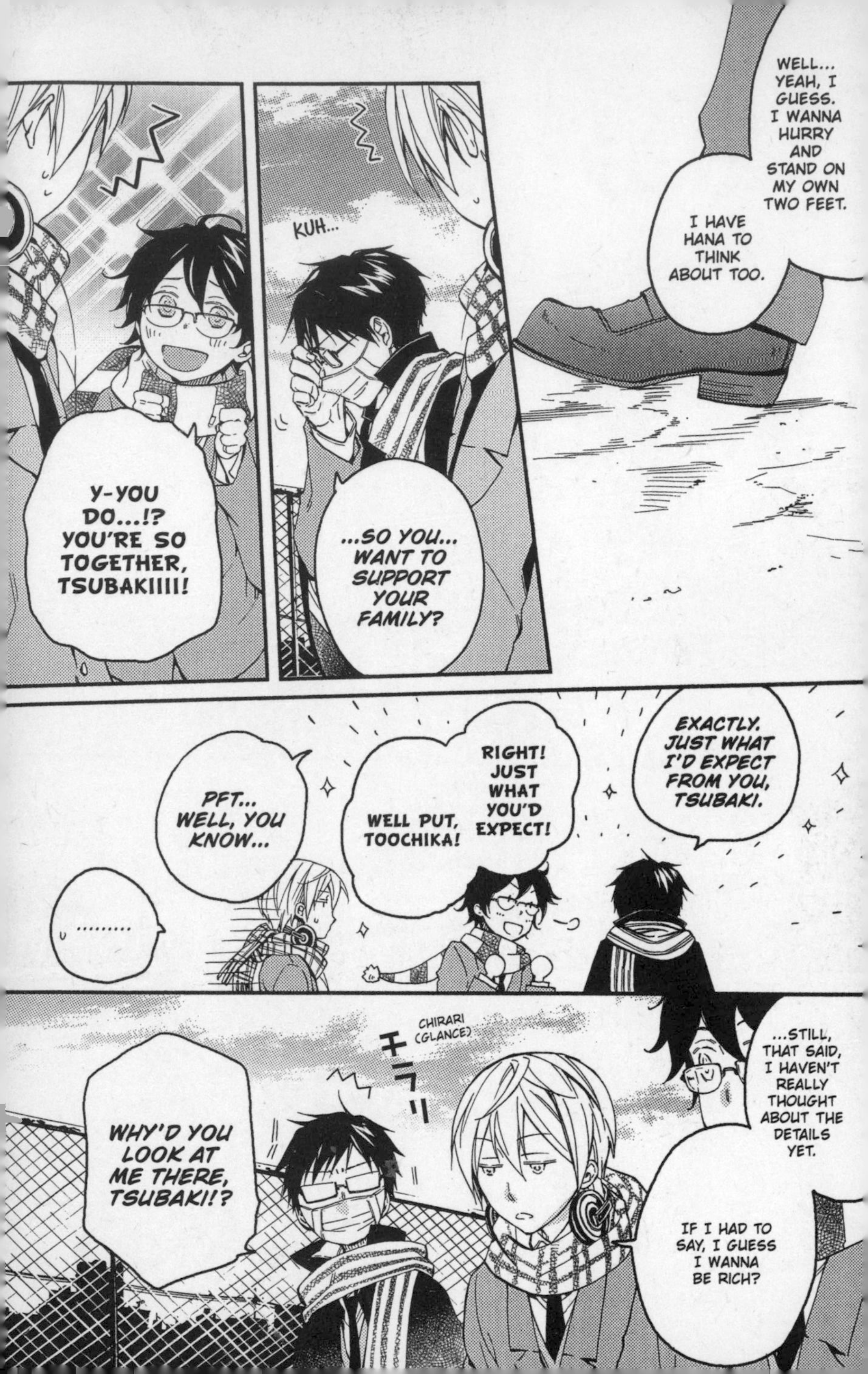
WELL... YEAH, I GUESS. I WANNA HURRY AND STAND ON MY OWN TWO FEET.
I HAVE HANA TO THINK ABOUT TOO.
KUH...
...SO YOU... WANT TO SUPPORT YOUR FAMILY?
Y-YOU DO...!? YOU'RE SO TOGETHER, TSUBAKIIIII!
EXACTLY. JUST WHAT I'D EXPECT FROM YOU, TSUBAKI.
RIGHT! JUST WHAT YOU'D EXPECT!
WELL PUT, TOOCHIKA!
PFT... WELL, YOU KNOW...
....
...STILL, THAT SAID, I HAVEN'T REALLY THOUGHT ABOUT THE DETAILS YET.
IF I HAD TO SAY, I GUESS I WANNA BE RICH?
CHIRARI (GLANCE)
WHY'D YOU LOOK AT ME THERE, TSUBAKI!?

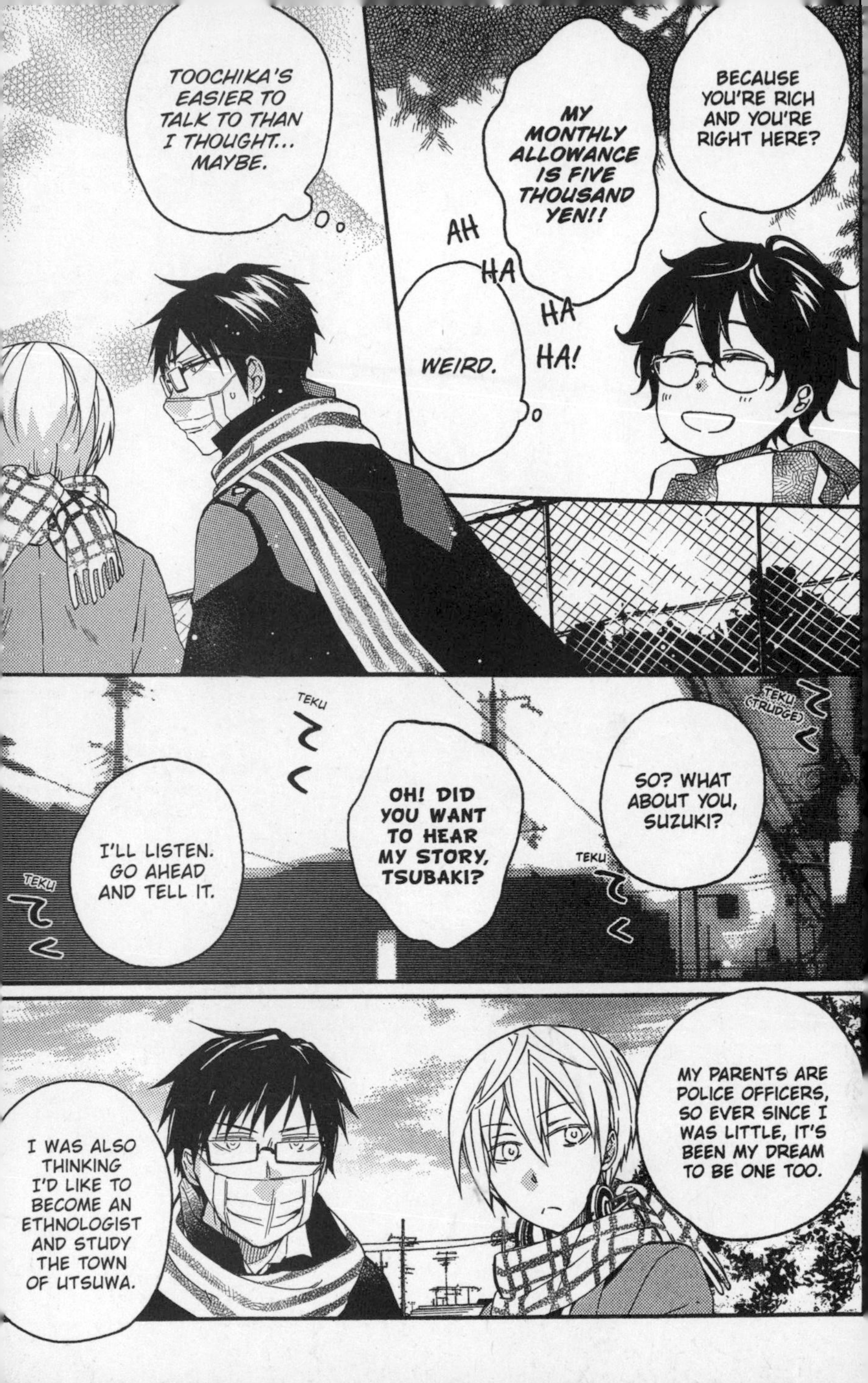
BECAUSE YOU'RE RICH AND YOU'RE RIGHT HERE?
MY MONTHLY ALLOWANCE IS FIVE THOUSAND YEN!!
AH HA HA HA!
WEIRD.
TOOCHIKA'S EASIER TO TALK TO THAN I THOUGHT... MAYBE.
TEKU TEKU (TRUDGE)
SO? WHAT ABOUT YOU, SUZUKI?
TEKU
OH! DID YOU WANT TO HEAR MY STORY, TSUBAKI?
TEKU
I'LL LISTEN. GO AHEAD AND TELL IT.
TEKU
MY PARENTS ARE POLICE OFFICERS, SO EVER SINCE I WAS LITTLE, IT'S BEEN MY DREAM TO BE ONE TOO.
I WAS ALSO THINKING I'D LIKE TO BECOME AN ETHNOLOGIST AND STUDY THE TOWN OF UTSUWA.

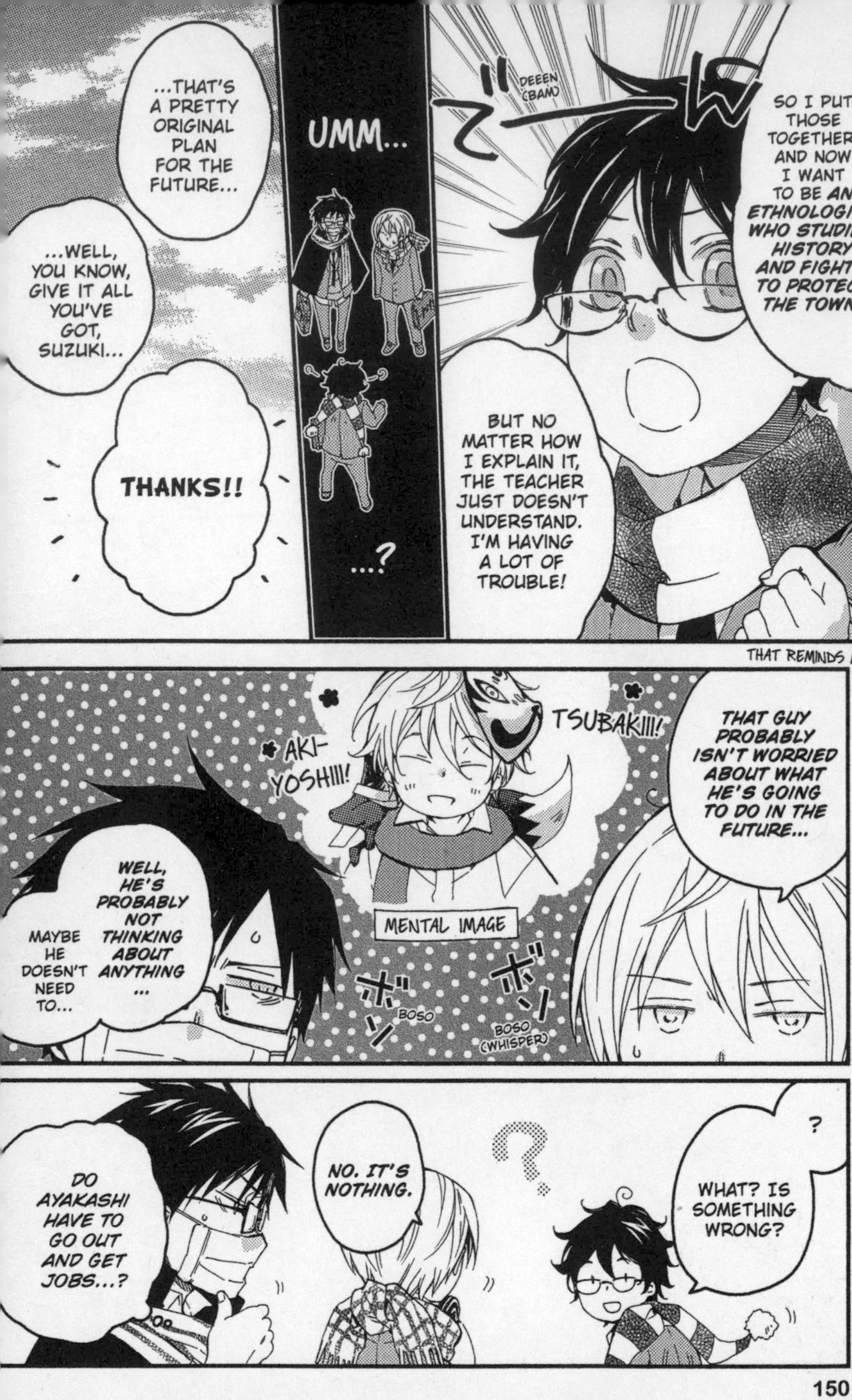
SO I PUT THOSE TOGETHER, AND NOW I WANT TO BE AN ETHNOLOGIST WHO STUDIES HISTORY AND FIGHTS TO PROTECT THE TOWN.
DEEEN (BAM)
BUT NO MATTER HOW I EXPLAIN IT, THE TEACHER JUST DOESN'T UNDERSTAND. I'M HAVING A LOT OF TROUBLE!
UMM...
...?
...THAT'S A PRETTY ORIGINAL PLAN FOR THE FUTURE...
...WELL, YOU KNOW, GIVE IT ALL YOU'VE GOT, SUZUKI...
THANKS!!
THAT REMINDS ME...
THAT GUY PROBABLY ISN'T WORRIED ABOUT WHAT HE'S GOING TO DO IN THE FUTURE...
TSUBAKIII!
AKI-YOSHIII!
MENTAL IMAGE
BOSO (WHISPER)
BOSO
WELL, HE'S PROBABLY NOT THINKING ABOUT ANYTHING ...
MAYBE HE DOESN'T NEED TO...
?
WHAT? IS SOMETHING WRONG?
NO. IT'S NOTHING.
DO AYAKASHI HAVE TO GO OUT AND GET JOBS...?

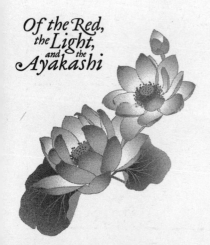

Of the Red,
the Light,
and the
Ayakashi

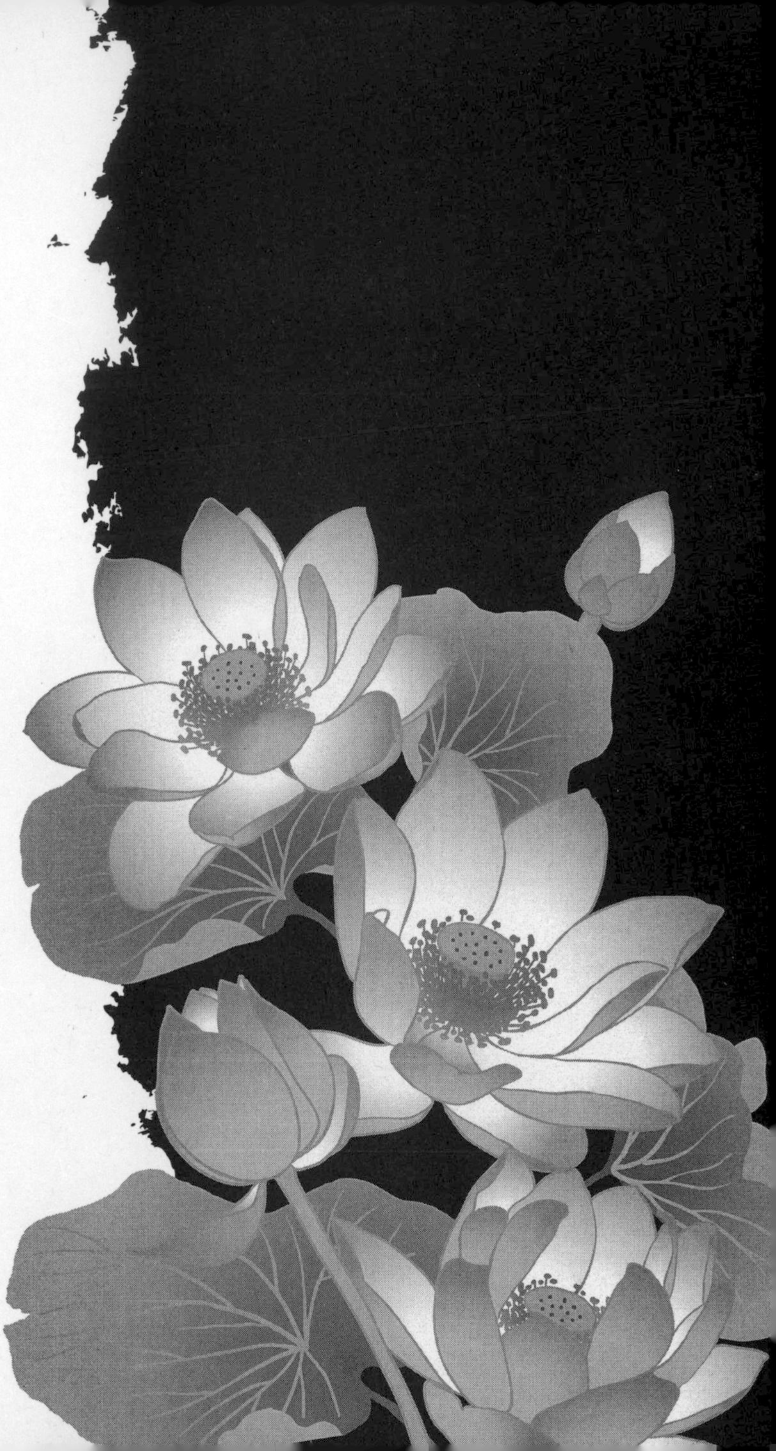

~ DIGRESSION ~
I'M HAPPY TO SEE BOY A ON THE BACK COVER.

WILL THE DAY EVER COME WHEN THE RABBITS—WHO NEVER GET TO GRACE THE BACK COVER, ALTHOUGH I SUGGEST THEM EVERY TIME—GET TO SEE THE LIGHT OF DAY? (THEY'RE SO CUTE IN ROUGH SKETCHES.)

SO CUTE! BUT WITH SAKU AND NAGI...
SUPER-CUTE!! BUT THIS TIME, IT'S US...

HELLO! HACCAWORKS* HERE.
YOU LOOK REALLY ROUGH, AKIYOSHI.
THE RAGING FIFTH VOLUME.
SO (SSP)
MASK
NANAO-SENSEI SOMEHOW MANAGED TO BRING A RIDICULOUSLY COMPLICATED PLOT TOGETHER ALL ON HER OWN (A GODDESS).
NOW THAT THINGS ARE IN THE FINAL STAGES, WE'VE ALSO BEEN INVOLVED IN THE DEVELOPMENT LATELY.
SORRY FOR ALL THE INTERFERENCE...
WE'RE SORRY THE ORIGINAL IS SO HARD TO UNDERSTAND...
NOTES
DO THIS HERE AND MAKE AKIYOSHI LOOK GOOD, AND THEN DROP TOUGO AND THEN THAT BLAH-BLAH.
WE MESS WITH THE PLOT SUGGESTIONS AND STORYBOARDS WE GET TO SEE.
THE LOOK ON SATOU-SAN'S FACE HERE IS A LITTLE FLAT, SO I CAN'T READ IT.
OH! I WANT TO SEE SATOU-SAN ON THE COVER...
GO THE KUROGITSUNE ROUTE HERE AND COME AROUND TO A GOOD REGROUPING.
STORY-BOARD
MOST OF OUR SUGGESTIONS ARE FUZZY AND EXCESSIVE...
MOTTO
N-NANAO-SENSEI'S SURE TO MAKE IT ALL WORK OUT.
WE JUST HAVE TO SAY WHAT WE HAVE TO SAY.
WE'RE REALLY SORRY.
THANK YOU FOR BRINGING SUCH WONDERFUL PERFORMANCES EVERY TIME!!

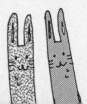

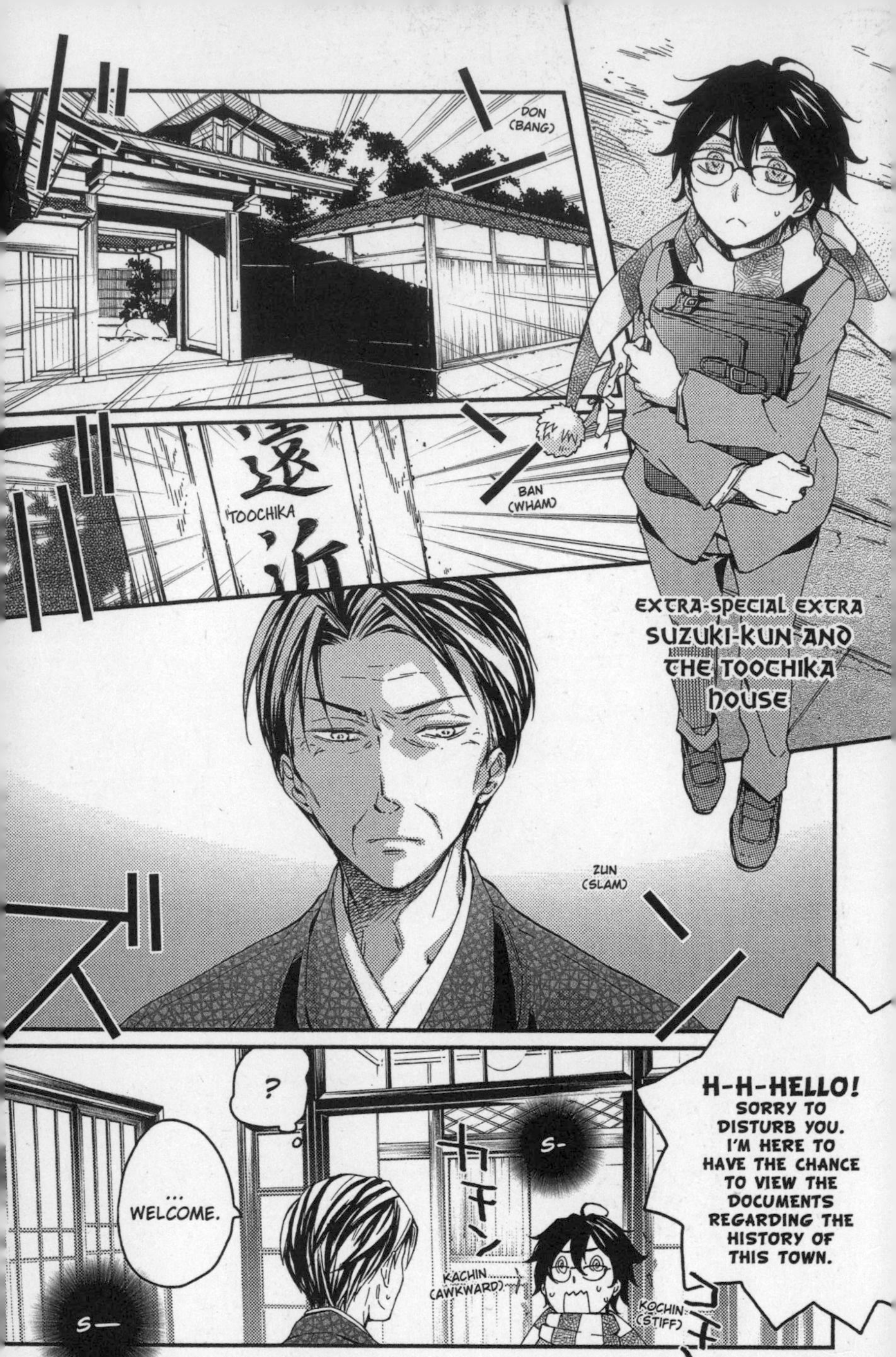
EXTRA-SPECIAL EXTRA
SUZUKI-KUN AND THE TOOCHIKA HOUSE
DON (BANG)
BAN (WHAM)
TOOCHIKA
遠近
ZUN (SLAM)
H-H-HELLO! SORRY TO DISTURB YOU. I'M HERE TO HAVE THE CHANCE TO VIEW THE DOCUMENTS REGARDING THE HISTORY OF THIS TOWN.
KOCHIN (STIFF)
S-
KACHIN (AWKWARD)
?
... WELCOME.
S—

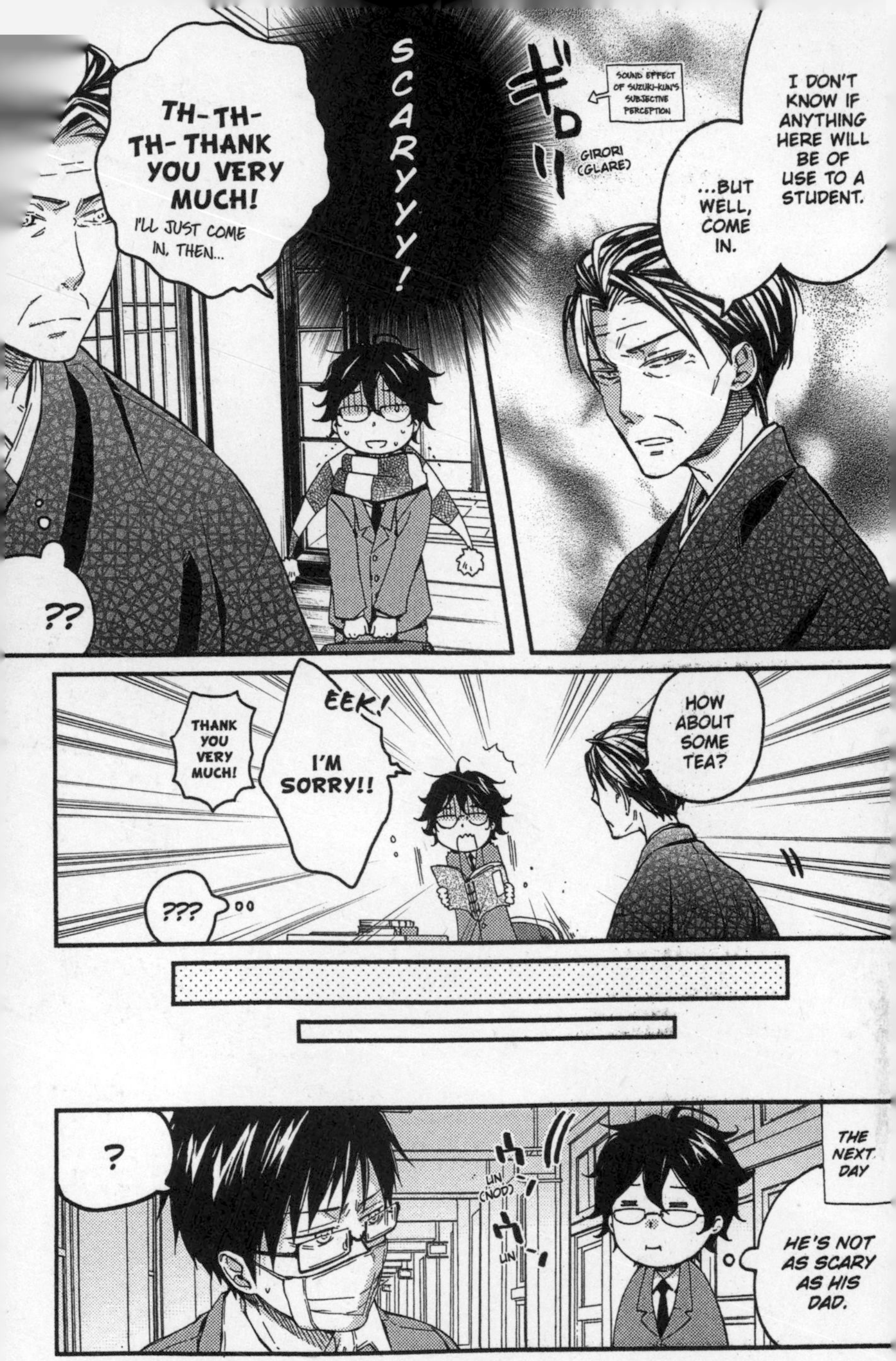
I DON'T KNOW IF ANYTHING HERE WILL BE OF USE TO A STUDENT.
...BUT WELL, COME IN.
SOUND EFFECT OF SUZUKI-KUN'S SUBJECTIVE PERCEPTION
ギロリ
GIRORI (GLARE)
SCARYYY!
TH-TH-TH- THANK YOU VERY MUCH!
I'LL JUST COME IN, THEN...
??
HOW ABOUT SOME TEA?
EEK!
I'M SORRY!!
THANK YOU VERY MUCH!
???
THE NEXT DAY
HE'S NOT AS SCARY AS HIS DAD.
UN (NOD)
UN
?

THANK YOU SO MUCH!! KURO

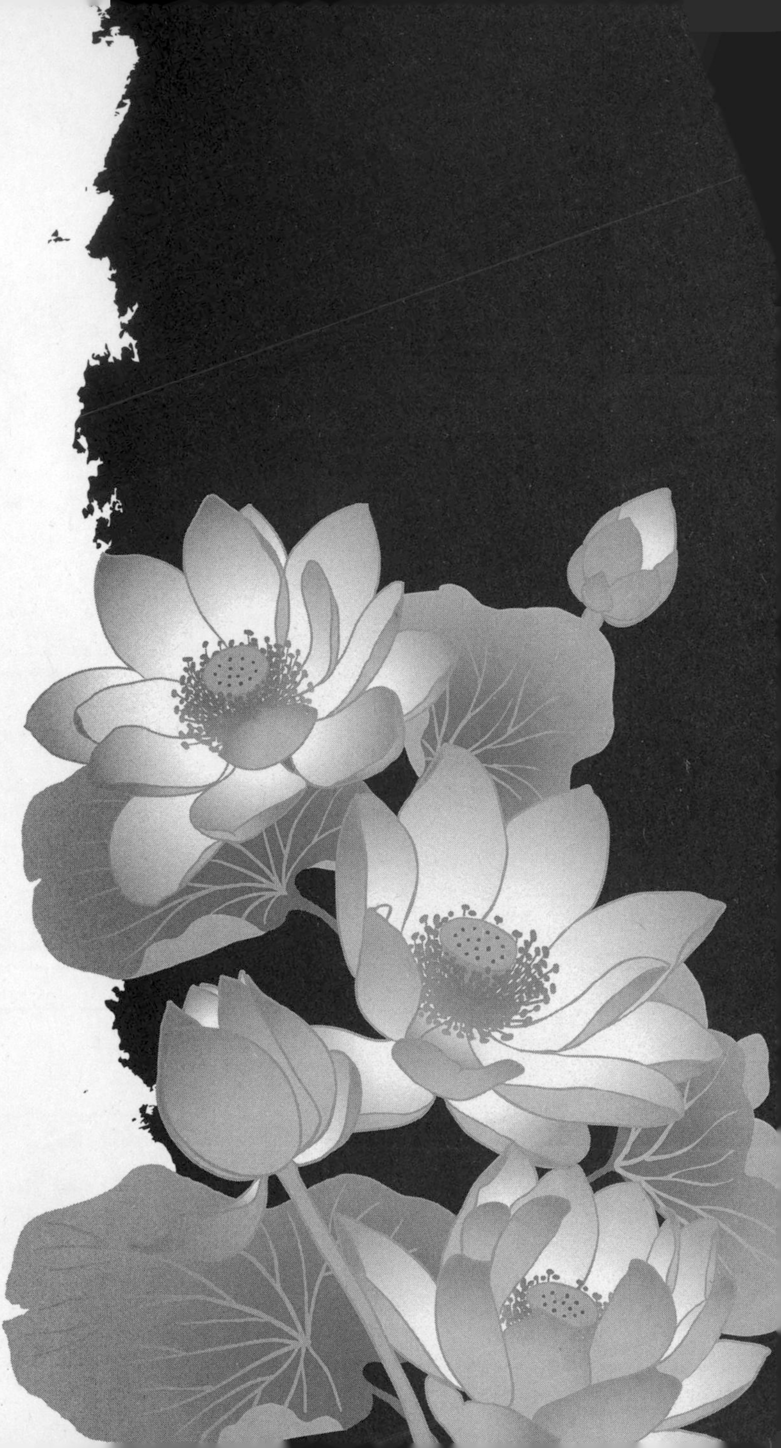

TRANSLATION NOTES

COMMON HONORIFICS

no honorific: Indicates familiarity or closeness; if used without permission or reason, addressing someone in this manner would be an insult.

-san: The Japanese equivalent of Mr./Mrs./Miss. If a situation calls for politeness, this is the fail-safe honorific.

-sama: Conveys great respect; may also indicate that the social status of the speaker is lower than that of the addressee.

-kun: Used most often when referring to boys, this indicates affection or familiarity. Occasionally used by older men among their peers, but it may also be used by anyone referring to a person of lower standing.

-chan, -tan: An affectionate honorific indicating familiarity used mostly in reference to girls; also used in reference to cute persons or animals.

Ayakashi is a general term for ghosts, monsters, haunted objects, mythical animals, and all sorts of uncanny things from Japanese folklore.

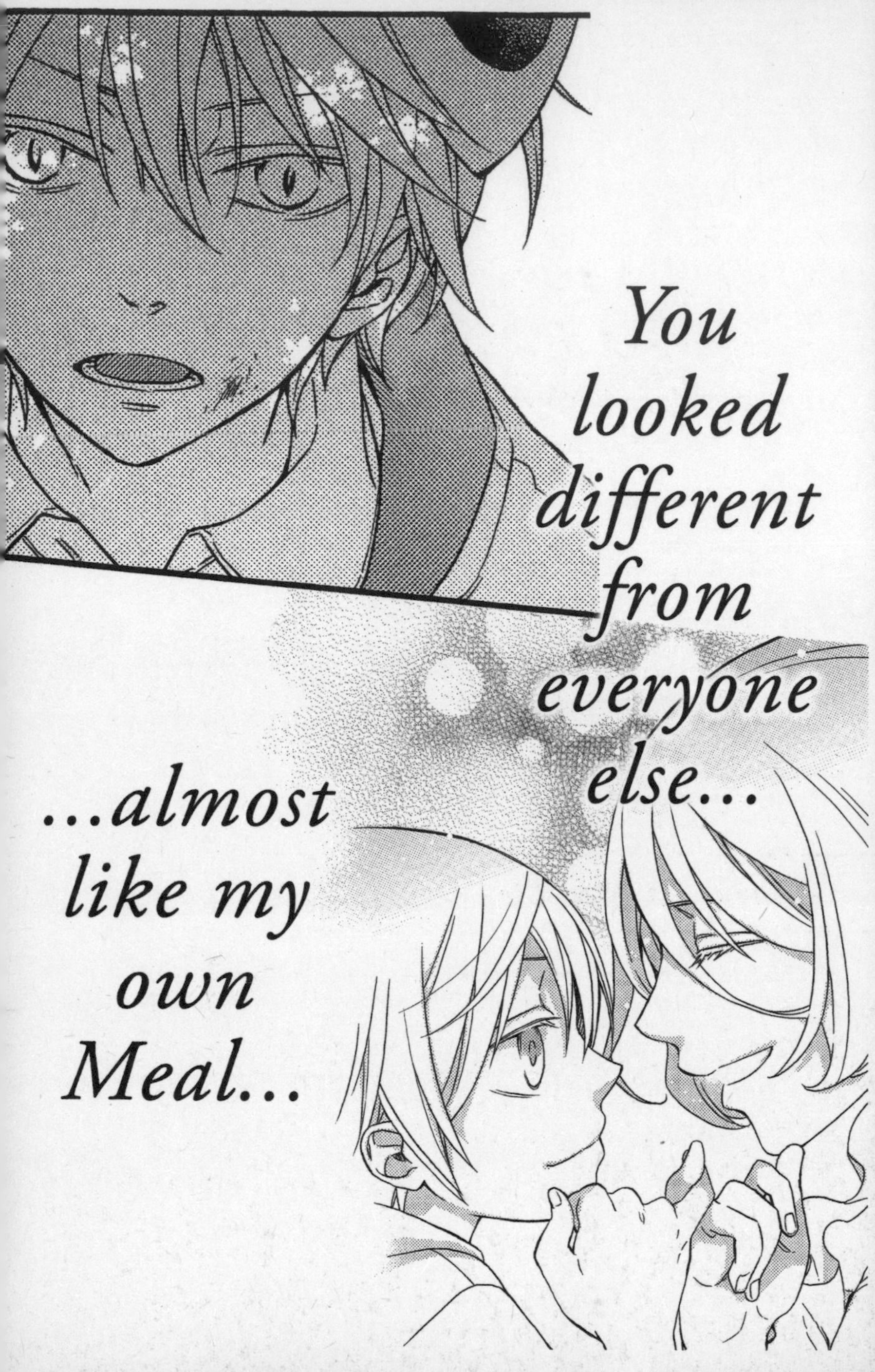
You looked different from everyone else...
...almost like my own Meal...

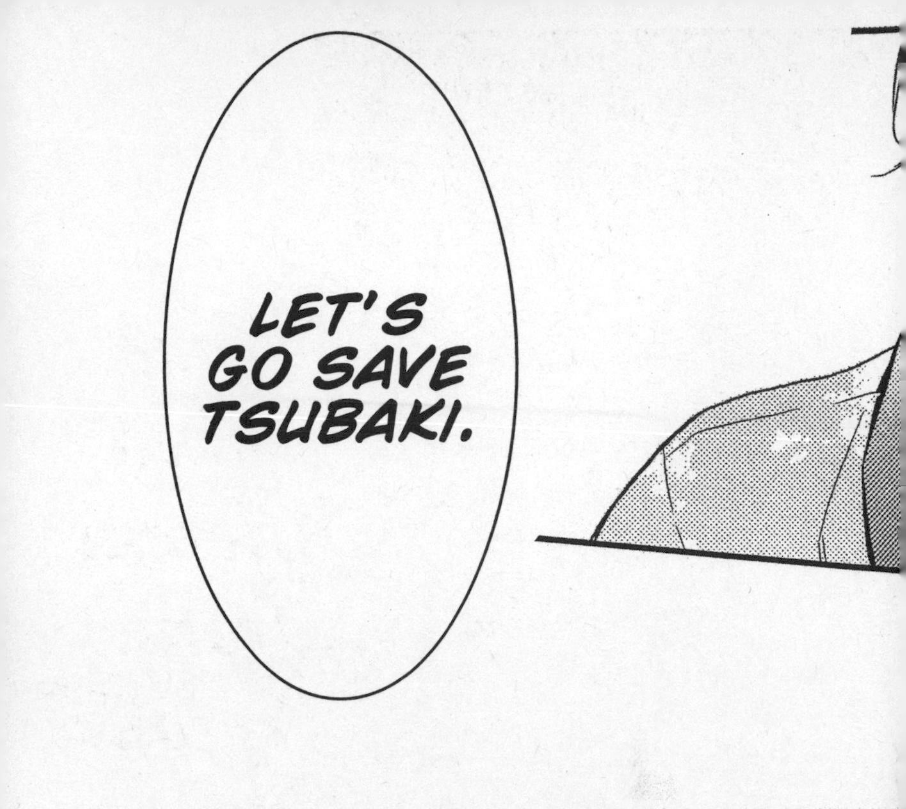
LET'S GO SAVE TSUBAKI.

"Come home, okay?"

Tougo's mother, Akane, and the song she sings...

Sins of the past, the feelings of others save the boys.

Of the Red, the Light, and the Ayakashi ⑥

COMING IN MARCH 2017

ENJOY EVERYTHING.

YOU SHOULD COME PLAY WITH YOTSUBA TOO!

Join Yotsuba as she delights in the things many of us take for granted in this Eisner-nominated series.

VOLUMES 1-13
AVAILABLE NOW!

Visit our website at www.yenpress.com.

Hello! This is YOTSUBA!

Guess what? Guess what? Yotsuba and Daddy just moved here from waaaay over there!

And Yotsuba met these nice people next door and made new friends to play with!

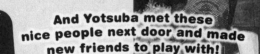

The pretty one took Yotsuba on a bike ride!
(Whoooa! There was a big hill!)

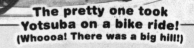

And Ena's a good drawer!
(Almost as good as Yotsuba!)

And their mom always gives Yotsuba ice cream!
(Yummy!)

And...
        And... OHHHH!

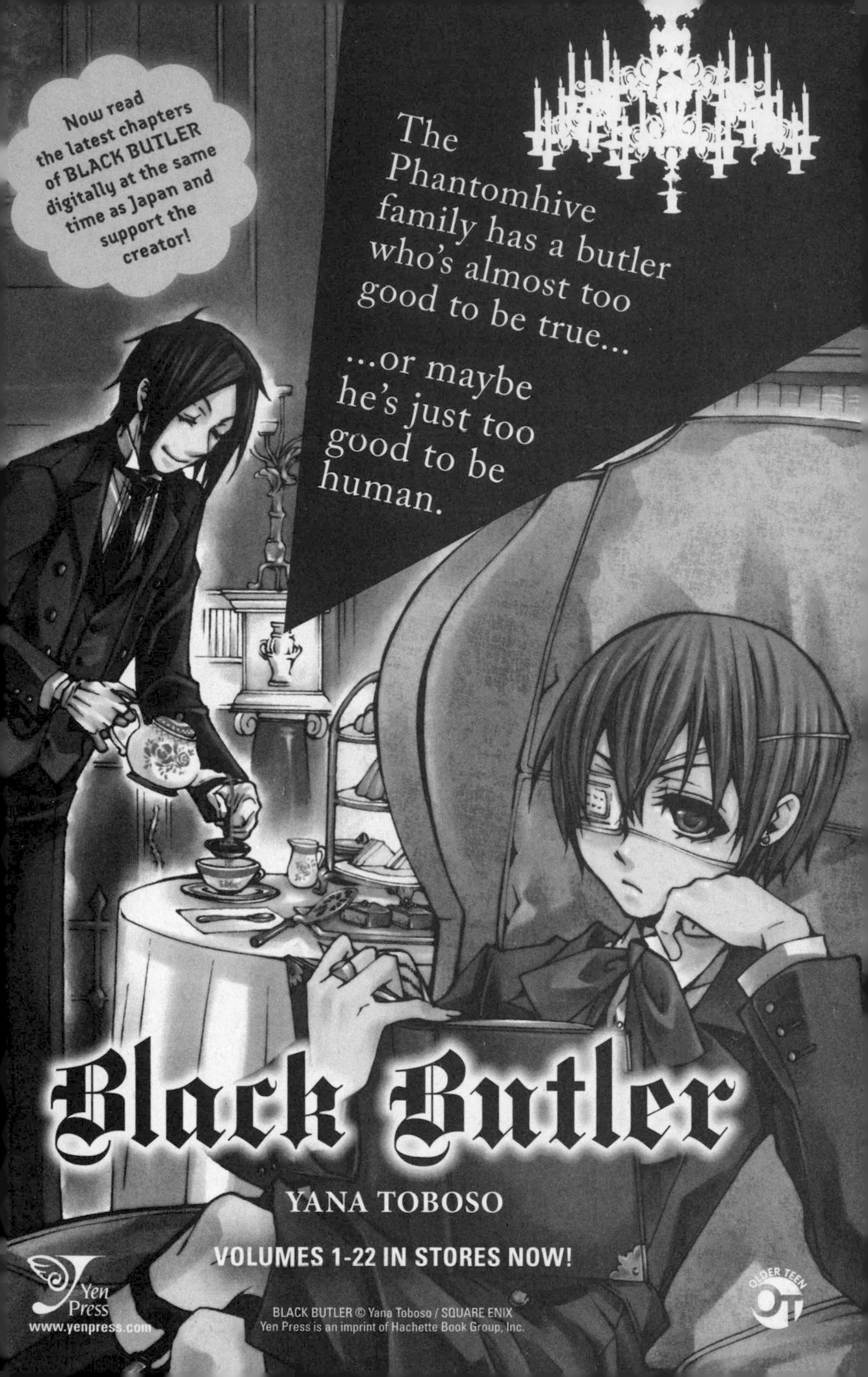

Now read the latest chapters of BLACK BUTLER digitally at the same time as Japan and support the creator!
The Phantomhive family has a butler who's almost too good to be true...
...or maybe he's just too good to be human.
Black Butler
YANA TOBOSO
VOLUMES 1-22 IN STORES NOW!
Yen Press
www.yenpress.com
BLACK BUTLER © Yana Toboso / SQUARE ENIX
Yen Press is an imprint of Hachette Book Group, Inc.
OLDER TEEN
OT

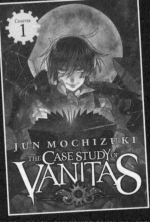

Of the Red, the Light, and the Ayakashi

ART BY Nanao
STORY BY HaccaWorks*

Translation: Jocelyne Allen ✦ Lettering: Alexis Eckerman

AKAYA AKASHIYA AYAKASHINO
© Nanao 2014
© Hacca Works* 2014
First published in Japan in 2014 by KADOKAWA
CORPORATION. English translation rights reserved by
YEN PRESS, LLC under the license from
KADOKAWA COPORATION, Tokyo through
TUTTLE-MORI AGENCY, Inc., Tokyo.

Yen Press
1290 Avenue of the Americas
New York, NY 10104

Visit us!
yenpress.com
facebook.com/yenpress
twitter.com/yenpress
yenpress.tumblr.com
instagram.com/yenpress

First Yen Press Edition: December 2016

Yen Press is an imprint of Yen Press, LLC.
The Yen Press name and logo are trademarks of Yen Press, LLC.

The publisher is not responsible for websites (or their content) that are not owned by the publisher.

Library of Congress Control Number: 2016932691

ISBN: 978-0-316-31021-5

10 9 8 7 6 5 4 3 2 1

BVG

Printed in the United States of America